FROM THE MAN-EATERS

nows Sharks, Suggests Precautions

R NATIVE AU

SATURDAY, JULY 15, 1916—TW

DEATH TO SHARKS

SHARK IN HUDSON NEAR TARRYTOWN

Monster Kept Abreast of the Berk-
shire for Ten Minutes, Says
Passenger.

What is believed to be the first shark
ever known to make its way up the Hudson River was seen yesterday in the
neighborhood of Tarrytown.

Robert Palmer, a business man of

Close to Shore

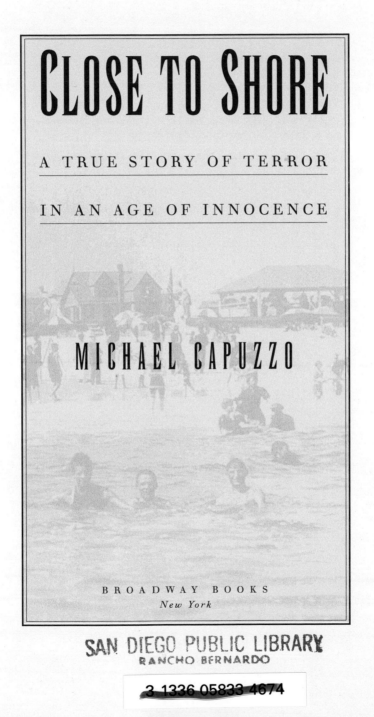

CLOSE TO SHORE

A TRUE STORY OF TERROR

IN AN AGE OF INNOCENCE

MICHAEL CAPUZZO

BROADWAY BOOKS
New York

To my father, William, who was born in the time of the shark and died while I was writing this story; my wife, Teresa, first ever in my heart, who turned the nightmares of predators into dreams; and finally Cosmo, a beagle, who sat on my lap all during the writing, watching for prey moving in the fields.

"The beach was such a novel experience that most were completely unfamiliar with the health hazards—and risks to life and limb—it posed."

—*Gideon Bosker and Lena Lencek,*
The Beach: The History of Paradise on Earth

"We're not just afraid of predators, we're transfixed by them, prone to weave stories and fables and chatter endlessly about them, because fascination creates preparedness, and preparedness, survival. In a deeply tribal sense, we love our predators."

—*E. O. Wilson*

Contents

❧

Author's Note

⤛⤜

This is a work of nonfiction. All characters are real, and their descriptions, actions and dialogue are based on newspaper accounts, interviews with family members, diaries, medical journals, and other historic sources. All of the shark attacks occurred as described in numerous contemporary newspaper accounts and interviews. To reconstruct the life of a shark in 1916 presented unique challenges. Its movements and the reasons for its unprecedented attacks have baffled scientists for nearly a century, and the mystery endures. I have given the most realistic and thorough account possible of the shark's actions based on the best available science, including interviews with ichthyologists and a study of current scientific literature. I have tried to make the individuals who play a role in this story come to life through the use of numerous historical and contemporary sources, and none utters a word, to the best of my knowledge, that he or she did not say. In rare and minor cases where the facts could not be discovered, for instance, whether a man took a hansom or automobile, I have used the same technique applied to the shark—to portray the most likely event based on extensive research of the time, place, and character. These few instances do not affect what I intended to be the most thorough and realistic account of the shark and the people and society it changed in 1916.

Michael Capuzzo
Wenonah, New Jersey
March 1, 2001

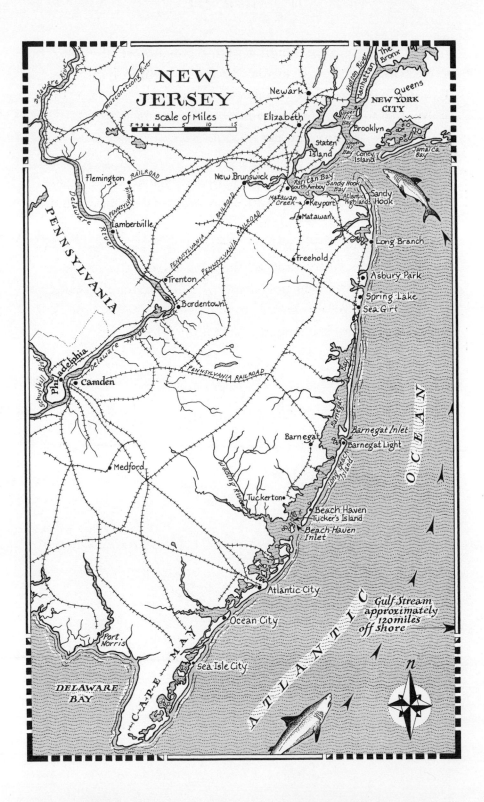

Close to Shore

The Last Man in the Water

~⚬~

The smell of the sea pulled him east. The Atlantic spread before him like a pool of diamonds, liquefied, tossing gently in gleaming tips and shards of changeable, fading bronze light. The sun climbed down toward dusk behind mountains of clouds swollen with moisture. The young man couldn't wait to get in the water.

The sandy beach stretched for miles. Behind him were seagrass-covered dunes, bleached fragments of shipwrecks, the shadows of Victorian turrets facing the sea. The warm wind carried the bark of a retriever, the faint perfume, so close, of the young women watching from the sands in their hourglass Gibson Girl dresses, their hair swept up high like the clouds captured in silk bow-tie ribbons. He was a handsome young man with slicked-back dark hair, a strong profile, a man who drew notice. He moved with the slight elbows-out jauntiness of a rebel, for ocean swimming was a new and godless pursuit, a worship of the cult of the body. The startling vision of a young man at the edge of the sea, Thomas Mann had recently written, "conjured up mythologies, was like a primeval legend, handed down from the beginning of time, of the birth of form, of the origin of the Gods."

As the young man paused to survey the beach, the dog came beside him and lapped his hand. The man put his toes in the water, then strode quickly into the shallows, the sandy muck sucking at his feet, for there could be no hesitation, no sign of timidity. Timidity was something he was determined to leave far behind, once and forever. The temperature of the water was sixty-eight degrees Fahrenheit, but he walked out thigh-deep, giving the impression it was a stroll in the afternoon air. As the water reached for his torso, he jackknifed his body and dove in. The lifesavers' rowboat, an old shore-whalers model, lay up on dry sand, beyond the seaweed line.

There were a few other swimmers, splashing and floundering near shore. Quickly, he was beyond them. He was strong and practiced, with a lean, muscular body, and he moved swiftly into deeper water. In the far distance, merchant steamers crawled northward on the warm, onrushing torrents of the Gulf Stream. He could hear splashing behind him, the dog playfully following. All eyes, he knew, were on him now.

He had tried out for the swim team at the university and failed to make it, but he was in his early twenties, at the cusp of manhood, and his endurance did not wane. Soon he had the water to himself, it was his ocean, he was without doubt the strongest swimmer of the hour, and he stopped, exhaled, and floated on his *back, a signal to shore that he had done what he had set out to do. He couldn't have known precisely how deep the water was beneath him, but, considering his distance from shore, he was certainly in far over his head.*

It is impossible to know what the young man was thinking as he floated, and the moments passed lazily into twilight. Perhaps he was thinking that he had come to a place of greatest ease, safety, and comfort. The whole summer stretched before him on the beach, with family and friends, not a care in the world but the European war "across the pond," which touched him not. His father had removed him from the mysterious and deadly plagues afflicting the lower classes in Philadelphia. He was engaged to be married in the fall. Perhaps he was pining over his absent love, his first and forever love, as a young man does under a summer sky with all of life ahead. The wedding was arranged. His whole future had been wonderfully arranged.

After a time, he realized he no longer heard the splashing of the dog. He turned over on his stomach and looked toward land: the beach was a distant, shimmering strip exhaling the day's radiant heat; the shadows had deepened in front of the turrets; ladies' parasols on the boardwalk bobbed like puffs of yellow cream against the darkening sky. He was the last man in the water. He heard the dog barking from somewhere, across the wind and waves, and was amused. He heard voices, as if from far away. He kicked vigorously, and began his crawl toward shore. He felt an exhilarating jolt of adrenaline lifting him onward and over the waves. Perhaps he mistook it for the thrill of being noticed, or a simple joy in his youth and strength—"He is a Mercury, a brown Mercury, his heels are winged, and in them is the swiftness of the sea," Jack London, one of his favorite authors, had written.

His form was perfect, arms arcing through the sea.

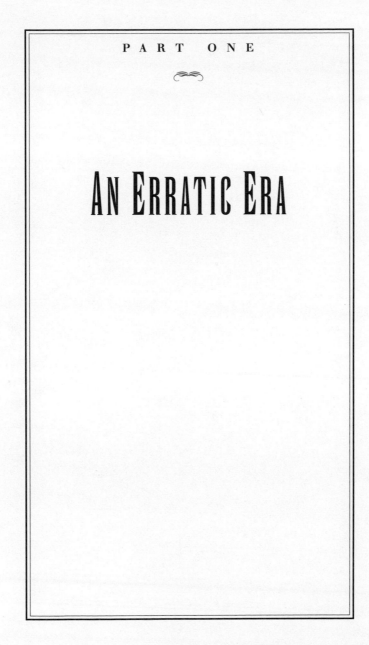

PART ONE

An Erratic Era

The Hotel

⁓

On an island off the southern coast of New Jersey, at the edge of the vast and desolate pinelands, stood an old, proud wooden hotel. The graceful spire could be seen far over land and sea and stole the flat horizon from the famous bygone lighthouse that was crumbling into the tides. Carved around the crown of the spire was a bas-relief of ocean waves rolling in endless and regal procession. The overall effect was of a Greek temple left to preside over a land of mosquitoes and greenhead flies. The Engleside Hotel was the grandest lodge on the deserted stretch north of Atlantic City, a world apart from the glamour of Asbury Park, where President Woodrow Wilson stayed that summer of 1916, running for reelection on the promise "He kept us out of the war." In Asbury Park, notable and fashionable people set the modish style, but the Engleside moved to the cadence of elegant and simpler days. With its somber turrets and long, low porches, the hotel had a noble and slightly melancholy air, like the last member of an old line.

The Engleside tower struck toward the heavens with peculiar immodesty for a structure built by Quakers. It rose in a series of four deep balconies, where guests in wicker rocking chairs watched white-sailed wooden craft play with the wind. On the beach were potato-in-spoon races, skits with parasols, violins, and leaping dogs—entertainments that diverted their guests from rumors that the kaiser's U-boats were trolling offshore. The hotel was a temperance house, but guests enjoyed the pleasures of reading, dining, dancing in the starlit evening, rowing on the moonlit bay, writing long, intimate letters, and waiting for the return mail. There was little else to do. On the porches by the sea there was Edith Wharton's popular *Ethan Frome* to read, and W. Somerset Maugham's *Of Human Bondage*. The children were in a tizzy over Kenneth Grahame's storybook *The Wind in the Willows*. The distant views were of twisted sea pine among the dunes, lonely golden eagles floating over the back country, and the water, thick with bluefish and striped bass, oyster and hard clam, which New Englanders called by the Indian name quahog and Philadelphians called Venus. Most of the guests of the Engleside, born to the Philadelphia aristocracy, read Latin and Greek. On clear days, the ocean appeared infinite before them. Long, gentle waves curled languorously onto miles of virgin beach and returned endlessly back to sea, but if the surf held the song of a Siren, it had long been resisted. For many years the Engleside's Victorian guests were too modest to disrobe to bathe. Philadelphians, changeless as their old and distinguished city, were reluctant or afraid to enter the water, for ocean bathing had not been done, and so for many years was not.

But late on the last night of June of that year, the deskman at the Engleside heard gentle splashing and frolicking in the water in front of the hotel. The young were challenging their Victorian parents with rebellious behaviors, and the latest fad was moonlight swimming. Perhaps the older generation was growing sentimental, aware of the looming shadows of the European mess. But many a deaf ear was turned that summer to the midnight air; the young were allowed to get away with it. The clerk that night heard nothing. The first cool air of the day blew through the hotel's open windows as the faint strains of hits such as "Don't Take My Darling Boy Away" spilled out over the water from the popular new portable camp and seashore Victrolas. The hotel's first five hundred electric lights glimmered and swam in the darkened sea. Deeper into the night, after the hotel was quiet and dark, the splashing and laughter in front of the Engleside lulled, and finally ceased.

Only yesterday, in the ancient life of the ocean fishes, had Leni-Lenape Indian kings led their warriors to the virgin beach to feast upon mountains of clams in preparation for autumn's wars; colonial sportsmen rumbled seaward on the carriage roads; Pennsylvania farmers rattled eastward by wagon, leaving crops behind for the annual "sea day." Never in the three human centuries at the shore, the eye blink that was the forty years of the Engleside, had so many people enjoyed the pastime of ocean bathing.

The tide surged in, free of human presence once again. The skates and rays and other fishes swarmed in their timeless feeding ways of the night sea, making subtle and unknowable adjustments.

At dawn on Saturday, July 1, the hotel and the ocean were united by the bright gold band of beach. Breakfast was served in the Engleside dining room by young Irish immigrant women from Boston, while the men read the Philadelphia *Public Ledger* and smoked Turkish cigarettes on the porches, and discussed the German march to Paris and the fall of the Philadelphia A's to last place. That was the summer the great Connie Mack affixed to the American language the axiom "You can't win 'em all." That weekend Mrs. Hetty Green, the world's richest and stingiest woman, would die, leaving $80 million and the notorious legacy of having refused to pay for an operation for her son, costing him his leg. By late morning, the sands were crowded with young men and women in the startling new swimming costumes, the women revealing inches of leg never before seen in public. In playful teams, men and women built sand castles, a new art in America and Europe that year. The shouting and flirting rose and fell like a nervous and reluctant tide, for this was all new, this lush and languid meeting of mankind and the sea, this joyful display of flesh.

In his office under the great spire, hotelier Robert Fry Engle reviewed the booking columns for the Independence Day weekend with great satisfaction. Engle, an artist and a gentleman given to tapered suits, Arrow collars, and the polished grooming of the new century (which included the new style of a clean-shaven face), shared his father's level-eyed Quaker pursuit of profit. For the second consecutive year, all one hundred and fifty rooms, rooms for three hundred people, were sold out from July Fourth straight through Labor Day. Engle, like his late father, born of old New Jersey stock, disapproved of the immoral and noisome behavior of some of his more modern guests, particularly those who tippled the stronger waters. But there was no denying the wonderful impact of the new horseless carriage and the railroads ferrying middle-class tourists en masse to the seashore, whatever their nouveau morality. The Engleside had never experienced such a boom. The great new century heralded a bright dawn for the hotel.

Other than their father-son business—an American tradition that was disappearing as the first generation of men dedicated their work lives to corporations—Robert Fry Engle seemed to have little in common with his father. Robert Barclay Engle, the Engleside's founder, was an immense, great-bellied Civil War veteran with a Whitmanesque Grand Army of the Republic beard. He was also a highly personable and witty innkeeper, a prosperous farmer, a shrewd and combative New Jersey state senator, and a dead-eye gunner. He was legendary for helping the leading men of his time, such as Jay Cooke, the great Philadelphia financier who bailed the nation out of the panic of 1873, shoot hundreds of wildfowl in a single day.

It was Robert Barclay Engle who possessed the pride, unseemly for a Quaker, to build a spire that thrust skyward; he who cleverly named the hotel by mixing the family surname with the ancient Gaelic word "aiengle," which his wealthy and literate guests knew meant "fireside" in the novels of Sir Walter Scott. It was Engle who had the guile to open his massive, remote hostelry in June 1876, less than a month before the centennial of the United States in Philadelphia, his primary market, as if daring the world to ignore him. (It didn't; wealthy sportsmen hired boats and knowledgeable guides to ply through the bays and marshes to his isolated lodge.) Engle, one of many Union veterans who made good after the war, sold Jack London fantasies to wealthy Philadelphia and New York businessmen in the Railroad Age already pining for the lost wilderness and rough fireside camaraderie of the war. But he had been born too soon. It was his son, born in the age of Rockefeller, who was poised to indulge in the big dreams and abundant capital of the twentieth century.

Yet, as a young man with artistic sensibilities, Robert Fry Engle was an unlikely candidate for the family business, and thus something of a disappointment to his father. Educated at elite Quaker private schools, he showed a rare feeling for the beauty of the ocean and dunes. Although he enjoyed hunting, he preferred aiming a camera instead of a Winchester at the wilderness. In the 1890s, graduating from the Kodak Brownie and its slogan "You push the button, we do the rest," Engle became one of America's first art photographers, imitating the evocative landscapes of the French Impressionist school of painters. In 1896, at the age of twenty-eight, Engle's photograph of a sunset over the bays of Long Beach Island west of the Engleside was included in the first art photography salon in Washington, D.C., which was praised by Alfred Stieglitz as the first American exhibit "worthy of international attention." Engle's photograph titled "The Summer Was Sinking Low" was subsequently chosen among the first fifty art photographs for the permanent photography collection at the Smithsonian Institution. The collection—sheep grazing in sun-hazed mid-west pastures, idyllic mid-Atlantic hills and valleys, the innocence of Victorian mothers and children in portraiture with nature—captured an American nostalgia for the wild places lost to the Industrial Revolution.

The celebrated young pictorialist traveled across America and into Mexico and Europe. He became a protégé of photographer Burton Holmes, the most famous travel photographer and lecturer of his day, and seemed likely to achieve Holmes's fame. But the ocean at Beach Haven, his father, the family business, kept calling him back. At the height of his artistic promise, he returned to the Engleside and never left, content to shoot portraits of his guests, the skits on the beach, the great spire looming over the sea. If there were two men in him, the artist and the bourgeois merchant, it was clear which one society valued most. The object of his career became business. It was the tenor of the times. Gusto, vitality, the bigness of big business, were the values of the young industrial republic already beginning to dominate the world. Sprawling, monstrous American capitalism was "The Octopus," said the rough-hewn California novelist Frank Norris. Theodore Roosevelt set the new American credo, but Norris expressed it best: "Vitality is the thing after all. The United States in this year of grace 1902 does not want and need Scholars, but Men."

There was big money to be made by the right kind of men. Inspired by giants like Henry Flagler, Rockefeller's partner at Standard Oil who opened the Florida wilderness with hotels and railroads, Engle was one of a group of Philadelphians who had invested millions of dollars to develop Long Beach Island into a similar paradise, a Florida of the mid-Atlantic. At the southern tip of the eighteen-mile-long, nearly one-mile-wide island was tiny Beach Haven, which would become known as "the greatest ocean city in the world." A sea metropolis lined with skyscrapers and humming with trolleys and tens of thousands of wealthy residents, it would outshine Atlantic City, its neighbor to the south, which, being closer to shore, had inferior ocean breezes, Engle claimed. Nothing less would do than a capitalistic conquest of the Jersey shore; men like Morgan, Carnegie, and Harriman set standards that were colossal.

After the tourist season of 1915, the most successful ever in Beach Haven, Engle could envision his great ocean city taking form, a paradise of comfort and ease for his guests, freed from the annoyances of nature. He could hear it in the roar of the new acetylene plant firing up the sixty-five goosenecked street-lamps that cast shadows on the four dirt roads and two dusty avenues of town; in the stir of the hundreds of newly planted saplings waving under the starlight to shade future tourists; in the rumble of Overland Tourers and tin lizzies plying the first automobile bridge to the mainland, which he had lobbied state politicians to build.

Progress was in the groan of cranes filling marshes to create land and digging miles of drainage ditches to defeat the mosquito, a notable pest of progress. A born salesman, Engle had what folks said was a "line" for the persistent "Jersey skeeter" problem. "There never was an Eden that the Devil did not try to get into," Engle said, "and the more perfect the Eden the more he tried to get into it."

Mosquitoes and flies buzzed and banged on the doors of the cottages facing the ocean, and flew straight in the open hotel windows, for there were no screens in those days. Another blemish on Engle's paradise that Saturday was the weather. The morning air clung like a limpid cheesecloth, a phenomenon the best scientific minds on the East Coast couldn't explain; the heat just wouldn't quit. White-clad figures on the tennis courts by the sea, where a youngster named Billy Tilden would play, moved at half speed. By late afternoon, many of Engle's guests retreated to the rustic comforts of their small, narrow, vintage seventies rooms, to the renewing balm of hot and cold seawater showers, the latest modern convenience. As dusk approached, a line of roadsters nudged quietly against the sand-blown ark of the Engleside, and Beach Haven was left to its timeless sounds of wind and surf that came, again, with the lingering twilight. The last of the sails tipped and skittered on the horizon as a handful of guests watched from the wicker rockers high in the tower. In his office far below, Engle set plans for Sunday's "ladies' softball game," where men played in skirts to even the odds. The laughter of the sea and of the swimmers subsided as the tide flowed out and young bathers changed in the Victorian bathhouses, leaving few swimmers in the water. There was a steady boardwalk parade back to the hotel of women who ducked demurely under sun umbrellas and cooled their porcelain faces with Chinese fans. In the lobby, men returned from fishing trips, grumbling there was nothing to be had; local guides were complaining of a mysterious disappearance of gamefish. From the formal dining room, lined with Corinthian columns and tropical murals like a European court, came the clink of china and silver and crystal, muting the distant call of gulls.

Other sounds, presently, drifted over wind and waves and echoed along the ramparts of the great hotel. In the beginning, the sounds were quieter than the dissolving hiss of sand castles, soft beyond the range of human detection, in fact. They were easily lost amid the languid noises of the summer colony winding down an ordinary afternoon in the wistful last days of the Edwardian period.

Yet the sounds would grow in intensity and travel swiftly, as sound does through water, and in time the reverberations would reach every corner of the grand hotel, around the globe, and across the new century, awakening something ancient and long forgotten in the human memory of the sea.

The Fish

The big fish moved slowly on the surface of the deep. Its dark top matched the leaden sea; its white bottom blended with sunshine reflected from beneath. The fish moved with grace and beauty remarkable for its size, in a cloak of invisibility fashioned from infinite silvery refractions of light. Unseen and unheard, it would swim for days without coming in sight of man or boat or another of its kind. Little about the scene had changed since the fish swam in the Age of Reptiles. The ocean was not yet watched by satellites or shadowed by the flying cross of airplanes. The fish had appeared before the continents divided, before there were trees and flying insects, enduring while nature underwent upheaval and extinction. The fish had survived and changed little.

The Victorian scientific lust, after Darwin, to classify and catalogue every living plant, animal, and human tribe had made no inroads on the fish's privacy. Indeed, extreme scarcity is one of its greatest survival gifts. It was in 1916—and still is, almost a century later—a once-in-a-lifetime experience for a fisherman or a sailor to see such a fish.

It was nature's plan for a minnow or a Maryland crab to be ordinary sights, but, like eagles in the sky and tigers on land, the great white shark sits atop the ocean's food pyramid, an "apex predator." Great whites must consume such massive quantities of flesh to survive, it would be unthinkable for them to be numerous. The great white is the largest predator fish on the contemporary planet that the laws of physics allow. It is, quite simply, too dangerous for there to be more than a limited number of its kind.

As a result of its great scarcity, little was known about the white shark in 1916. Most Americans had never seen a shark, except for scattered photographs in newspapers and drawings such as the comically nearsighted "grand chien de la mer," vaguely resembling a great white shark, in Jules Verne's bestseller *Twenty Thousand Leagues Under the Sea.* The sailors' myth of a "man-eating fish" persisted in the machine age as a hoary, vaguely dubious relic of the Age of Sail. Herman Melville had witnessed ferocious sharks on his Pacific whaling trips and wrote in *Moby Dick* of the white shark's "transcendent horrors, its elusive . . . terrible . . . whiteness." But Melville had died penniless in New York in 1891, his big book an antiquated flop in the modern age of steamers and telegraph cables, Ahab's great sperm whale, the nineteenth-century sea monster, driven nearly extinct by man. All the sea monsters of the ancients were shrinking in the deductive glare of science: "It's scientific" would soon be the magic phrase that settled all parlor arguments, as Frederick Lewis Allen would write in *Only Yesterday*. The ship-grappling kraken turned out to be the giant squid, huge, mysteriously shy, tucked away harmlessly in the depths. The "man-eating giant octopus" was neither, simply a large, inky cephalopod; the mermaid, mythic Siren that lured sailors to their doom, was the far less perilous, if less comely, manatee. Well-read Victorian and Edwardian men were determined not to fall prey to excesses of ancient myth or modern "pseudo-science of the Jules Verne sort," as Mark Sullivan noted in *Our Times*. A man was wary of being duped by the newspapers, notorious fabricators that trafficked in "perpetual motion, rain-making, pits dug through to China, messages from Mars, visitors from outer space." To turn-of-the-century men, the man-eating shark, like the sea serpent, seemed just such a myth.

Jules Verne himself faithfully reported the Victorian skepticism in 1870 in *Twenty Thousand Leagues Under the Sea*: "Even though fishermen's stories are not to be believed it is said that in one of these fish was found a buffalo head and an entire calf; in another, two tuna and a sailor still in uniform; in another, a sailor with his saber; and in yet another, a horse with its rider. It must be said, though, that these stories seem a bit doubtful." Myths of the sea had a way of enduring, however, even in the most rational men. It would fall to the 1890s, to a new class of men, men who controlled and manipulated nature like none before, to expose the myth. In 1891, "monopolies," "trusts," and "robber barons" entered the American language and men were seized by an awe and fear of bigness—big railroads, big money, big men like Rockefeller and Harriman. Yet if ordinary man was small and had to bow to "nature's noblemen," as the robber barons much preferred to be called, he could at least be at ease and equal in the ocean, swimming—a sport "we all from cats to kings can enjoy." For in the 1890s, the largest oceanic predator, the man-eating shark, was proven to be a specious fable, a fish no match for any man, and surely not the colossus of the day.

On a warm, windy afternoon in July 1891, the luxury yacht *Hildegard* steamed east in the Atlantic far from the dark New York skyline. The day was fair with a reluctant sun, and now and again a wave crested. The *Hildegard* ran trim with teak and brass gleaming but lacked the whimsical grace of the old sailing yawls; the new coal-powered yachts of the Gilded Age were low and slick. Against the gray emptiness with only petrels for company and an occasional distant steamer, the ship buzzed and glowed with the faint nimbus of a Gay Nineties party. Cigar smoke curled beyond the gunwales, and the sports chewed tobacco. Cigarettes were a sign of sissiness to the men, or low breeding, for the men aboard the *Hildegard* were the "upper crust," as the newspapers called them then. Smoking was verboten for women and the showing of an ankle a scandal, yet the gentler sex aboard the *Hildegard* displayed a decadent and empiric sensuality. In swan dresses and broad hats bedecked with ostrich feathers, they moved in a shifting constellation of diamonds—diamond hatpins, tiaras and diamond-encrusted lizards, insects, and bees, all the rage. Steam had given the rich for the first time in history the ability to sail away to the deep, to float to nowhere in particular for sporting amusements or the pleasure of squandering time and space as if there were no greater refinement. The wastes of ocean were a final barrier distancing gentlemen from the rabblement. "You can do business with anyone," said J. P. Morgan, "but you can go sailing only with gentlemen."

Leaning over the railings that afternoon were men in Prince Albert suits and ties and glistening soft shoes, sportsmen like William K. Vanderbilt, Jr., the captain's brother-in-law, who would reciprocate with invitations to come aboard his family's 291-foot yacht with twenty staterooms and crew of sixty-two. The younger Vanderbilt, dark and mustachioed and handsome, was in the process of reducing his grandfather Cornelius's railroad fortune in a manner that would directly inspire the coining of the 1890s term "conspicuous consumption." Parties aboard the *Hildegard* routinely included such men as the captain's friend Charles Dana, publisher of the *New York Sun;* his newly hired architect, Stanford White; his boon drinking companion at Delmonico's, Theodore Roosevelt, seven years away from leading the Rough Riders up Kettle Hill. The captain himself, Hermann Oelrichs, had also donned a suit and vest, yet neither silk nor gabardine could conceal the enormous power of his torso, nor deflect the admiring looks cast his way. In those days of titans of industry and sensation-seeking socialites and the obsequious gentlemen of the press, all were drawn to Hermann Oelrichs.

Oelrichs stood nearly six feet, more than two hundred pounds, a giant of a man for the time, broad-beamed and narrow-waisted with a great handlebar mustache and shining, arrogant eyes. An international shipping mogul, Oelrichs was one of America's richest men, and had won the hand of the finest catch of the late Victorian Age—"bonanza heiress" Teresa Fair, a California senator's daughter in line to inherit the Comstock Lode. An avid sportsman, Oelrichs helped introduce polo and lacrosse to the United States. He was also acclaimed as the best amateur baseball player and hammer thrower in New York City and the finest amateur boxer and swimmer in the country. Yet there was about Hermann Oelrichs, too, the ache of promise unrealized. He remained aloof, declining offers to run for both mayor of New York City and president of the New York Athletic Club. "Hermann Oelrichs was so richly endowed by nature and so perfectly equipped both mentally and physically," opined *The New York Times*, "that his friends have been almost unanimous in declaring that had he so chosen he might have made for himself a much larger place in life."

Yet that afternoon, as the *Hildegard* steamed east, Hermann Oelrichs made perhaps his greatest contribution. As his crew fed the leaping fires of the boiler, as servants distributed food, and the men called out, "gimme a smile" (a gentleman's term for a drink), and grew loud and expansive and joined in a raucous sporting mood, there arrived a moment, on the edge of dusk and the continental shelf, freighted with the nineties need for spectacle. In that moment Hermann Oelrichs declared he was looking for sharks.

If a shudder overtook the *Hildegard*'s passengers scanning the iron-colored sea, they could have been forgiven. Sharks were widely feared in those days as ferocious man-eaters, based on terrifying tropical legends of which Oelrichs, like his friend and fellow world-traveler Roosevelt, was especially familiar. Despite the skepticism of science, dread of the shark persisted in 1891 in tingling hairs on the back of the neck. In the publication that year of "Song of Myself," Whitman celebrated all the universe except the "leaden-eyed" shark, the ominous crease in a wave "where the fin of the shark cuts like a black chip out of the water." That afternoon, as ripples of anticipation traversed the ship, Oelrichs announced, as he often had back in the parlors of Gilded Age New York, that so-called "man-eating" sharks were a fable of the ancients. Sharks were in fact cowardly, he insisted, and he would frighten away the largest of them that surfaced from the fathoms.

That year Oelrichs had offered in the pages of the *New York Sun* a reward of five hundred dollars for "such proof as a court would accept that in temperate waters even one man, woman, or child, while alive, was ever attacked by a shark." Temperate waters he defined as the East Coast of the United States north of Cape Hatteras, North Carolina.

In the rollicking spirit of the times, Oelrichs—like his brother-in-law, Vanderbilt, who hosted America's first motorcar race to further "scientific development of the automobile"— seemed more interested in a good show than in advancing science.

But the audacious wager by a captain of the shipping industry "started the papers all over the country to discussing sharks," *The New York Times* reported. "Mr. Oelrichs contended that the ancient and widespread fear of sharks had little or no support in the shape of verified or verifiable cases in which they had killed or even injured a human being . . . He limited the offer to temperate waters because he had little knowledge of shark habits in the tropics, but even there he thought them harmless scavengers."

Now, on this summery afternoon at the edge of the century of human progress, the validity of shark attacks would be settled to the satisfaction of intelligent men once and for all.

If any man in the Gilded Age could best the shark, it would be a man who possessed Vanderbilt's wealth and Roosevelt's vigor and an unsurpassed reputation for prowess at sea. Such a man was Hermann Oelrichs. He was American director of the prestigious North German Lloyd shipping company, which would soon produce the world's first luxury superliner, the *Kaiser Wilhelm der Grosse*. According to historian Lee Server, the 655-foot-long, two-thousand-passenger German ship "held a place of pride in the human spirit" rivaled only by the big city skyscrapers as a "remarkable emblem . . . of a remarkable era . . . and of the seemingly limitless progress of science and technology." Before the *Mauretania* and *Lusitania*, *Normandie* and *Titanic* were built in an effort to duplicate the glory of the *Kaiser Wilhelm der Grosse*, Oelrichs hosted elaborate dinner parties in the middle of the Atlantic in the stateroom of the world's greatest ship, regaling his wealthy friends with tales of his long swims and encounters with sharks.

In an era when the first modern oceanographic research from the 1870 voyage of the HMS *Challenger* was just being published, Oelrichs's captains, who traversed the seven seas in steamships, reported to him that in their combined years of transoceanic travel they had neither seen nor heard reliable evidence of a man-eating shark. And the tycoon confirmed as much to be true from his own extensive observations.

The millionaire director of *Norddeutscher Lloyd Bremen* was indisputably one of the world's great long-distance ocean swimmers. At a time when ichthyologists researched sharks by waiting for dead species to be brought ashore by fishermen, Oelrichs had swum in the presence of countless sharks in deep and shallow waters and never been attacked. Although he never swam the Hellespont like Byron, as he had dreamed, New York newspapermen spread his fame. One wrote, "Some of the trans-Atlantic skippers used to say . . . that upon nearing the American coast they would look for Hermann Oelrichs, and would then know that they could not be very far from land." Every summer for years he had made legendary five-mile "shark-chasing" swims off the New Jersey coast, from which he returned to shore and *New York Herald* headlines like "Oelrichs Scares Away the Sharks."

A generation before the Roaring Twenties rise of professional sports, Oelrichs was a star of heavily publicized sporting stunts for which the public hungered. He challenged the champion John L. Sullivan to a boxing match, putting up a $10,000 purse of his own money. Sullivan declined. Fighting an adversary who had no choice in the matter, Oelrichs wrestled a caged lion to a draw, to the thunderous approval of the press and his fans. Many of the passengers of the *Hildegard* had no doubt seen Oelrichs in the Atlantic off Newport, Rhode Island, demonstrating he was stronger than any fish in the sea. As the press and the cream of New York society, including Whitneys and Vanderbilts, crowded the cliffs over the ocean, Oelrichs challenged a fisherman in a boat to reel him in as a "human fish." For twenty minutes the fisherman struggled and failed to reel in the stout sportsman on a line fastened to his waist, providing society with what newspapers called "the most interesting incident of the Summer."

Now, aboard the *Hildegard*, a hundred miles from shore, several large sharks appeared starboard. Conversation ceased as the big fish moved silently, fins slicing high through the waves. Whispers traversed the deck as Oelrichs quickly changed to his bathing clothes, murmurs growing to shouts as the sports in the crowd urged him on. Oelrichs directed his hands to move the ship closer, and approached the railing. While side wagers were made, men snatched their white boaters against the wind, and women leaned over the railing to watch, long dresses whipping erratically. Others averted their eyes as the water received the powerful athlete.

Oelrichs disappeared for a moment, then surfaced between heaving four- and five-foot waves. Shaking the water from his brow, he stroked away from the boat, knifing through the waves atop a thousand feet of ocean. In ways unknown by the boating party, the sharks detected the presence of a large mammal thrashing noisily in the water and began to move in eerie concert.

Yet to the astonishment of the shipboard party, Oelrichs thrashed boldly in the presence of the sharks, quickly scattering the most fearsome-looking fish in the sea as if knocking out a dozen John L. Sullivans at once. As the sharks disappeared into the deep, Hermann Oelrichs, flushed with pride and exertion, climbed back aboard his yacht, victorious. The passengers of the *Hildegard* cheered wildly, waving boaters, handkerchiefs, and scarves in the briny air. It is not known whether it was a harmless species or dangerous makos or oceanic whitetips that had fled into the deep. A century later, scientists would not have been surprised to see any of these sharks avoiding a man, not preferred prey in such a chance encounter. The big sharks attack in stealth or in defense, and a small, sluggish, finless mammal would hardly represent a threat. The truth of the encounter was impossible for men to discern that afternoon in 1891, and couldn't compete with the legend that reached New York City that evening: Hermann Oelrichs had conducted an experiment, man versus shark, and the outcome was plain for any man to see. The sportsman had swum among ferocious sharks, and sent them fleeing.

The great fish were no match for a man.

The moment would have been emphemeral, a parlor trick at sea, yet Oelrichs, like the fish he challenged, possessed his own qualities of myth. Fifteen years later, in November 1906, Oelrichs was crossing the Atlantic on the *Kaiser Wilhelm*—returning to New York from "taking the waters at Carlsbad" to recover from the exhaustion of assisting in the relief efforts of the San Francisco earthquake—when he died, at age fifty-six, of a dissipated liver. He was eulogized on the front page of *The New York Times* as a major figure in the city's life for a quarter century, who might have contributed far more to society. Yet the Gilded Age mogul-sportsman went to his grave knowing he had won his wager. Indeed, his position on man-eating sharks had grown more convincing to the scientific community with each passing year. By 1906, the Wright Brothers had flown, the newly invented marvel of neon lights lit Broadway (where George Bernard Shaw opened with *Man and Superman*), Jack London had written *The Sea Wolf.* Yet scant more was known about the true nature of sharks. No one since 1891 had come forward with proof of a shark attack on man in the temperate waters on the East Coast. As the widowed grande dame, Mrs. Hermann Oelrichs, and an aging William K. Vanderbilt, met Hermann's body at the port of New York, the shark wager had fully outgrown its vaudevillian beginnings as a feature in New York's yellow journalism wars, a summer diversion for the Four Hundred who graced Mrs. Astor's and Mrs. Oelrichs's ballrooms. It was now respected scientific data. Ichthyologists at the American Museum of Natural History in Manhattan, a world leader among the new and serious museums, were quoting Hermann Oelrichs's bet as compelling evidence that man-eating sharks did not exist. On the question of shark attack in the new twentieth century, it was the best science there was.

By the summer of 1915, when Bell in New York spoke to Watson in San Francisco in the first long-distance call, and Ford developed the marvel of a farm tractor (and made his one millionth car), the editors of *The New York Times* adjudged it time, long overdue, for society to acknowledge the modern and scientific view of sharks.

In an August 2 editorial, "Let Us Do Justice to Sharks," the *Times* decided it was "time to revive the controversy . . . [Hermann Oelrichs] excited" and put the issue to rest once and for all. Almost a decade had passed since Hermann Oelrichs's death, the *Times* noted, a quarter century since his famous wager, and no verifiable shark attacks on man on the East Coast had yet been reported. The editors were puzzled at the persistence among modern people of an irrational fear of sharks.

"To this day there is nothing that will so quickly set a crowd of swimmers scurrying for our beaches as the sight of a shark's fin in the offing," the *Times* lamented. Such fears were baseless and unreasonable, the newspaper's editors wrote. While the *Times* allowed that "the bitter hate that every sailor feels for the whole shark tribe can hardly be wholly baseless, for hate is always the exact measure of fear, and all fears have reason of one sort or another," the only evidence of such an attack was a single photograph, reportedly taken from a steamer in the Red Sea, "seeming to be a shark in the very act of closing his jaws on a man." Given Oelrichs's uncollected reward and the paucity of other evidence, the *Times* concluded "that sharks can properly be called dangerous, in this part of the world, is apparently untrue."

In the spring of 1916, the great white swam on the surface of a world that perhaps knew less about its nature than it had in several centuries. Even in the twenty-first century, the white shark remains largely a mystery. The force of its bite has never been measured. The bite of a six-foot lemon shark has been calculated at seven tons per square inch. The great white, at nearly twenty feet, three thousand pounds, will not submit to dental examination, and will not accept confinement. The fish is too big, too violent, beyond control. Man has never been able to keep the great white in captivity. When this has been attempted, the giant shark batters its head against its prison, unable to accept boundaries, hammering at the metal stays in the concrete that it senses electromagnetically. All that is known about the jaw power of the great white is that it must be immeasurably stronger than a small lemon shark's.

In 1971, Jacques Cousteau postulated that the white shark

had poor vision. Now it is known that its eyesight is so remark-able that it can hunt, in rare cases, more than half a mile deep, its expressionless black eyes absorbing the faintest light. Until the late nineteenth century, scientists did not believe life existed at such a depth, concluding that the ocean floor was a lifeless plain. But when the transatlantic telegraph cable was hauled up for repairs, the thick cable swarmed with heretofore unknown creatures, a new universe. The first ocean scientists to explore the depths of that universe were alive in 1916, but their discoveries were decades away. They could not have known what was coming.

The fish's arrival was choreographed by nature to be mys-terious—a survival advantage—a mystery that only height-ened human ignorance and fear.

The Doctor

≈

A hundred miles from the sea, not far from the bank of the Schuylkill River in West Philadelphia, was a large yellow brick Victorian. The fine golden façade was popular among the city's nouveau riche. The house at 4038 Spruce Street was four stories with a mansard roof, nine Ionic columns supporting a sweeping front porch, and a marble staircase with a wrought-iron banister curving inward to the street. From its east wall sprouted its identical twin at 4036 Spruce, creating the impression of a huge nineteenth century mansion with the arms of a sphinx. A dozen four-story brick sphinxes huddled side by side on the block, scores of gray predawn windows concealing the enormous families and energies of the new bourgeois Edwardians. Once rolling farms and estates during the Gilded Age, the neighborhood was now a horsecar suburb for professional people fleeing industrial Philadelphia across the Schuykill. One of the first suburbs in America, it was a Victorian dream of nostalgia and nature in an ordered state. Halos of gas lamps smudged the coal-sooted shadows of English gardens and finely forged gates; sprawling Norman castles, Tuscan villas, other reverential manors of Old Europe commanded broad swathes of lawn down to the dazzling brightness of the river.

In the early morning the dusky outlines of the factories of Baldwin locomotives and Rohm & Haas Chemicals, Stetson Hats and Disston Saws, Whitman's Chocolates and Breyer's Ice Cream appeared in a lacework of smoke and coal dust and telegraph wires draping the "workshop of the world." In refinery and foundry, warehouse and mill, men and thousands of children under ten worked in the gray clerestory light before dawn. Across from the city, in the fashionable town of Camden, New Jersey, Walt Whitman had not so long before boarded the white river ferry *Wenonah* and crossed to Philadelphia and back for hours, marveling at the "long ribands of fleecy-white steam, or dingy-black smoke," glorying in the roar of progress and industry that he proclaimed the muscle of the great American era. "I cross'd and recross'd, merely for pleasure—for a still excitement. What exhilaration, change, people, business . . ." During Whitman's last years in the 1890s, the shad in the river had acquired the "peculiar taste" of coal oil. Now, on this morning in 1916, in a mystery to men of the time, the fish were almost gone. The process by which chemicals and human and animal waste consumed the oxygen fish needed to spawn was not then known. By 1916, Philadelphia had developed and dammed its rivers for commerce for parts of four centuries, expressed in a popular nineteenth-century sculpture "Allegory of the Schuylkill River," depicting a wild-bearded river god in chains.

Shortly before daybreak, a slim and dapper gentleman of a certain age descended the marble steps of 4038 Spruce for his morning stroll. Dr. Eugene LaRue Vansant sported garb of the last century—beige seersucker suit, heavy gold watch fob, shore-white pants, white Oxford shirt, white shoes, panama hat, and bow tie, trailing a nimbus of fine cigar smoke. The doctor had dressed for the seashore, where the food was grand, the air delightful, a doctor could act like a man, and a man, if he wished, a boy. Eugene hoped to escape the restlessness and fatigue that had dogged him for days. Nervousness, he called it, or if his patients pressed him for the scientific name, neurasthenia. It was the epidemic of the new century, the disease of modernity. Insomnia, hypochondria, skin rashes, hay fever, premature baldness, and nervous exhaustion were its symptoms, and William and Henry James, Edith Wharton, Theodore Dreiser, and Theodore Roosevelt were among its sufferers. That neurasthenia implied a certain elevated sensibility, culture, and status was no consolation to Eugene during the nights he couldn't sleep.

Dr. Vansant heard it often said in America after 1900, "a man had to run faster just to catch up." But for an Anglo-Saxon gentleman raised in the frontier days of Abraham Lincoln and Andrew Johnson, there was hardly time to catch a breath. Just as a man was getting used to a few things—macadam, alarm clocks, elevators, unconscious thoughts, evolution from apes, telephones, pizza, frank talk about sex, big cities, mass magazines, movies, "the problem of the young," the first concrete baseball "park," the death of God—the scientists announced that time and space were illusions. The key paper of Einstein's general theory of relativity, smuggled into England in the spring of 1916, created confused fears not only over the collapse of Newton's laws but of the moral foundation of the Judeo-Christian world. In time, Dr. Vansant's son Charles's generation would postulate modernity: There were no absolutes—of time and space, of good and evil, of right and wrong. "Anarchy," William Butler Yeats wrote in 1916, had been "loosed upon the world."

Fretful thoughts and forebodings had kept the doctor up in the feather bed in the second-floor master bedroom. Nineteen sixteen was the most unsettling year he had known, as the pace of bad news in the *Ledger* raced unabated. Recently, the American Medical Association, based in Philadelphia then, had called for "preparedness" camps to train eight hundred American doctors to take army mules into the field (ambulances hadn't yet been invented) in the event of American entry into the European war. The doctor's friends and colleagues at the AMA had been heroes and medical legends in the Civil War and Spanish-American War, but he had been too young to serve. Privately, Eugene's colleagues filled him with stories of the futility of medicine in the face of weapons that butchered men beyond repair. That year, a Victorian gentleman's worst fears about the modern age were realized: Tens of thousands of soldiers died at the Somme in an unleashing of "all the horrors of all the ages," wrote a young war correspondent, Winston Churchill.

Lying awake as he had many nights since the snow melted, Eugene Vansant ruminated about his own inability to serve his country once again, this time because he was too old. And about his son Charles, who was old enough to be called to the European front should Wilson fight the kaiser. The hot weather made sleeping difficult. Next to him, Louisa slept fitfully. The doctor's wife was fifty-six, elderly for a Victorian woman, wearied from bearing him six children, two of whom died in infancy. She was heavy-set and the heat was hard on her. Moths and mosquitoes blew in on the warm night air from the bay window over the street.

In the morning, Eugene could feel moist tropical airs sweeping into the city, air associated, in the doctor's training, with disease. Vansant had been alarmed by reports in the *Ledger* the previous week of a rapidly spreading epidemic of "infantile paralysis" in New York City that had killed hundreds of children and young adults. Panicked authorities, who closed schools, theaters, vaudeville houses, stadiums, and hotels, hadn't a clue how the disease traveled—through dirt, physical contact, perhaps the hot, humid air. It would be thirty-nine years before Jonas Salk, then one year old in New York City, would develop the vaccine for the disease, later known as poliomyelitis, or polio. The epidemic was spreading to northern New Jersey and Pennsylvania.

Dr. Vansant had treated a number of cases in past years, as the terrible affliction began, and often ended, in the throat, and parents turned to him, a specialist in the emerging field of laryngology, as a savior. A sore throat, headaches, fever, and nausea were followed by paralysis of the limbs—including the muscles of the larynx, causing death by asphyxiation. Dr. Vansant was powerless to stop the course of the disease, and it had broken his stoic reserve more than once to watch a child die. It brought back painful memories from his youth in the nineteenth century, rattling in the City Hospital horse cart to the river tenements, where rag-shrouded creatures shrank from his touch. Doctors were considered agents of death, and the poor went to hospitals to die; the agony ended in the dead house with a coroner performing a candlelit autopsy. Dr. Vansant had no desire to revisit the dark days of medicine, when all a physician could offer was mercy.

As one of the leading laryngologists in the United States Vansant was familiar with the foremost medical thought on infantile paralysis: The best way to protect a child was to remove him from the city to the countryside for the tonics of isolation, rest, and clean air. And the cleanest air in the United States blew pure and free across the Atlantic and over the lovely New Jersey shore, Dr. Vansant and many Americans believed.

Dr. Vansant was looking forward to a long, soothing, and restorative stay. The shore was a place to escape the crowding and disease of civilization. By autumn, when the cool weather blew in, the epidemic would be a distant memory, and perhaps Wilson's neutrality would hold.

If any age could cure the disease of infantile paralysis, Dr. Vansant believed, it was his era of scientific "modern medicine," the age of miracles. "Scientist" was a new word of the nineteenth century, replacing "natural philosopher," and Dr. Vansant was exceptionally proud to be a scientist in the days when that distinction was worn like a title at court.

Eugene Vansant was a practitioner of the most powerful science of all in the new century, that of medicine. He practiced in the golden era of American medicine, when doctors enjoyed a new and radiant status. The turn of the century was not just the grand scientific age of ocean liners and telegraph lines, moving pictures and the electric light; it was a time of medical marvels. Pasteur discovered that microorganisms caused disease; the British surgeon Joseph Lister developed antiseptic surgery; vaccines sent into retreat such ancient scourges as typhus, smallpox, yellow fever, cholera, and the black death. By 1900, human populations were booming; men were living longer. Nature itself was under control in the great age of science and optimism. And of all the men who symbolized mankind's control of nature at the turn of the century—industrialists like

Vanderbilt, engineers such as Brooklyn Bridge-builder Roebling, inventors like Edison and Ford, Progressive politicians who would improve the very nature of man—physicians were beginning to surpass them all. The ancient dreaded practitioners of leeching and bloodlettings had become, in the new century, the "saviors of humanity."

In the winter of 1916, Eugene Vansant turned fifty-seven years old, an age when most men at the turn of the century had died of old age or were putting their affairs in order. But Dr. Vansant was fit and wiry-strong, walked briskly without the aid of a cane, and had not a hair that was white. He was a small, fine-boned man easily underestimated by other men, but his firm jaw and large, noble forehead were said to be scientific evidence of fine character and intelligence (a dozen fellow Philadelphia scientists had weighed their colleagues' brains after death to test the principles of phrenology). His walrus mustache was a relic of a different time, but it gave him a certain Rooseveltian force. Those who noticed a likeness to T.R. kept it to themselves, as the doctor was not known for his sense of humor. Wire-rimmed spectacles framed startling, intense blue eyes, a habitually nervous, icy gaze difficult for men to meet. The piercing eyes enhanced Dr. Vansant's reputation as a brilliant if imperious physician, innovator of Victorian treatments and tools for the ear, nose, and throat—confident a scientific approach could cure anything.

His fine reputation earned Dr. Vansant referrals from doctors in Philadelphia as well as from outlying towns and other cities. His thriving practice allowed him to acquire many pieces of Philadelphia real estate in addition to his stately home on Spruce Street, substantial holdings in railroad stocks and bonds, and a seashore house in Cape May, New Jersey, a fashionable enclave of Baltimore and Philadelphia society, where the family summered. He belonged to the Union League, one of the nation's most prestigious private clubs, where he dined with actors, titans of industry, and statesmen such as President Rutherford B. Hayes. The doctor's wife, Louisa, the former Louisa Epting of Pottsville, Pennsylvania, was an heiress to one of the great fortunes in the Age of Coal, and a grande dame of Philadelphia society.

But when he counted his blessings, the doctor placed his family ahead of his material bounty. He was a devout member of Walnut Street Presbyterian Church, where the pastor denounced the excessive materialism of the modern age, and Dr. Vansant hewed to the Victorian conviction that home, his wife, and four children were the sacred harbor in the tempest of the world. There were, contrary to modern perceptions, emotional and playful Victorian fathers, but Dr. Vansant was not one of them. To his three daughters and son he turned the stoic, disciplined countenance of nineteenth-century manhood. Yet there is little doubt, according to family members, that Eugene Vansant shared the Victorian sentiment for family. As English author John Ruskin's father, a wine merchant, once wrote: "Oh! How dull and dreary is the best society I fall into compared with the circle of my own Fire Side and with my Love sitting opposite irradiating all around her, and my most extraordinary boy."

The Biter with the Jagged Teeth

❧

The shark's life began with a male and female entwined. Other fish reproduced without touching, but for the shark's parents there had been courtship, albeit in its most rudimentary form—chase. In ancient times Aristotle was struck by the intimacy of shark mating, but the union of great whites has never been witnessed by a human being. Scientists can reconstruct the moment only based on their understanding of other sharks.

Somewhere in the Atlantic, male and female circled each other with supreme grace. The male grabbed the pectoral or side fin of a female and the brutal choreography began. Each would have been at least twelve to fourteen years old to be of sexual maturity—huge, practiced predators. The male, equipped with two claspers, or pseudo-penises, inserted one sideways into the female's cloaca, the reproductive opening. If there is implied intimacy in union, the tenderness ended there; biting and slashing left the female bleeding like the victim of an attack. Her remarkably tough skin protected her from some of the worst of the biting during intercourse.

The union produces something rare in the ocean: the embryo of *Carcharodon carcharias*, named from the Greek *harcaros* (teeth), *karcharias* (shark), sometimes translated as "the biter with the jagged teeth." The embryo shared a family tree, a phylum, and a subphylum with *Homo sapiens*. The shark was an individual, nurtured in a womb, attached to its mother by an umbilical cord. Like man, the developing cells of the embryo differentiated into a symmetrical form, vertebrae, a brain, a jaw, intestines, dermal skin; from the same layer of embryonic tissue that produced the dermal skin arose distinct teeth. The shark shared the womb with eight to ten other "pups," all attached to individual umbilical cords, all being nurtured by their mother. During gestation, the shark's brain triggered a simple equation: life=food=life. The life was very close, and the shark attacked—killed and fed, devouring its mother's fertilized and unfertilized eggs. So the shark began life as a kind of *in utero* cannibal. Twelve to fourteen months after conception, it emerged having won the most elemental of sibling rivalries—the privilege to be born.

The shark began not, as most fish did, as a helpless egg, one of millions adrift in the sea to be plucked by predators, a good-luck-to-you discharge, a primitive lottery drawing for life. It came out of the womb four to five feet long, fifty to eighty-five pounds, hunting. The shark had no air bladder for buoyancy, like most fish, so it had to keep moving, moving and killing and eating, or it would sink to the depths and die.

There was no playful puppyhood, no more nurturing from parents, no innocent gamboling with brothers and sisters. The newborn shark fled them as one would an enemy—fled its mother, especially. Her instinct was to eat the nearest food source. Nature pumped her full of hormones that diminished her appetite temporarily. Mother's parting gift to her pups was to give them a brief window of escape before she devoured them.

The waters off Long Island were cool, to the shark's liking. Even to scientists in the twenty-first century, the birthing of *Carcharodon carcharias* is veiled in mystery. Yet the great white was probably born off Montauk, as early as 1908, one of the few places scientists have seen populations of pups.

In the Atlantic, off the eastern tip of Long Island, the fish moved at the speed of a walking man, so slowly it seemed hardly to be swimming at all. The slow speed was vastly deceptive. When aroused the fish was alarmingly quick, capable of speeds of perhaps thirty miles per hour. It darted and fed gluttonously on small fish and squid in the early months, but grew slowly. Its pyramidal head carried rows and backup rows of smallish teeth—baby teeth. Speed was its chief defense at this size, when the shark was young and vulnerable to larger predators. Like a mackerel or tuna, it flew on the power of a sickle-shaped tail, but unlike them its skin was covered with thousands of tiny sharp denticles, miniature teeth that aided speed and stealth. The navy tried to emulate this design for its submarines but was unable to duplicate it. Speedo, the swimsuit manufacturer, succeeded in mimicking the denticles in its full-body suits to give swimmers added speed. But there were important differences. On the shark, the denticles were like razor-sharp sandpaper. A man who brushed against them would be instantly bloodied. The baby fish was a missile of teeth.

As winter approached, the waters south of Long Island gradually cooled. As a large predator, the great white needed a huge home range to find big prey, and cooler waters expanded its range. Soon the shark began to migrate south as far as the cooler waters and available prey would take it—in the winter, as far south as Florida. Come late spring and summer, the warm, wet season in the subtropics, the shark, preferring cooler water, headed north.

All its movements were in shallow waters now, near shore. As a full-grown adult, huge and unassailable, the great white would be capable of open-ocean migrations—in the deep where prey was scarce—capable of crossing between continents in search of new hunting territory. Yet now it stayed near shore, near familiar and abundant prey. The shoreline was its world, the natural habitat of *Carcharodon carcharias*. The young shark would range out in waters as deep as sixty to eighty feet and swim into waters four feet deep—or shallower, if it was chasing something. It chased seals up on the rocks. The young shark was equipped to follow its prey wherever it fled, almost all the way up onto shore.

To Be Different from What Has Been

❦

Butchers' carts and icemen's carriages moved sluggishly behind the great houses as Dr. Vansant strolled back toward his home. The Gothic towers of the University of Pennsylvania, modeled after Oxford and Cambridge, swam high in the brightening sky. A neighborhood park was still but for wrens flitting between trees and the statues of Charles Dickens and Little Nell. The peace of Saturday morning reigned at the City Hospital and Almshouse, where the doctor had interned and knew well the nightly bellowing from delirium tremens in the drunk wards and the miserable shrieking in the madhouse. Dr. Vansant's colleagues, the alienists, believed mental illness could be cured by cleansing blasts of cold water and a stay in the sylvan country. Whether this was true or not, the suburbs now surrounded the Hospital for the Criminally Insane.

Dr. Vansant hurried along, his mind wandering with protective concern for the children, especially the girls sleeping in close, hot quarters on the third floor—Mary Eugenia, twenty-two; Louise, seventeen; and Eleanor, eleven. The doctor was heartened that his son Charles, the oldest, a month from his twenty-third birthday, had his own house now in West Philadelphia and could take care of himself. The boy was showing the independence of manhood, and even, to the doctor's delight, had a "special girl" who would soon become something more.

Early risers respectfully tipped their hats to the doctor, whom they saw often in dark suit and derby hat, carrying his black bag, making his rounds in a hansom cab. His seersucker summer going-to-the-seashore suit was a sign of wealth. Lightweight suits were unheard of at the turn of the century outside the deep south. Most men possessed only one trusty, heavy blue serge.

Number 4038 stood in the deep shade of American sycamores. Behind the wrought-iron fence rose the perfume of a small English garden. The Packard, one of the first automobiles on Spruce Street, was parked in back, at the servants' entrance. The house was only twenty feet wide, yet, reflecting the hunger for space as the first professional class sprawled westward, it was immense beyond the façade, stretching a hundred and twenty feet back, an imposing five thousand square feet in all.

In the kitchen the doctor found the plain cook, who handed him a cup of café au lait, the American breakfast drink of choice, although sometimes to settle his nerves the doctor sipped the new decaffeinated brew, Sanka. Hearty aromas rose from under the hand of the fancy cook—a breakfast of grilled plover or filet mignon, littleneck clams, mushroom omelets, and robins' eggs on toast was typical in the Vansant household, where the doctor broke the fast in the traditional nineteenth-century manner, with locally harvested foods. Boxes of Post Toasties and Kellogg's cereals were on hand for the children: John Kellogg's Corn Flakes in particular had taken over the American table in the past decade with claims of healthfulness and efficiency for the twentieth-century family in a hurry.

Louisa, too, had succumbed to modern touches: one of the first electric refrigerators, new from Chicago; an electric stove; a toaster. The whole country marveled at the gadgets science had supplied for the kitchen. The servants baked fresh bread each morning, but the bin also was stocked with "white bread," one of the new "pure" factory-made foods said to be an improvement on nature itself, a wonder of machine efficiency, milled with the wheat germ removed. Not until the next year, when half of American men weren't healthy enough to fight in World War I, were white bread's nutritional deficiencies recognized. Dr. Vansant had never heard of a "vitamin," nor had anyone else.

As the lilting voices of the girls trailed through the rambling Victorian, Charles clattered into the kitchen, joining the family for breakfast. The children were uncommonly excited that morning, and Dr. Vansant responded severely. He commanded the dining room table with stern visage, demanding silence while the servants brought silver trays of food. "If the children were not sitting at the dining room table before Dr. Vansant himself was seated at the head of the table," a relative recalled, "they were sent to their rooms without eating. The doctor was a true Victorian patriarch."

As breakfast commenced, Dr. Vansant, without lifting his

eyes from the *Ledger*, swiftly corrected his daughters' posture. The hollow of their backs could not touch the chair. A man was the lord of his castle and his domain extended not just over the children. Were Louisa to venture a comment at table, it was not unusual for Dr. Vansant to silence his wife with an abrupt "Ta-ta, Lulu, I don't believe it was your turn to engage in conversation."

Mary Eugenia bristled at her father's dominance of her mother. That year she marched in a suffragettes' parade in downtown Philadelphia. She cheered when President Wilson, in a speech in Atlantic City, promised his support for women's right to vote. Dr. Vansant had little sympathy for the rights women were claiming in those days. His plans for the futures of Mary Eugenia and Louise were one year of finishing at a fine college in Massachusetts (Wellesley for the former, Smith for the latter), then back to Philadelphia to attend the Pierce Business School until the right man came along. It had been necessary only for the boy, Charles, to receive a full university education.

It was a man's world in 1916. Father answered his divine calling by working outside the home, providing for his family while also serving society's greater good. Eugene was part of America's first bourgeoisie, the white Anglo-Saxon professional class whose sons would prosper in the Ivy League, on Wall Street, and in corporate boardrooms in the first half of the twentieth century, who would entrench their families as the American elite. At 4038 Spruce Street, all such dreams rested on the boy.

Mother's mission was in the home, the sacred crucible of Victorian life. Louisa was the family chronicler, creating meaning and a sense of place. In her home she expressed the richness and variety of life in a wealth of different rooms that were just beginning in those days to be swallowed up, one by one, by the modern "living room." There was the music room, where Mary Eugenia, Louise, and Eleanor practiced the piano lessons published daily in the women's section of the *Ledger*, and there was the library, study, and conservatory.

But it was in the parlor, where strangers and social inferiors were not invited, that the story of the family was told. In the parlor the woman of the house expressed, through carefully chosen antiques, heirlooms, photographs, daguerreotypes, travel curios, and *objets*, a series of complex and interwoven feelings intended to be experienced as art—a room telling a silent story that only family and dear friends of fine sensibilities were entitled to hear. The story told in the Vansant parlor, typical of the Victorians, was of the preciousness and loss of children. Photographs of Mary Eugenia, Louise, and Eleanor in a rowboat with Dad and Patty, the family terrier, on the lake in the Poconos, the lake where Father proposed to Mother. The girls in long white dresses at the summer home in Cape May. A grinning Charles and his friends from prep school, arm in arm on the deck of the steamer *Belfast* in morning suits, white pants, black vests, Arrow collars, and ties, sailing the Atlantic for a grand tour in 1912, after the *Titanic* sank. There, too, were black-rimmed photographs of two sons, Eugene, Jr. and William, who had succumbed to pneumonia and whooping cough in infancy.

Louisa was so firmly rooted in the sturdy brick fortress on Spruce Street, it was difficult to leave to set up housekeeping in a hotel, and the shore itself was vaguely threatening. Young Americans in 1916 rediscovered swimming as it was invented by the Romantics—not to traverse water but to explore every sensation of the soul. The serene and reclusive sought Lord Byron's "rapture on the lonely shore/there is society where none intrudes/by the deep Sea, and music in its roar." Sensualists "rolled in the sea, shouted like a savage, laved [their] sides like a bull in a green meadow, dived, floated and came out refreshed." Romantic artists and poets threw themselves upon the waves "for the thrill which the very real possibility of drowning offered."

There was little wonder the late Victorians of Old Philadelphia were uneasy in the presence of the great heaving form of the sea and the restlessness it inspired: It was so un-Philadelphian. In the terra firma of Louisa's parlor on Spruce Street was a life inscribed by a constellation of virtues, certainties as fixed and brilliant as the stars. Philadelphia was the most comforting of big cities to call home. It proudly termed itself "the most Chinese of American cities," changeless behind a great wall of contentment and ritual and shared belief. Louisa believed in love, beauty, honor, duty, piety, and honest work. If God didn't exist (and many since Darwin were sadly skeptical), the morality of the Holy Bible was nonetheless absolute. England and France were suitable addresses, after which the sole civilized point on the map stood, according to turn-of-the-century Philadelphia writer Christopher Morley, "at the confluence of the Biddle and Drexel families . . . surrounded by cricket teams, fox hunters, beagle packs, and the Pennsylvania Railroad." Law or medicine, her husband's profession, were the solid occupations, followed by banking and insurance. The military or national politics were out, for they removed a man from Philadelphia. Louisa knew with certainty that the social Five Thousand never divorced. (And in the rare case that someone did, it was not with the indiscretion of the middle class).

Novelty was frowned upon, be it embodied by Whitman, Audubon, Eakins, or Joseph Leidy, who had introduced to the world the idea that a species of monstrously large reptiles not described in the Old Testament had existed on the far shore of the Delaware River. From a backyard in nearby Haddonfield, New Jersey, Leidy assembled the bones of a creature taller than a house, which he said had the pelvic structure of a bird, the tail of a lizard, and walked upright like a man, foraging with armlike limbs. This, Leidy said, was a *Hadrosaurus foulkii*, what he called a dinosaur, whose existence suggested the unimaginable idea that the world was millions of years old and had not been made exclusively for human beings.

Philadelphia in 1916 defined itself proudly as a place lost in time, an island of Victorian virtue in a sea of American change. That year a journalist from *Harper's Weekly* visited the city and found the forces of tradition resolute, the nibbles of modern erosion few. "The one thing unforgivable in Philadelphia is to be new, to be different from what has been."

When Philadelphians ventured beyond the wall each summer, they moved in flocks to safe and sedate places favored by other Philadelphians—Northeast Harbor, Bar Harbor, Mount Desert, Maine, and Cape May. The classic Philadelphia outing—in the words of Dr. Vansant's colleague Dr. S. Weir Mitchell, contemporary of Freud and famed founder of the "rest cure"—was a leisurely walk in the woods after which "the servant busied himself with the lunch, and put the wine to cool in the brook."

It was an unspoken rule that a proper Philadelphian did not swim in the ocean. The upper classes rode horseback, painted portraits, went on hikes and walking parties. To swim was decidedly middlebrow, messy, and perhaps dangerous. The sea held mysteries a Quaker saw no sense in divining. Philadelphia's first Jersey shore summer refuge was Long Branch, and there, according to Charles Biddle, father of Nicholas Biddle, president of the Second Bank of the United States, occurred "the archetypal confrontation of Quaker caution and the wild waves."

In Louisa's day, it was frowned upon for both sexes to be in the water at the same time, even a body of water as big as the Atlantic. Ocean swimming was chaste. In her time European women entered the ocean in horse-drawn "bathing machines," small, roofless cabins on wheels complete with windows and drapes, where a modest woman could enjoy the healing waters of the sea free from prying male eyes.

The modern beach was a hedonistic Xanadu that shocked her and Dr. Vansant. In the caress of the warm sea (which the Romantics equated with sex), the styles and mores of the past were relaxed, flesh bared, the cult of the body risen, Pan idealized, Venus reborn. To the sea, young men and women vanished in roadsters, entwined in the privacy of a movable parlor. At the ocean they kissed in the seaside bathhouses where burlesque postcards were sold. Women sheared their hair, smoked cigarettes, and drove automobiles. Young women bared arms and shoulders to the sun and waves. The power of the female form inspired gawkers, shocked or aroused. There was alcohol, dancing, suggestive songs. Lousia and Eugene, like many Americans, could deny "the problem of the young" until F. Scott Fitzgerald raised the banner for wanton youth in 1920 in *This Side of Paradise*, revealing that most nice girls in fashionable cities had kissed *many* boys. Yet at the seashore in 1916 there was ample evidence of the new freedoms to worry them. The dissolution of the formal nineteenth-century world they knew was first revealed at the beach, as if the restive ocean were the agent of change and the shoreline the advance guard.

The most shocking development was in the water, where the rising hems of swimming costumes became a battle line drawn by the Victorian establishment. In that summer of 1916, there was a cultural revolution over the ideal female form—the cover-all Victorian skirt-and-trouser bathing costumes gave way to lithe, form-fitting swimsuits, and the modern American image, practical and sensual, was born. The appearance of languorous female arms, legs, and calves as public erotic zones roused a national scandal. On Coney Island, police matrons wrestled women in the new clinging wool "tube" suits out of the surf. In Chicago, police escorted young women from the Lake Michigan beach because they had bared their arms and legs. In Atlantic City, a woman was attacked by a mob for revealing a short span of thigh. The American Association of Park Superintendents stepped into the fray with official Bathing Suit Regulations, requiring trunks "not shorter than four inches above the knee" and skirts no higher than "two inches above the bottom of the trunks." Police took to the beaches with tape measures and made mass arrests.

Louisa, reading the newspaper, worried about the potential ruckus awaiting at the Jersey shore. Atlantic City—the glittering sea metropolis of four hundred hotels and fifty thousand guests only ten miles south of tiny Beach Haven—was a seat of the rebellion, the *Philadelphia Evening Bulletin* reported. Under the headline "Startling Hosiery Fad Rules the Beach," the *Bulletin* noted that ladies wore bathing socks rolled down instead of up, *exposing the knee*. This moment was a turning point in American fashion; once that line was crossed, more flesh and less fabric became the style of the twentieth century. "The very modish thing . . . is reminiscent of the Highland laddies in the wee kilties, which permit the air of Heaven to play freely on their braw limbs," the *Bulletin* noted. "The mode is popular among the damsels who have dimples in their knees . . . The lifeguards are primed to remonstrate if the craze continues. 'It draws too many sharks,' they explain."

It was Dr. Vansant's masculine privilege to read the *Public*

Ledger uninterrupted each morning at breakfast. Sometimes he retired to his Morris chair in the library, a cozy, dark, wood-paneled room decorated specifically for the man of the house, who had time for the leisure of reading. Here were displayed his fine old books, his busts of Shakespeare and Aristotle, his collection of minerals (to illuminate his interests in learning, history, and the natural sciences), his humidor, and his stack of *Saturday Evening Post*s to be perused as he sat by the small fireplace, swept clean of the ashes from December's chill. The furniture and *objets*—heavy wooden European pieces, silver ice bucket with carved lion's-head handles—expressed the grandeur of the past.

The newspaper lay on the ottoman, raising a dusty smell of lead ink, and Dr. Vansant could not have been blamed if he lifted the broadsheets with trepidation. Big headlines, photographs, advertising, telegraph dispatches from Europe—it was all new, as startling as the messages it conveyed. The narrow columns of gray nineteenth-century type had never revealed a world so consistently urgent, not during Reconstruction or the bank panic of 1893 or even the assassination of President James A. Garfield in 1881, during Vansant's first year of medical school. For much of the nineteenth century, the Philadelphia *Public Ledger* had greeted Eugene like a genial friend, the voice of Republican saneness. A visitor at the turn of the century observed: "Philadelphia has its own dry drab newspapers, which are not like any other newspapers in the world, and contain nothing not immediately concerning Philadelphia. Consequently no echo from New York enters here—nor any from anywhere else." Lately, the *Ledger's* companionship had failed the doctor.

Across the Atlantic, south of Neuve Chapelle, France, the British were firing a million shells a day, lighting the night sky for thirty miles "brilliant as if with the glare of the aurora borealis." The Germans, in a triumph of military science, had recently turned air into a weapon, poison gas. The federal income tax, levied for the first time in 1913, was soon to be doubled to pay for increasing government expenses, including construction of the Panama Canal. The Treasury Department announced a new tax on inheritance over $50,000, and the doctor's fortune far exceeded that. The tax would compromise the legacy he planned to leave his children.

The doctor thought of his son when he read that Wilson was being pushed toward war on two continents. Declaring he would rather be judged by the "verdict of mankind" than by the election of November 7, the President had dispatched the 1st and 2nd infantries of the Pennsylvania National Guard from Philadelphia to Texas on troop trains as a protection force against the border raids of the Mexican Pancho Villa.

In Philadelphia, forty thousand machinists were expected to strike that morning for the rights to an eight-hour workday and overtime—unheard of and excessive rights, the doctor believed, advocated by the Democrat Wilson. What had happened to the rugged, self-reliant Republican nation Dr. Vansant had known? The city grand jury was investigating the "slaughter" of sixty-three pedestrians by motorcars in the past six months. Angry motorists were running down staid pedestrians and poky horse-carriages in a war over the streets. Many men and women simply didn't know how to operate the fast, jerky machines. Motorcar salesmen were supposed to provide five lessons before letting a man leave the dealership, but salesmen often skipped the last few sessions, the *Ledger* reported gravely, inspiring the newspaper to publish a daily driving lesson. That morning's tip concerned a fundamental element of driving in reverse: One must stop before moving ahead for "the car cannot move in two directions at once."

The doctor found no succor from the sports columns either.

Grover Cleveland Alexander suffered a rare loss to the New York Giants as a Phillies infielder "stuck his finger into a hot grounder and was added to the hospital roll." The proud Philadelphia Athletics were walloped by the Yankees 7–0 despite the presence in the A's lineup of the game's greatest slugger, Frank "Home Run" Baker. (Babe Ruth was a pitcher for the Boston Red Sox in the World Series that fall, and was said to have a promising swing.)

Dr. Vansant was proud of his famous neighbor, Professor William Curtis Farabee, who returned from South America having discovered "the Garden of Eden of British Guiana." The explorer added to the archaeological museum's peerless collection a few shrunken heads of the Jivaro and measurements of the limbs of the Macusl, Wapiatiana, Prokoto, Zapara, and Asumara tribes. But Dr. Vansant was astonished to read that many Americans were disappointed in Farabee's expedition. It was a great age of exploration, when Peary reached for the North Pole, and many believed Farabee had set out to find "the lost world" of Jurassic dinosaurs on a remote Amazonian plateau discovered by the British Professor Challenger in 1912. Dr. Vansant was mystified that the average man didn't seem to understand that both the Jurassic dinosaur and Professor Challenger were fictions in Arthur Conan Doyle's 1912 bestseller *The Lost World.* Indeed Dr. Vansant was frequently struck by the ignorance of the public in scientific matters.

Aside from the report on infantile paralysis, which, to his relief, had not reached the southern Jersey shore, the doctor was keenly interested in the War Department's recent analysis of the new class of German U-boats, said to be the most devastating marine weapons ever invented. They were capable of crossing the Atlantic entirely underwater, and according to the

Ledger, mid-Atlantic seaports such as Baltimore, Atlantic City, Wilmington, and Cape May were the most likely targets of attack, for much of the nation's coal, iron, oil, and munitions was produced within an eighty-mile radius of Philadelphia.

The family had been disappointed when the doctor announced that they were not going to their summer home in Cape May, with its Baltimore and Philadelphia society, Queen Anne mansions, and familiar rhythms. Charles was especially dejected; he cherished his hours sailing in his own boat. Louisa, however, was relieved, for she fretted about her son's safety in the sailboat, far at sea. Given the headlines in the *Ledger*, Dr. Vansant thought Beach Haven, a remote, little-known family resort, was a prudent choice—the safest possible place.

An editorial in another newspaper that summer left the doctor pondering the new century. Noting an unusual occurrence of wars and revolutions, strange crimes, divorces, heat waves, and unforeseen hurricanes, the editorial writer pondered the possibility that technology had destroyed a natural equilibrium, setting something amiss in this "erratic era":

> Mariners tell of strange storms arising, seemingly, from convulsions beneath the deep rather than in the heavens above. Can it be that the forces of destruction let loose by man have been mighty enough to throw the terrestrial adjustment off its balance and put the universe out of whack? Is it possible that our submarine prowlings and torpedoings have disturbed the Atlantic currents, or displaced the Spanish mainspring? Something certainly is wrong somewhere, and it would seem to be up to the geodetic gentlemen to solve the matter 'ere we monkey further with forces that may turn upon us to our complete annihilation.

The Most Frightening Animal on Earth

Fortunately for everything else that swam, the great white grew slowly. Its body stiffened along three parallel muscles that ran from snout to tail. With the new bulk came a decline in speed, and the shark's narrow teeth, once ideal for snaring fish, broadened out so that catching small fish grew almost impossible. Adaptation was not difficult. The shark's size and strength were enormous advantages now, and its speed still remarkable for its size.

Like an infant child, the shark's head had rapidly achieved adult size, expanding massively. Twenty-six teeth bristled along its top jaw, twenty-four along the bottom jaw. Behind these functional teeth, under the gum, lay successive rows of additional teeth, baby teeth that were softer but quickly grew and calcified. Every two weeks or so, the entire double row of fifty functional teeth simply rolled over the jaw and fell out, and a completely new set of fifty rose in its place. White and new, strong and serrated. Broken or worn teeth were not an issue for the apex predator.

Little is known about the shark's appetite, except it was enormous, and like a man who didn't know where his next meal was coming from, the fish gorged itself. The waters of the subtropics, off southern Florida, had lured the shark that winter, emerald shallows crowded with prey. As the shark grew, its appetite shifted from small, cold-blooded fish to large, warm-blooded creatures, luscious with blubber and fat, rich with the oil that it would store in its liver for long periods to prevent starvation. It was a lesson in survival, and the shark was survival's star pupil.

With quick thrusts of its dorsal fin, the shark plunged to the bottom of the ocean, huge eyes widening to absorb light from the gloom. On the surface it tore great hunks of blubber from the carcasses of whales. It was capable of astonishing leaps out of the water, rocketing almost vertically to the surface, the huge fish hanging in midair, oyster-black top and glistening white bottom separated by a ragged line, like a child's charcoal drawing, unusually small triangular teeth set in a crude pointed snout, and round, fist-sized, expressionless black eyes.

The shark was designed hydrodynamically, and with its new bulk it moved with the majesty of a Boeing 747, master of the seas. After eight years, the shark had nearly doubled in size—to almost eight feet, and more than three hundred pounds. It remained years away from sexual maturity, less than half grown. It was a shadow of the nearly twenty-foot goliath that would bite big sea turtles cleanly in two, shell and all—it was merely a juvenile. Yet already it was as close to invincible as a living thing can be.

The shark knew, instinctively, not to fear the behemoth shadows of the blue whale—the largest creature in the sea—who had somehow bypassed the laws of scale of predation and grazed on plankton and plantlike krill. There was nothing to fear, either, from fifteen-foot tiger sharks, formidable man-eaters that attacked almost everything else. Already the shark was larger or more powerful than almost anything else in the sea; it was, according to Harvard naturalist E. O. Wilson, "with the saltwater crocodile and Sundarbans tiger the last expert predator of man still living free . . . by all odds the most frightening animal on Earth, swift, relentless, mysterious and unpredictable."

Only two creatures in the sea, scientists believe, would be emboldened to attack a seven- or eight-foot great white aside from another, much larger, great white. The first is speculative, but ichthyologists believe the huge sperm whale, armed with impressive teeth and already documented as an attacker of the giant megamouth shark, must also seize great whites from time to time. The second attacker of great whites does so rarely, it is believed, but an attack is documented. In October 1997, veteran biologist Peter Pyle was riding his seventeen-foot shark research whaler near California's Farallon Islands when he witnessed "a very amazing sight . . . [an] orca with a ten-foot white shark in its mouth." Two female killer whales—the smallest one twelve to fifteen feet long—had been seen killing and eating a sea lion when apparently the white shark investigated and was not welcome. An hour later, the orca was seen pushing the shark along as it writhed in its mouth. But the orca did not consume the white. Instead the whale eventually dropped the eviscerated shark and it sank, while gulls began a "feeding frenzy on the liver and other bits of the shark floating to the surface."

Yet the juvenile shark cruising in the subtropics knew no natural enemies and felt no fear. Perhaps it felt something resembling curiosity, or excitement, as it searched ceaselessly for appropriate prey, but not fear. The great white sliced through the cool, shallow waters of southeastern Florida with princely arrogance that winter. Amberjacks, dolphins, other sharks, and small whales fled its approach or died swiftly for their mistake.

In the late spring the shark was swimming slowly several miles off the coast of southeast Florida, somewhere between the Keys and West Palm Beach, when it was seized by a current much warmer than its liking. The shark resisted, but the current was unimaginably powerful, a mighty river that swept the shark away from the shallow, familiar coast. The force of billions and billions of gallons of water tumbling with trillions upon trillions of tons of plankton and algae and uncountable fish—wahoo, tunas, dolphins, flyingfishes, and billfishes—bore the shark away from shore. The current was miles wide and rich with prey, but the water was uncomfortably warm and deeper than it liked, and in this new environment the juvenile began to struggle. The young shark coursed through the rushing water, stalking yet somehow unable to kill or eat. The shark was not engineered to know fear, but perhaps for the first time in its life it experienced prolonged failure, failure leading to hunger. The shark was still formidable and could sustain itself without food for days. It battled the current, but the current whipped along like moving walls, providing the shark yet another alien experience—powerlessness. As it swam and tried to adjust to this new environment and grew hungry, the Gulf Stream, warm and wide and inescapable, carried the shark north.

A Train to the Coast

⤲

Warm air baked in waves from a sea of rooftops across the city. Crowded tenement rowhouses were steeped in odors of sweat and boiled cabbage, laundry motionless over dank alleys where children and dogs made retreat. The wealthy drowsed on a sticky Saturday morning, while the gentlemen of the press, dark stains under serge vests, reported "complete stagnation of the normal action of the human race" with outbreaks of "intense suffering" among the poor and destitute.

A baby died in the arms of her mother waiting in the office

of the overseer of the poor to charge her husband with deser-
tion. Another infant perished from sunstroke at the moment of
victory in the Sixtieth Street Business Men's Association baby
parade. A dockworker collapsed and died receiving a ship at
port. A man had a heart attack reaching for the front door of his
house. A young police officer suffering "acute mania from
heat" climbed to the top of a five-story building and jumped
off. July would transform Philadelphia into a tomb sized for a
thousand new corpses, most of them destined for the local potter's field.

The warming air disturbed the order of nature at all levels.
The Cruelty Society sent out a water brigade as thirty thousand
horses faltered at their wagons. A crazed bulldog jumped back
and forth between two porches, trapping the families inside
until it collapsed and died. Three men braved the deadly currents of the Delaware River to cool off—and drowned, one with
his head stuck in the bottom on a dive. A mystery arose on the
river: A severed human foot, size seven and a half, surfaced near
shore—a murder victim, police said, or a swimmer eaten by a
large fish. What fish was capable of such a feat, police hadn't
a guess.

By midmorning on July 1, the migration to the sea began.
Across downtown Philadelphia, thousands of Italian, Irish,
Jewish, and Polish immigrants and working-class men, women,
and children, laden with rope-tied rugs and straw hampers
stuffed with towels, bread, and sausage, bottled water and beer,
made their way to the trams. Crowds thronged to Broad Street
Station, where the Pennsylvania Railroad crossed the Delaware
River to Atlantic City, Cape May, Asbury Park, Ocean Grove,
Beach Haven. Newsboys on street corners shouted, hawking
copies of the *Bulletin:* "Record Thousands Rush to Shore," the
headlines declared. They were day-trippers who would return

before nightfall, blistered and sunburned but proud to have participated in the new fashion of beachgoing. The luckless, unfamiliar with the Jersey shore's legendary undertow, might not return at all. But the exclusive hold of the affluent on the ocean had fallen. It was the largest migration to the shore in the city's history. The railroads of the Industrial Age had opened the seashore to the masses.

Twenty blocks west of downtown, the Vansants' servants hoisted great steamer trunks into two automobiles parked behind Number 4038, near the rear entrance reserved for domestics. The trunks were laden with hand-fashioned silk and cotton clothing, damask linens, new wooden tennis racquets, swimming costumes, photographs and paintings, the portable Victrola. Both vehicles were filled to the rails (there were no roofs on cars in 1916) with luggage—and with the doctor and Louisa, their four children and friends, maids, cooks, servants, and nannies in tow. The Vansants traveled in the grand style of the last century, a time when old-moneyed Philadelphians packed carriages and boats to simple, elegant resorts to spend the entire summer. They were not especially comfortable with the invasion of the multitudes. In the words of Old Philadelphia social icon Sidney Fisher, "The masses in this as in everything else have destroyed all decency." Suddenly, one rode a railroad car "crowded to excess with all sorts of people," Fisher said. "This I have never seen before."

The masses made travel an ordeal. Motorcars and carriages, electric trolleys and wagons, jammed the narrow seventeenth-century lanes of William Penn's old city. The roar of the new machines mingled with smells of gasoline and horse dung. Over Broad and Market Streets floated a murky brown haze that Dr. Vansant had noticed only recently—the exhaust from the city's growing number of automobiles.

As the Vansants motored east on Spruce, Independence Day flags festooned every shuttered business window, every rowhouse porch, giving the procession an odd mixture of a festive and funeral quality. It was a massive show of support for England in the European war. The newspapers this year were campaigning for a "safe and sane" Fourth. One hundred and eighty-five Philadelphians had been seriously injured in 1915 by fireworks, cannons, firearms, gunpowder, torpedoes, and toy pistols. The doctor was glad to remove his children from such dangers.

Ahead loomed a highlight of the trip for Charles—Broad Street Station. The mammoth redbrick station was the railroad hub of America, sending its Tuscan-red locomotives emblazoned *Pennsylvania* to thirty-eight states. Some of Charles's most pleasant memories were of riding the Pullman to Boston and New Haven with hundreds of his classmates to watch Penn play football against Harvard and Yale.

Red-capped porters with an ethereal grace led the Vansants to a Pullman, while the hordes of passengers crowded the regular trains. To ride a Pullman on the Pennsylvania Railroad in the summer of 1916 was to experience the golden age of passenger railroading. More Americans rode the rails in 1916 than they ever had before, or would again, and never was an American railroad as mighty as the Pennsylvania. The "Pennsy" was a nation unto itself, with factories, boats, hotels, coal mines, grain elevators, and telephone and telegraph companies, revenues greater than some countries—and twenty-eight thousand miles of tracks that served almost half the nation's population by rail. A man on the overnight Broadway Limited from Philadelphia to New York to Chicago could enjoy all private car accommodations, sip Manhattans in the bar-lounge observation car, dine on roast duck à l'orange in the dining car, and get a morning trim in the barbershop.

The Vansants were bound for none of these civilized points on the map. By devouring all of its competitors, the Pennsy could take a man to the end of the world, or close enough for a connection there. By lease arrangements, the Pennsy's influence extended to smaller railroads, the tiny cross-hatched lines in the farthest corners of the map, such as the New York & Long Branch (N.J.) Railroad, and its subsidiary, the Tuckerton & Manahawkin Railroad. Through the aegis of the obscure Tuckerton & Manahawkin, the mighty Pennsylvania Railroad controlled service to Long Beach Island, New Jersey. There, at the southernmost point on the island, was the barren, easternmost point of the Pennsy empire, reached by the new service, the Beach Haven Express.

The express offered a service to the Jersey shore that would not be equaled in the rest of the century—four daily round-trips between Philadelphia and tiny Beach Haven, only two hours away. With the improved service, Dr. Vansant planned to join his family at the seashore every few days, while still working the entire summer. He would be more available to his patients, and able to return to the city quickly in case of an emergency. He would also enjoy hours on the train in the company of his son. Charles planned to commute from the sea to his job as a salesman at Nathan Folwell and Company, the textile manufacturer. Dr. Vansant was looking forward to time alone with the boy. He thought his son needed his guidance and more masculine influences. He was hoping vacation, too, would toughen up the boy. Away from the effete society of Cape May, in rustic Beach Haven his son could meet the rugged challenge of the sea. While mothers worried about the dangers, Victorian fathers considered the ocean a portal through which a boy became a man—a test of the social Darwinist doctrine of the day that "only the fittest survive."

The doctor's love for the boy was not immediately apparent. His conversations with his son were formal and distant, fissures in a glacier that bound father and son together yet separated by cold, refracted spaces. A stern patriarch, Dr. Vansant had little patience for the foibles of his oldest child, yet he felt a love for his son he could not express. To read their relationship as distant would be a modern failing, for beyond clubs and sports and masculine rituals, their bond concealed hidden power. It was from father to son that the family inched over the landscape of generations and time.

In the person of Charles, Dr. Vansant harbored aspirations far greater than his own rise from the merchant class to the bourgeoisie. Being visited late at night by the doctor, in dark suit and black bag, making his rounds by horse and carriage in the nineteenth century, it would have been impossible not to sense his austere determination. Eugene could trace his American lineage back to 1647 and the Dutch colony of New Amsterdam. Indeed, he was himself a culmination of the line, the best-educated Vansant in the family's long history. But the Vansants were *nouveau arrivé* in Philadelphia, having come in the 1830s. So it was that the doctor possessed a rather time-honored ambition: to establish a distinguished Philadelphia family, an enduring legacy, as permanent a mark as a man could leave in a restless, modernizing country. If it seemed quixotic to modern sensibilities—Americans in 1916 were motoring everywhere on the map, claiming no fixed home, no memory of the past—it was perfectly normal in Philadelphia, an old city with the most deep-rooted of American aristocracies.

For Dr. Vansant the first step in making a legacy was to introduce Charles, known to family members as "the shining only son," to the world of men. The doctor invited him after his twentieth birthday into the retreat of the smoking parlor at 4038 Spruce, where the men retired for billiards, political discussions, and cigars while the women sipped tea in the parlor. Upstairs was a small exercise room where father and son lifted weights together, following the new and popular regime of German bodybuilding. Father and son took the roadster to the prestigious Cape May Country Club, where amid the endless marshes and scrub pines by the ocean, Eugene taught the boy the recently imported Scottish game of golf.

Through formal ritual and a thousand unspoken ways, Eugene tried to shape his son's view of being a man, of being a Vansant, from an identity to a calling. After Charles graduated from Penn, Dr. Vansant introduced his son to the prestigious Order of the Founders and Patriots of America, of which the doctor was the national treasurer-general and Pennsylvania governor. Charles, carrying forth the line, would be a member. In addition, the boy was warmly welcomed to the Union League, one of the most elite private clubs in America. The doctor's timely word with Nathan Folwell, whose textile mill was one of the country's largest, landed Charles his first job in 1914 as a salesman.

Charles was among the first wave of American men to climb the corporate ladder. He was eager to prove to his father that he was a "go-getter," a new and popular American phrase. He never suffered the despair of the Lost Generation. A contemporary of Charles Epting Vansant's, Francis Scott Fitzgerald—another young man born to a white Anglo-Saxon Protestant family in the 1890s, a Princeton man to Vansant's Penn—would write in another four years in *This Side of Paradise* of the disenchanted young "grown up to find all Gods dead, all wars fought, all faiths in man shaken." But not now, not yet, not in this summery interlude before America entered the Great War.

Charles had grown up in a time of American hubris, iron and steel, certainty and progress. He was excited by his generation's idealistic dreams of the future, and particularly enjoyed a fanciful poem written by one of his prep school classmates in 1906, titled "In 1999":

> Father goes to the office
> In his new bi-aeroplane
> And talks by wireless telephone
> To Uncle John—in Spain
> Mother goes a-shopping
> She buys things more or less
> And has them sent home C.O.D.
> Via "Monorail Express."
> Sister goes a-calling
> She stays here and there a while
> And discusses with her many friends
> The latest Martian style
> And when her calling list is through
> She finds a library nook
> And there with great enjoyment hears
> A new self-reading book.

Although Dr. Vansant was immensely proud of his son, it was pride that masked a certain uneasiness or even shame. The boy, just like his sisters, had inherited his mother's looks and charismatic, creative personality. The doctor's concern was a classic one in the Victorian age, faced by the German burgher Thomas Buddenbrooks in Thomas Mann's popular novel of the turn of the century: how to hand his thousand-year mercantile line to his artistic son? The doctor knew that there had been two personality types in the Epting and Vansant lines for many generations: the stoic and the creative, the latter manifested in a famous Vansant opera singer who collapsed on a Paris stage during a performance. All four of his children, even "baby"

Eleanor, eleven years old, were precociously creative, and the doctor knew from his colleagues at the Hospital for the Criminally Insane and experts in melancholy, that such gifts could be unhealthy and unproductive, especially in a boy. Discipline, self-denial, honor, and duty, strength in deeds and not words were the elements of Victorian manhood.

In the demanding way of a patriarch who has invested great expectations in his son, Dr. Vansant had groomed Charles from an early age to carry the family torch. He enrolled the boy at age thirteen in a prestigious prep school such as no Vansant had enjoyed—the Episcopal Academy in Philadelphia, whose venerable stone halls were a passage not only to manhood but to the Ivy League and the Philadelphia oligarchy.

But Charles struggled to fit the model. A thin and fragile boy, he failed to hold up to the rigors of baseball, football, cross country, or any of the varsity sports that allowed a boy to proudly wear the E on his sweater. Instead, he tried hard to position himself as the rakish class wit. In his graduation picture for the class of 1910, he is wearing the standard dark suit and high starched Arrow collar, but he is the only one in the class sporting a gold watch fob and chain—styling himself in an acceptable masculine image of the day, the Edwardian dandy. Later at Penn, Charles tried out for the French Club and German dramatic society.

Thus the doctor, seeing in his son a feminine spirit, urged him into business, and pressed upon him the need to develop stoicism through physical, manly pursuits.

The central question for the doctor involved the boy's manliness. Eugene Vansant wasn't alone in his worries. His colleagues at the club shared a deep concern for the femininity of their own sons. It was a larger concern, too, of the President. In the Industrial Age, Woodrow Wilson said, young men lost the attachment of a father and work that bound them through history. Men left the farm, the stable, and smithy for the factory and office, leaving their sons home in the company of women. Concerned about the softening of boys in the Victorian age, Baden-Powell founded the Boy Scouts, where "manliness was taught by men, and not by those who are half men, half old women." All-boy prep schools soared in popularity to provide surrogate fathering: to remove a boy from the world of his mother and five o'clock teas, "from the contagion of his sisters' company . . . and thence to Rugby."

Feminine softness was a difficult reputation for any young man, especially in an age when President Roosevelt rallied the nation to the "strenuous life." By 1913, the best-known and highest-paid author in the world was Jack London, the adventure writer who believed life was a "testing ground of the strong." Size, strength, and gusto were paramount—the bigness of bridges and railroads, steamships and skyscrapers, the Standard Oil Company, the big stick of American imperialism abroad. Life was a competition of beasts, a social Darwinist struggle for supremacy, with mankind prevailing over the lower orders and superior men triumphing above all others. Charles and his friends could quote by heart the new naturalist philosophy, from Frank Norris, from Upton Sinclair—and from Jack London's *The Sea Wolf*:

> I believe that life is a mess. It is like yeast, a ferment, a thing that moves or may move for a minute, an hour, a year, or a hundred years, but in the end will cease to move. The big eat the little that they may continue to move, the strong eat the weak that they retain their strength. The lucky eat the most and move the longest, that is all.

The Sea Monster

⤬

The great white shark swimming in the warm waters of the
Gulf Stream was adapted to live anywhere in the world, in
the Gulf of Alaska and the Mediterranean, off the coasts of
Formosa and southern Chile. In cooler waters, its vascular system warmed the blood flowing to its eyes and brain, a genetic
response enabling it to live and hunt in waters of widely vary-
ing temperature. Its migration north along the eastern seaboard
of the United States was a thoughtless, instinctual action, but
the shark was not the pea-brained creature it is often portrayed

to be. The great white, in fact, possesses a large and complex brain. Theoretically, it could be trained, were the task not unthinkably dangerous. As it swam and grew, the shark adapted and learned by experience, but the ability to reason, suggested some experts, was beyond it. "Reasoning implies the ability to integrate experience, forethought, rationality, learning . . . into a complex decision-making process," ichthyologist George Burgess of the University of Florida's Museum of Natural History says. "Sharks, like most animals, simply react in predetermined ways that, from an evolutionary standpoint, are clearly effective—or else they wouldn't be here any longer! That's why white sharks don't hold grudges, and don't spare women and children . . ."

Most of its brain is given over to enormous olfactory lobes, and thus it has been called a "brain of smell." It can smell prey a quarter-mile away. Sharks have been observed, writes Thomas B. Allen in *The Shark Almanac*, trailing bathers in the shallows who had scratches on their legs. According to the zoologist A. D. Hasler, "We are concerned here with a sense of such refined acuity that it defies comparable attainment by the most sensitive instruments of modern chemical analysis."

Bathers with cut fingers may have been a mild curiosity to most sharks, but the young great white faced more pressing problems now. Competition among the large predators in the Gulf Stream was intense.

After days, the great current passed on without it. The Gulf Stream plunged north, roiling past the coasts of New York, Massachusetts, New Hampshire, and Maine, turning east at Nova Scotia to cross the Atlantic to England. Somewhere approximately seventy miles east of New Jersey, a looping wave, a fluke current, whirled the shark out of the mighty stream. Suddenly, the crowds were gone. Even surrounded by prey in the Gulf Stream, it had failed to sustain itself. And now, the crowds had gone. The small pelagic fish, the helpless prey, had disappeared.

Six hundred feet beneath the shark, the continental shelf was lush in bottom fishes—rake and cod, ling and porgies—a short dive for a great white, but this shark had grown used to hunting the surface, and passed over the bottom feeders.

The young great white was lost, pulled by a stray plume of the Gulf Stream. Of all the fish in the sea, it was the deadliest, yet, ironically, the first to suffer from damage to the ecosystem, the most likely to go extinct. It was the cost of scarcity: For the ecosystem to remain in balance, the great white must forever skirt extinction.

The great fish's environment had not just diminished, it had disappeared. Perhaps it was attacked and injured by a larger predator. What motivated it is unknown. What is known is that it became a rare "rogue" member of its species—a deranged individual apex predator, a behavior seen in man-killing lions and elephants in Africa. And in human beings. "It was the equivalent," says George Burgess, "of a serial killer." At the dawn of the twentieth century, this comparison was not yet available, as human serial killers were not known. In the parlance of the time, it was a sea monster.

Soon other currents and scents, like the ones that had snatched it into the giant stream, began to work on the young shark, pulling it west. Prey was still scarce, its hunger growing, but the water was getting shallower, and all its senses told it that this at least was a good thing. It was nearing shore and its more abundant prey.

It was sometime in late June when an especially powerful and new scent began to flow from the coastal streams of New Jersey into the sea. The shark picked up the scent and decided to investigate. If the scent was foreign—the shark may never have encountered human beings—it would have induced caution along with interest. In all encounters it was governed by a rule born inside it: Never start a fight you can't win. In such moments, the shark did not rise much above its customary sluggish pace, reserving all energy for the moment of attack.

Paradise

⮑⮐

Trailing a pennant of thick black coal smoke, the Beach Haven Express steamed toward the glittering sky, the freshening breeze. Five miles from the coast, over the Manahawkin meadows, Charles and his sisters were forced to shut the windows as mosquitoes, gnats, and greenhead flies swarmed the car. The Pullman grew suffocatingly hot.

Straight ahead, set against the horizon and the sea, defining the center of human presence, stood the tall, conical spire of the Engleside Hotel. The great wooden arc had weathered forty years of hurricanes and storms that had ruined many islanders; it was said misfortune never met the Engle family. Just south of the Engleside was Reuben Tucker's community of Tucker's Beach, once America's fashionable first sea resort, now in the course of becoming a ghost town and being consumed by the ocean. In a few years a gale would blast Tucker's Beach clean off the tip of Long Beach Island, creating Tucker's Island, whereupon the waves would complete the process of slowly engulfing two hotels, post office, school, lighthouse, Coast Guard installation, and eighteen homes, until not even the birds had a place to stand.

The Pennsylvania Railroad's Beach Haven station rose nobly from the quagmire like the colonial seat of a distant new territory—a small Queen Anne hymn of dormers and shuttered windows overlooking awesome stretches of sea grass and swamp. A porter from the Engleside rushed forward to hoist suitcases and steamer trunks onto the island's first motorized vehicle, an extended Model-T with a green canopy and ENGLESIDE AUTOBUS stenciled on the door. As Charles disembarked, he posed for a photograph he no doubt planned to treasure as a keepsake. In the photograph he is wearing a black double-breasted suit and boater hat and standing proudly next to the giant black Pennsylvania steam engine, his eyes bright with summertime joy. He is carrying a suitcase in each hand for a long and leisurely stay.

Seeing his son, tall now and filling out, standing by the railroad engine, pleased Dr. Vansant, for the boy was at last coming into his own. After the dandyism of his early years, the male camaraderie and roughhousing he enjoyed in college had hardened him. Charlie, or "Van," as his Penn friends called him, had thrown himself, half naked, into the freshman class fight, and taken a good beating while shouting the class motto, "Wring their necks; smear 'em green; Pennsylvania nineteen fourteen." Like Amory in Fitzgerald's *This Side of Paradise*, he viewed college as a place to "go in for everything" to "see what he was made of." What Van was made of was not just the French Club and German dramatic society, the humor magazine, literary journal, and year-book, but also golf and cricket, baseball, soccer, and crew. He mourned a classmate who died on the *Titanic*, shared the outrage over a plan to make the university coed—"desecrate not the sanc-tity of bachelor hall!"—and drank his way through the senior class banquet with the rest of them, carousing through a revelry of ragtime and vaudeville and feasting, a night memorialized in a ditty he fondly recalled: "Bouillon of clam, filet of sole, a brew made by Anheuser/We see them coming home next day—A lit-tle pale Budweiser." He wasn't the best at anything, except the Wireless Club, of which he was made president senior year, but the young man who disembarked at Beach Haven was a grown man, not just clever but capable and athletic, a fine swimmer, a son a father could be proud of.

If Dr. Vansant felt a wave of foreboding, he could have been forgiven, for the entrance to Long Beach Island recalled his memories of the island as a tragic place in the Age of Ships. Walt Whitman, the bard of Camden, New Jersey, and a fre-quent visitor to the island, wrote of mountainous waves con-cealing "unshovelled ever-ready graves." The doctor knew the shoals off the Barnegat Inlet as the graveyard of the Atlantic in the seventeenth, eighteenth, and nineteenth centuries, the watery tomb of four hundred to five hundred ships and men beyond counting. The schooner *Powhatan* breached by a wave that swept to their deaths all twenty-nine crew and three hun-dred and eleven passengers, German immigrants bound for New York; a passenger ship from Liverpool, grounded on the bar in a winter gale, thirty souls perishing from the cold; the New

Orleans packet *Auburn*, loaded with cotton and hemp, lost with nineteen of her crew; the schooner *Surprise*, of Baltimore, down with another thirty men. By the bay was a mass grave of fifty souls who had washed onto the beach from the *Powhatan*, including a mother and baby who were still said to haunt the island.

Miles Carey, the Engleside's porter, signaled the official start of vacation as he cried, "Engle-siiiiide!" ushering the final stragglers aboard the autobus. Woody, his rival from the New Baldwin Hotel, boomed "New Baaldwin!" It was a beloved annual ritual to the Philadelphia summer colony that ended up in the local newspaper and letters home and memories long after other events faded. Adding to the majesty of the scene was a new feeling of importance for the summer colony at Beach Haven. The four-times-a-day Pullman from Philadelphia to Beach Haven was truly extraordinary. The newspapers boasted of the future of Beach Haven as a great coastal city now that the mighty Pennsylvania Railroad had reaffirmed its importance. Beach Haven was six miles at sea, advertised as farther from land than any New Jersey resort, free of "land breezes" and pollen. The American Medical Association had endorsed it as one of the finest resorts for sufferers of hay fever on the East Coast. Promoted by Quakers for its rustic and healthful appeal, it billed itself as "the only practical resort in America."

Soon the Vansants were motoring down Beach Haven's main street, Beach Avenue, a baking promenade of sand and crushed shells lined with kerosene lamps and bayberry bushes. Mosquitoes hovered everywhere despite the fortune spent on drainage ditches west of town. To the surprise of Dr. Vansant, who often recommended the island as an escape from allergies, ragweed sprouted on every corner, and goldenrod surfaced in the middle of the street. The railroad had unknowingly imported the seeds with carloads of gravel for the first paved roads. Domestics slowly moved in and out of small shops in the heat, buying fresh meats and groceries for their masters in the hotels and cottages, for there was no refrigeration, and ice-boxes were inadequate. The servants called the street Mosquito Alley.

In a few blocks the autobus turned left into a large park a block long, and there, at the end of the park, facing the sea, was the massive Victorian "stick" architecture of the Engleside. Bunting draped the long veranda on the front of the hotel, American flags flew from porches and peaked roofs, streamers rose from the portico to the turret five stories above. Dust whirled on Engleside Avenue as Packards and Model-Ts, Overlands and Pierce Arrows moved in a continuous stream in front of the hotel. Gone were the lazy days of ships. Robert Engle, eager to build his business, had pressed politicians to build the automobile causeway to the mainland in 1914. Now Beach Haven had an enormous parking garage, and Bay Avenue was called "the automobile speedway through the heart of Beach Haven."

Through the portico, under a wooden sign hand-lettered in Gothic script announcing THE ENGLESIDE, was a changeless world, an Edwardian parlor by the sea. Out on the veranda, gloved waiters served English tea and pastries and offered Philadelphia newspapers. Gentlemen and ladies in promenade dress took a stately constitutional, enjoying the grandeur of the sea from the boardwalk, lifted safely above the muddle of sand and tide. Tennis players volleyed on the clay courts by the ocean, near the grand bathing pavilions, and as the light deepened just so, two or three men and women could often be seen practicing the new fad of *plein-air* painting, recording azure and sapphire seas. The sea breeze carried the pollen and mosquitoes away.

Porters escorted Louisa, the girls, servants, and nannies to the Vansant suite of rooms. In the lobby, Robert Engle warmly greeted his old friend Dr. Vansant. The doctor felt at ease in the refined atmosphere of the Engleside. Two blocks away rose the Victorian turrets of the massive New Hotel Baldwin, owned by a Philadelphia railroad mogul. The Baldwin catered to the sporting and drinking crowd, a "modish" set that made the doctor uncomfortable. At the Baldwin, wine flowed at every meal, dances were held nightly, and women taught the latest ragtime steps such as the grizzly bear, the turkey trot, and the bunny hop. The new music out of New Orleans, jazz, was heard there for the first time that summer of 1916. The Baldwin Grill foamed with German beer at all hours, and during Prohibition, would be a speakeasy disguised as a café, where swells sipped whiskey in teacups. The Engleside remained, to the doctor's taste, a temperance house.

A raucous spirit prevailed at the Baldwin that put a Philadelphia gentleman ill at ease. In the marshes west of the hotel, sportsmen raised Winchesters and Parkers and shot birds out of the sky before such practices were outlawed. Riflemen stood on the shore and picked porpoises off in the surf as cheering crowds watched. Dr. Vansant preferred the quiet elegance of the Engleside, and its emphasis on wholesome exercise, particularly ocean bathing. The doctor recommended swimming and exposure to sea air for a variety of ailments.

A gentle breeze fluttered the white cotton draperies on the windows over the sea, a placid silver-gray mirror glinting here and there in the late sun.

The Engleside tower faced directly on the Atlantic, but the long, narrow body of the hotel stretched back perpendicular to the ocean in respectful retreat from wave and gale. None of the eighty-eight windows on each long side faced the sea, but "every room has a view of the ocean," Engle advertised, "many of both ocean and bay, none with objectionable outlook. The rooms on the third sleeping floor have a large attic between them and the roof." This mercifully let hot air rise beyond the guests in the days before air-conditioning. The hotel was built in 1876 with no electricity, plumbing, or heating, and guests had used candle-lanterns to find their rooms at night; now it boasted new electric lights, a bath on the west end of each hallway, spring beds and hair mattresses in every room, and running water for toilets and sinks in some of the suites. The rusticity summoned pleasant childhood memories for Louisa, for it was the height of elegance of her summers past in the Railroad Age.

In contrast to their surroundings were the elaborate clothes the servants unpacked—cottons, georgettes, silks, and delicately printed satins with gauzes and eyelets and décolletage, the new "modish" checks and stripes and solids, gauzy evening dresses— enough for the Vansant women to change four to six times a day during the summer, which they fully intended to do given the heat and demanding social occasions.

As the servants set up houskeeping, Louisa couldn't escape the niggling sense that something was wrong. Louisa was a flamboyant personality whose highs swept the children into joyful adventures of art, music, and play, and whose lows demonstrated the depths of a mother's concern. She was never quite comfortable at the shore of the new century. Old Philadelphians never warmed to the modern concept, borrowed from the Romantics, of ocean swimming as hedonistic expression of the beauty and freedom of the body. In Louisa's day, the beach was best experienced from the veranda or boardwalk; to enter the water was to risk encounter with undertow, sea creatures, or moral failing, flesh improperly exposed. Louisa's misgivings were more than Victorian prudishness. Many men and women at the turn of the century didn't know how to swim yet threw themselves into the currents and undertow to join the fad. Often, a resort afternoon ended in a drowning.

It was a normal maternal instinct she experienced every day, most acutely in the nineteenth century, when the children were babies and their breathing faltered or their appetite waned and there was nothing she could do but pray until the fear passed. Over the years she had learned to feel secure as the children grew and life amassed its comforting rhythms of normalcy. Yet now the prickle of unease returned.

Charles also unpacked, but didn't linger with his mother and sisters. The temptation to join the first seating for dinner was strong for young men. Robert Engle advertised exclusively in Boston newspapers for summer help, and the dining room was filled with a fresh crop of attractive young Irish waitresses with lilting accents, many of whom the young men ended up dating. But Charles decided to attend the second seating at eight. He said good-bye to his sisters and mother and headed down to the bathhouses.

As the day came to its end, Louisa, wearing a long dress and a wide-brimmed hat, lifted her train and led her daughters downstairs for the customary twilight stroll before their 6:30 seating for dinner. A lady appearing for the evening was an event. Women in long, flowing dresses, corsets pinching in the abdomen and thrusting out the bosom, strolled regally with veils and broad-brimmed hats bedecked with ribbons and towering arrangements of flowers and feathers, the fashionable Gibson Girl style. Many women spent the entire day inside the hotel, attending morning concerts, whiling away the afternoon over whist or bridge, retiring upstairs to rest their delicate constitutions. More adventurous women were directed to the gentler waters west of the hotel, to go crabbing in the bay or sailing with their children across the bay, or to Tuckerton for a picnic along the shores of lovely Lake Pohatcong.

The ocean was the realm of men. The masculine ideal was Richard Harding Davis, the Philadelphia and New York war correspondent and icon of Anglo-Saxon dash and derring-do, the young Ernest Hemingway's hero. It was the custom for a man to take a dip in the ocean every day of his vacation. Many made a hardy show of heading down to the beach during a strong rain or big storm to challenge the waves. It was de rigueur for young men, upon checking into their hotel, to take an immediate dip in the ocean—morning, afternoon, or evening, no matter how cold the water or how rough the weather. It was a test of mettle. To shy away from the ocean was to break the masculine code of a strenuous life set by ex-President Roosevelt.

Louisa found her son on the wide beach playing with a dog. At this hour the sea was nearly deserted. Sand whipped across the boardwalk and beat against the bathing pavilions; dusk was gathering on the horizon. The sea was empty of swimmers. Louisa cast an appraising eye on her son's one-piece black bathing costume, a standard she accepted. Louisa disapproved of the new men's suits that bared the chest, and often, in 1916, got a man arrested. But Louisa's mood lightened. Charles, frolicking with a large, energetic retriever, had drawn attention. The few people on the boardwalk and veranda were watching, amused.

It swelled Louisa's heart to see her son, young and handsome, relaxed and at play for the first time in many months. She was struck by what a fine young man he had become, but it was a bittersweet sight too; it was Charles's last summer away with the family before he married and started his own family, his own life.

Louisa and the girls joined the doctor on the boardwalk. The Vansants, proud of their athletic son, stood looking out over the sea, enjoying the light breeze, the balmy twilight air, the grandeur of the ocean, and the knowledge that a fine dinner and a comfortable bed awaited. The moment was crowned by the joyful sight of Charles charging into the surf, and, to the delight of the small crowd, the dog leaping after him into the waves. Splashing and kicking in tandem, trailing a wake of bubbles and froth, both of them, man and dog, began to swim.

Twins of Darkness

~≈~

Toward the eastern horizon the tide flowed out, away from the sun, and the Engleside tower chased the fleeing waters with its shadow. The great wooden tower lifted lazily toward the summer clouds tinged in burnt copper, its honeycomb of open-air balconies shading wicker rockers. Men with spyglasses stood in glassed-in observation rooms on the rooftop for a last glance of three-masted schooners in the lonely distance. The hundreds of sailing craft that adorned the coast during the day had vanished. In the floors below, guests drew hot baths as the hotel windmill spun, pumping water from an artesian well. Women donned fresh corsets and hoop skirts, desperate that each dress be different from their neighbors', while the men all endeavored to dress exactly alike in white flannels, blue blazers, and neckties. Nannies and servants herded the young upstairs to be dressed for the children's dining room, from which the children would graduate, at age five or six, to dine with the adults.

Robert Engle strolled through his hotel in a crisp Oxford shirt and bow tie. The windows to the sea revealed knots of guests on the veranda, isolated strollers returning on the boardwalk over flattened dunes—all the fruits of a booked hotel, clear weather, and tranquil seas. Guests admired his photographs on a folding screen by the front desk—tennis players on the hotel courts, the wreck of the Sicilian bark *Fortuna* from '08, the lighthouse, claimed by the tides, toppling into the sea. Late-arriving motorists were checking in after a rugged journey across the state over the dirt roads of the Pine Barrens. Their eyes were rimmed with dust in the shape of goggles.

In the oceanfront dining room, with hunt scenes on the walls and chair backs in the shape of lyres, waitresses in crisply starched white uniforms and bobbed hair prepared for the 6:30 dinner seating. There was a small hubbub surrounding a group of sportsmen with sunburned necks and brine-smelling clothes who spoke slightly louder than necessary. The day fishermen had returned grumbling. Beach Haven fishing was legend. Robert Engle trumpeted the abundance of marine life off his beach. But now there was a scarcity that men struggled to explain.

Beach Haven's fish stories were eye-popping in those days, and supported by fact. The ocean abounded, unpolluted and primordial. Mrs. Charles W. Beck caught 258 weakfish in the bay in two and a half hours, including two on a double hook thirty-eight times. Through the inlets whipped great ocean species that were mistaken in those days for "sea monsters": huge manta rays, eight-hundred-pound ocean sunfish. One morning in the summer of 1907, Charles E. Gerhard, a musician with the Philadelphia Orchestra, and his wife waded ankle-deep into the ocean in their bathing suits and discovered the sport of big-game surf fishing. Gerhard cast a line and landed a twenty-pound channel bass. Then came a fifty-five-pounder. Robert Engle had a new activity to promote at the Engleside, with a double benefit: The dining room became famous for fresh fish.

Unknown at the time, thirty-five miles from shore—far out of sight of the rooftop spyglasses—rose an underwater mountain range of huge sand dunes ten miles long and a mile wide: a submerged island from the last ice age. In the 1920s, charter captains would discover this remarkable "Barnegat ridge" swarming with countless squid and other small fish being fed on by bonito, tuna, and false albacore. Rich men on Zane Grey holidays, sailing motor yachts resplendent in mahogany and brass, would be astonished by the tropical species close to the Jersey shore, giant marlin and wahoo. The first blue marlin from the tropics caught on the New Jersey coast was landed at Beach Haven. A visitor to Beach Haven landed a twelve-foot, 1,150-pound mako shark—the largest fish caught, at the time, anywhere in the world.

As men experimented with the new sport of game fishing, they became aware, and wary of, an unpredictable Beach Haven current that doomed the fishermen. During otherwise fine fishing weather, coastal currents would suddenly shift in their flow from a southerly direction to a northerly one. Strange as it seemed, this immediately chilled the coastal waters, and fish refused to bite or left the coast until the current switched and flowed southward, warming the waters again. Such currents were frustrating the fishermen that day. Cool water had moved in along the coast, driving off the menhaden, a southerly species of bait fish that migrated to New Jersey in the summer, drawing game fish. Although it had yet to be discovered, the cool coastal waters were a magnet to *Carcharodon carcharias*, the great white shark.

That evening, as dusk approached, the young shark swam west toward shore. Thrown off by a whirl of the Gulf Stream, deep water where it failed to thrive, it had passed right over the abundant prey of the continental shelf and was becoming a hungry creature, moving slowly toward its natural habitat, the coastline, where the water was rich with enticements. As it approached, there were strong offshore upwellings of cold water common to Long Beach Island in the summertime, chilled water that would attract the big fish yet chase away other species—some of whom no doubt fled, as they always did, upon the arrival of the apex predator. The large prey fishes it had fed on in the shallows or the subtropics were gone.

Seven miles from shore, the shark began to pick up a stream of information. It smelled the rich cocktail of organisms washed to the coastline from rivers and inlets swollen with heavy summer rain. This triggered a genetic message: prey. But it smelled something else, something that didn't fit the automatic profile to hunt, but required what the great white would experience as a mild curiosity . . . a strong, disconcerting lure. Human waste, the product of urban development, was being pumped off the New Jersey coast then for the first time.

Two to three miles from shore, its progress was halted by a vast net suspended perpendicular to the coast, stretching six miles straight out to sea and covering every inch of potential passage from the surface to the bottom of the ocean. This was the first of some twenty-five fish "pounds" strung like a series of labyrinths along the coast of Long Beach Island. The pound fishermen hung the net from a series of ninety-foot poles of North Carolina hickory buried in the ocean bottom and rising above the waves like the masts of a shipwreck. The pound was framed on the three sides and bottom with great nets, forming an immense boxed trap. The island's thriving pound industry, second only to tourism, landed ten million pounds of fish a year. Even if the traps were empty, given the scarcity of fish, the surrounding coastal waters were habitually flush with the by-product of industry—guts and offal from cleaned fish— a cocktail of the living and the dead that drew the shark toward shore.

Something else, people of the time believed, attracted the shark. Another "sea monster," black and torpedo-shaped and glistening with dark water, surfaced on the East Coast later that night. It was the German U-boat *Deutschland*, 315 feet long, the largest submarine ever built and the first to cross the Atlantic. It inspired awe and fear, and the press described it as having "eyes like a monster sea dog"—an ancient reference to the great white shark.

The *Deutschland* slipped beneath the English blockade and four thousand miles of waves while the crew drank French champagne, read translations of Shakespeare and Mark Twain, and played selections from *Peer Gynt* on the phonograph. Although it was carrying only cargo, not weapons, as a German U-boat it alarmed Americans—the previous year a U-boat sank the passenger liner *Lusitania*, killing 128 Americans. For the rest of the summer of 1916, the great white shark and the German U-boat would be linked, in editorials, cartoons, and letters to the editor, as invading twins of darkness on an innocent American shore. People speculated that the submarine attracted the shark as they shared the same waters, but in fact if the shark ever spied the U-boat—thirty-five times larger than itself—it would have simply fled.

Sensing intense organic activity, the young white picked up speed, perhaps to five miles an hour, in the direction of shore.

Red in Tooth and Claw

◄ ❧ ►

Charles stood knee-deep in the shallow surf, feet planted on the soft golden sand, the outgoing tide gently swirling about his calves. His feet were pale from indoor work and fully visible in the cool, clear water. The breeze was mild, the sun pale and forgiving in the late hour, the ocean bottom free of seaweed. This was why people from the great West, as far as St. Louis, rode the Pennsylvania Railroad to the bather's paradise of the Jersey shore. It was a place of legendary beauty, a place to feel *alive*. Even with calm weather and high blue skies, Charles could feel the whisper of an undertow, the faint rocking motion of distant waves, the immense tug of the sea. He looked out at the flat surface of the ocean, which concealed the softly sloping coast for which South Jersey was famous. Ahead bobbed the diving platform Robert Engle had installed in front of his hotel for the new season; in the distance floated a line of salmon clouds. The water was chilly, but in a few moments Charles would be used to it. Behind him he could hear the dog splashing and paddling toward him. It was a red Chesapeake Bay retriever, the only American breed in the American Kennel Club, a rugged, tireless seventy-five-pound bird dog. Charles recognized the breed on sight, for any man who handled a rifle—and Charles had been a member of the gun team at the university—admired the beautiful water hunter of the vast Maryland bay. The Chessie had the steadiest of retriever personalities, sound of judgment, biddable but not silly, a stout worker bred to partner with man. He and Charles bonded instantly. There really was no way, once the dog bowed deep into its front paws to signal play, that the dog could be prevented from following him into the water. Or that Charles could resist the charms of the Chessie. He had grown up with dogs and longed to have one again.

The dog was paddling hard now, approaching fast. Charles could hear the splashing and knew without looking—an instinct all mammals share—that something was bearing close, and he reacted instinctively and dove to stay ahead of the dog: two species playing, communing across the waves. With a rush of coolness along his torso, the man swam, joining the blissful tumble of the deep, falling into the master stroke of the nineteenth century, which he was taught was the most natural form in the water, an imitation of the frog: the breaststroke. It was fashionable in Charles's time to celebrate the effortless, instinctive nature of being in the water, the first human home. It was said that the ocean flowed in the veins, that blood was nearly the consistency of seawater. In the ocean a man escaped the Industrial Revolution and rediscovered his eternal self, was fully human again. After a few strokes, as he adjusted to the water, Charles stretched into a crawl, the master stroke of the new century, recently popularized for its speed and power. The dog followed.

As man and dog swam out in a line, they joined the sweeping canvas the ocean offers the shore, the portrait of white-tipped sea that stirs feelings the Romantics believed only artists and poets could experience. The ocean swelled to meet them, waves lifted them up and rolled on toward the coast, where they broke on the sands and withdrew with a prolonged hiss. Charles closed his eyes as his face turned rhythmically into the sharp, cold brine, feeling the rush of coolness along his torso, eyes stung with saltwater as he stroked in measure with the cadence of the swells. The dog kicked with all four legs beneath the surface, a force that lifted its head above the waves and left its shaggy tail floating in a trail of froth. At the same time, unseen beneath the surface, other waves traversed the shallows and the deep, waves of differing lengths and speeds but all of the same flawless contour and pattern of the breakers—underwater waves shooting across the spectrum in multichannel cacophony.

Far out at sea, swimming steadily, the young shark received a faint signal. Currents were washing against the thin steel cable that rooted the diving platform of the Engleside Hotel to the bottom, causing it to vibrate and issue infinitesimal waves of sound from its anchorage one hundred feet from the beach. These waves exploded seven miles out to sea in less than eight seconds, moving at more than three thousand miles an hour, rhythmic, constant, reaching a sensitive line of nerves embedded in the head of the fish, the head that turned slowly side to side to improve the chances of favorable reception. The faint sound waves grew stronger, more regular, and the shark made a tiny adjustment in direction. The great fish swam directly into the wave of sound, which broke and scattered over its huge pyramidal head, as it began, ever so slightly, to move faster.

Emerging from the deep, in perhaps fifty feet of water, the shark sensed something different. Long, powerful, irregular noises began to batter its conical head, a wild mixed signal. A suprahuman detective, it cruised at fifteen miles an hour while instantly processing information across the spectrum. An image appeared in its brain, an electronic projection, a pulsing outline of two objects moving near the surface. The shark could detect microscopic urine particles in the water: *Mammals.* Each movement broadcast sounds and scent and an electronic trail, an aura of impulses.

Charles was the strongest swimmer in the water now, his arms and legs indicating one thing to the shark: *Large prey.* Then there was the dog. It is now known that a man who swims in shark-infested waters with a dog greatly enhances his odds of being attacked by a shark nearby, according to ichthyologist George Burgess, who directs the International Shark Attack File, a compilation of well-known shark attacks. "The irregular swimming actions of animals are extremely attractive to sharks. The front paws doggy-paddling, creating a maximum splash, the rear legs bicycle-pedaling, four rapidly moving legs making a blending motion at the surface couldn't be a whole lot more attractive." In 1987, off Panama City, Florida, a man jumped from his boat to go swimming. His girlfriend lowered his poodle into the water, and within moments a large bull shark removed much of the man's leg, killing him instantly. The Shark Attack File is filled with accounts of sharks drawn to human victims by the erratic thrashing of a paddling dog. That afternoon in 1916, sound waves from the seventy-five-pound dog drummed on the great fish's head with feral intensity, a jagged, broken signal of distress.

The shark swam nearer, preparing to launch its signature attack—sudden, surprising, relentless. Charles stroked smoothly and happily, unaware he was being profiled. The great white was closing in.

A small crowd on the beach watched as Vansant, a strong swimmer, stroked out beyond the breakers. They were as a group in that moment, standing on the edge of time in 1916, wise in ways moderns are not, educated in the classics and myths, more in touch with the sea. Sperm whales were the oil fields of their time, the ocean the highway. But these people lived before modern oceanography, before radio and television, and were no more prepared to witness the first man-eating shark in American history rise from the waves than to see Captain Nemo's *Nautilus* surface from the abyss. Who could blame them if they saw a "sea monster"?

There were other ghosts of antiquity the Edwardians saw along the beach that evening, visions that enchanted them in the pleasing form of a young man and dog at play in the simple theater of the sea. The virile young athlete was an Edwardian icon. Dorian Gray, *The Wind in the Willows*, *Peter Pan*, and the Boy Scouts revealed the cultural worship of Pan, who "is not dead," Robert Louis Stevenson declared. In reaction to industrialism and Victorian repression, the young man who never grows old led "the whole earth in choral harmony." Charles was eager to prove his vitality, and there was no finer place to do so than at the beach, his form and vigor on display in society as they were nowhere else. "The surf," according to beach historians Lena Lencek and Gideon Bosker, "emerged as an area in which the strong were separated from the weak, where young males played out the drama of natural selection before the eyes of discriminating females."

In the late afternoon of July the first, Charles was swimming the Atlantic to see how far he could go. Long-distance swimming was an adventure that enthralled the public. Charles did not slow his stroke when he and the Chesapeake retriever had passed all the swimmers in the water. This earned a small cheer from shore. Unknown to Charles, he had entered a wilderness, and his desire to set himself apart led him to violate a fundamental rule of nature: Stay with the group. A lone mammal, exposed and vulnerable, invites a predator. In a study of great white shark behavior by George Burgess and Matthew Callahan using data from the International Shark Attack File, no other humans were within ten feet of the victim in 85 percent of the attacks. As Charles was being feted and admired from the beach and boardwalk, he was being observed, as well, underwater.

Fifty feet away, in deeper water, the great white was mulling whether to attack. Far from our image of a mindless killer that overwhelms its victims, the great white takes no chances when challenging prey. Once a great white decides the odds favor it, the decision is beyond appeal, the attack relentless.

As the crowd on the beach studied the tableau of man and dog, suddenly, with no apparent reason, the retriever turned back toward shore. Witnesses thought the dog tired out, simply swam too far. Charles was the victor in the amusing play.

Charles turned around, too, treading water, and called out to the dog, enticing it to return. But the retriever, climbing onto the beach, shook itself off and remained on the sand, looking out at the man in the water. On the boardwalk and beach, people waited for a resolution to the drama. The Vansant girls saw Charles give up the game. He was coming in.

But as Charles swam toward shore, a bystander on the beach noticed something odd. A dark fin appeared in the water behind the young man. At first it was mistaken for a porpoise, a sight people were accustomed to then. But porpoises were known to roll in schools parallel to the coast; this fin was alone and moving swiftly toward shore in the direction of the young man. Someone on the beach cried across the waves, "Watch out!" As the fin approached, the chorus grew: "Watch out! Watch out!"

But Charles could not hear the warnings. He was turning his head in and out of the water in a rhythmic crawl. The great white could see his prey now moving underwater with startling clarity, making what followed even more unusual. For in the great majority of shark attacks on humans, sharks are hurtling through roiling, cloudy water in which they must strike quickly to seize their prey. The flash of a pale foot resembles the darting of a snapper, a belt buckle winks in the sun like a fish scale, and the shark bites. But the great white saw Charles Vansant clearly and kept coming. In the last instant, some researchers have suggested, it detected the final confirmation of mammal: the blood pounding through Charles's veins. *The thumping of his heart.*

In that moment, an awful feeling swept over Vansant as the continued cries, louder now, "Watch out!" rang from the beach. Seconds before the attack, a shiver traveled down his spine—humans are gifted, as are all large mammals, with the instinctive ability to detect that they are being hunted. As the creature's shadow merged with his on the bright, sandy floor of the sea, Charles experienced an adrenal explosion, the overpowering natural urge to live. He was in only three and a half feet of water, close to shore. Safety was at hand. But it was too late.

The great jaws rose from the water, a white protective membrane rolled over the eyes, fifty triangular teeth closed with more than six tons of pressure per square inch, and man and fish splashed in a spreading pool of blood. One bite. One massive, incapacitating bite tearing into the left leg below the knee. Charles screamed in mortal agony, a scream that resonated to the beach and tennis courts and veranda. The attack had taken less than a second, but now time began to slow down. His parents and sisters and the crowd of onlookers stood transfixed in horror and disbelief.

Charles still screamed, numb with terror, trying to free himself from the vise of fifty large serrated teeth, but he, too, had little idea what was happening to him. He went into shock, and even as shock subsided, despite the gruesome wound, he felt, incredibly, a minimum of pain. As strange as it seems, it is common for shark attack victims to experience "painless torture"—to greatly underestimate the severity of their wounds. Some experts suggest the first bite produces massive nerve damage or somehow numbs the victims of pain. One neurophysiologist calls this phenomenon "non-opiate stress-induced analgesia." A body of anecdotal evidence compiled over many years suggests that under great stress, soldiers, athletes, and other people don't seem to "feel" pain—perhaps, experts say, because pain in the most life-threatening situations is not advantageous for the survival of the species.

People onshore had no frame of reference for what was happening. "The young man was bathing in only three and a half feet of water," remembered W. K. Barklie, a Philadelphia businessman on the beach that day. "We thought he was joking until we saw the blood redden the water."

Charles fought valiantly, but his struggle to free himself only tightened the shark's grip on his femoral artery: the great teeth ground down to the bone. Witnessing their son being devoured by a predator, Dr. and Mrs. Vansant were numb with shock and pain that would shadow them for the rest of their lives. But Louise, the middle sister, kept her wits about her as she witnessed a sight she would never forget: "Everyone was horrified to see my brother thrashing about in the water as if he were struggling with some monster under the surface," Louise recalled. "He fought desperately, and as we rushed toward him we could see great quantities of blood."

Then, as if a spell were broken, men entered the water to rescue the young man as shouts arose from the beach.

What followed baffled shark researchers for decades: The great white backed off in the red-tinged surf, pieces of Charles Vansant's calf and femoral artery in its mouth, and appeared to be waiting. Twenty years later, in the summer of 1936 in Buzzards Bay, Massachusetts, a great white provided a clue to the shark's behavior in Beach Haven in the summer of 1916. That summer, a fourteen-year-old boy swimming in shallow water was savagely bitten by a great white. As the boy screamed and floundered in a balloon of blood, the shark was observed "standing off in the blood-reddened water but a few yards away, seemingly ready to make another attack—and why it did not is inexplicable."

The reason is brutally simple, according to John E. McCosker, director of San Francisco's Steinhart Aquarium. The great white employs a classic predatory technique once practiced by the saber-toothed tiger. The extinct tiger hunted the woolly mammoth by biting it once and standing back. So, too, soldiers are trained to make an easy shot for the stomach instead of the trickier shot to heart or head. The sure, deadly shot echoes the primitive logic of the massive first bite and retreat. Avoid needless confrontation. Expend no more energy than necessary. Take no chances.

The great white was waiting for Vansant to bleed to death.

First to reach the surf line was Alexander Ott, an excep-

tional swimmer, who later became a champion and a swimming showman with Johnny Weismuller in the 1920s. His decision to enter bloodied water where a shark was taking its prey
took extraordinary courage. Ott swam swiftly, but by the time
he reached Vansant in waist-deep water, the fight was over. The
young man was struggling not to drown in a cloud of his own
blood. The shark had vanished. Quickly Ott hoisted Vansant
under the arms and began to tow him to shore. It was then that
Ott felt a powerful tug in the opposite direction, and realized
with horror that the shark had hit Vansant again and fastened
to his thigh. The shark and Ott were in a tug-of-war with
Vansant's body. The shark appeared to Ott to be black, ten feet
long, and five hundred pounds. It was unimaginably strong, he
thought. He cried for help.

More men rushed into the water and formed a human
chain with Ott, frantically trying to free Vansant from the jaws
of the shark. Vansant was still conscious, struggling to escape,
but the great teeth held fast; the creature was an eating
machine of inconceivable power. The human chain had succeeded in pulling Charles nearly to the beach—but the great
white followed, its massive conical body scraping the sands. The
monster was *coming onto the beach*. Then, suddenly, it was gone,
a whirl of foam trailing the dark fin as it submerged. "The
shark held on until it scraped bottom," Barklie recalled, "then
it let go and swam away." Profound shock had momentarily
seized the people on the sands. They had no context for what
had happened; there was no way for them to know that sharks,
in other times and other lands, followed their human victims
right up onto land. It was unthinkable, alien, awful confirmation of a Darwinian truth the Victorians had long denied:
Nature was "red in tooth and claw." There was no way for them
to know that the popular new sport of recreational swimming,

fueled by expanding wealth, industry, and human population, had brought the nightmare of centuries of sailors to shore.

Charles lay crumpled on the beach, bleeding profusely. Men and women rushed to his side, some out of love, others out of morbid curiosity; still others, unable to look, turned away.

Louise Vansant, who had kept composure during the attack, almost fainted when she approached her brother. "The terrible story was revealed," she said. "His left leg had been nearly torn off."

A Doctor in the House

❦

D r. Eugene Vansant flew down the boardwalk steps, onto the sand, and rushed to the fallen figure of his son. Ott and Barklie moved aside to make room, and Eugene kneeled on the beach and took Charles's hand. The young man was lying on his back, his left leg a bloodied mass, blood pouring from the wound and pooling with the soft, receding tide. His face was a ghastly white, and he moaned in pain, reeling toward unconsciousness. Eugene put his fingers to his son's wrist; the boy's pulse was weakening. His eyes signaled that he recognized his father. There was little time.

Dr. Vansant removed his jacket and vest, rolled up his sleeves, and ordered that no one touch the wound. Germ theory was one of the principal findings of Dr. Vansant's lifetime, and Vansant operated in sterile whites instead of a black business suit, as he had once done. But no modern supplies were available now. The doctor's mind raced as he was thrown back on his training in nineteenth-century medicine. He had never seen such a wound. What in the Lord's name had caused it? Was it suffused with animal poisons? It appeared like a wound of war, but it was a bite. He recalled the wisdom of his teachers—men who were legendary doctors from the Crimean War, the Civil War, and the Spanish-American War. His mentor, Dr. Samuel David Gross, wrote *The Manual of Military Surgery* in 1861 at the request of Lincoln and Ulysses S. Grant. It became the classic Union guide to amputations on the battlefield, using chloroform and a bone saw. Confederate doctors used it too, adding a sip of brandy to soften a man's will for the procedure. But now there was little available but brandy, and nothing could be done, Dr. Vansant realized, until the bleeding was stopped.

Alexander Ott, the heroic swimmer, tore strips of fabric from a woman's dress to use as a tourniquet, but the rush of blood barely slowed. Soon Dr. Herbert Willis, a future mayor of Beach Haven, joined Dr. Vansant at his son's side, along with Dr. Joseph Neff, former director of public health in Philadelphia. The three medical men inspected the wound and conferred. A fish bite of such magnitude was outside their experience. The bleeding was so profuse that the doctors feared Charles wouldn't survive an automobile ride to the nearest hospital in Toms River, thirty miles northwest.

Engle suggested they move the young man back to the hotel, where there was water, soap, and bandages. Dr. Vansant helped carry his son to the hotelier's office. There the men quickly unscrewed the hinges of Engle's office door and laid it across two desks as an operating table, a familiar sight to Dr. Vansant, for it resembled the legendary old wooden operating table in the Jefferson Hospital operating theater. But little else during the crisis was familiar, and it was soon evident that in the hour of his son's direst need, Dr. Vansant wasn't quite sure what to do. This pained him terribly, both as a father and as a physician, dredging up memories he would rather never have re-encountered. For many years, it was suspected by his peers in nineteenth-century medicine that Vansant wasn't properly trained to handle an emergency. The criticism may have been unfair, but it weighed heavily on him since his main critic was the legendary Dr. Gross, the venerable "father of American surgery."

Gross was immortalized in the most famous medical painting of the nineteenth century, Thomas Eakins's masterpiece *The Gross Clinic*, in which the renowned professor stands in black street clothes, raising a bloody scalpel to make a lecture point, having made an incision in a young man's leg without sterilization procedures, which were unknown. In the gloom of the operating theater—lit only by skylight—a black-cowled woman, apparently the boy's mother, covers her face in agony.

Vansant heard the grandiose white-haired professor's admonitions in his dreams. Gross had warned that to leave the ranks of legitimate practitioners for a narrow specialty was to forgo the proper education of a medical man, to risk inability to recognize general problems in the major organs and extremities of the body, to be helpless in a crisis. Gross once introduced the most distinguished laryngologist of the nineteenth century, Dr. Jacob da Silva Solis-Cohen, to a lecture hall as a man "who devotes most of his time to a cubic inch of the human anatomy," adding, "Someday I suppose we will have specialists confining themselves to diseases of the navel."

The sight of his son also recalled and magnified the feelings of doubt and helplessness Dr. Vansant had suffered upon the sickness and death of his other sons, Eugene Jr. and William. In Engle's office, Dr. Vansant assisted in cleaning and bandaging the wound, but the bleeding remained profuse. He discussed with the other doctor transporting Charles to a hospital by motorcar, but the wound was so severe, they agreed he would not reach the hospital in time. Half a century later, Vansant's wound would have been considered relatively minor for a shark attack, medium-severity arterial damage, which "the victim usually survives if correct [modern] treatment is administered on the beach," according to South African doctors D. H. Davies and G. D. Campbell in *The Aetiology, Clinical Pathology and Treatment of Shark Attack*. But that evening, at 6:45, an hour after he entered the water for a swim, Charles Epting Vansant died of shock and massive hemorrhaging on Robert Engle's office door. Dr. Eugene LaRue Vansant looked on helplessly as his son died.

Within a year, grief would age him terribly, turn his hair completely white, and leave him a stooped and beaten man.

That evening a hush fell over the Engleside dining room. But after dinner, hotel guests cornered fishermen and baymen and other wizened veterans of the shore who drifted on and off of the veranda all night long. The red trails of pipes and cigars waved in the night, and the number of people who had witnessed the attack seemed to grow by the hour. Robert Engle tried to remain stoic and calm as reporters from Philadelphia newspapers scuttled about the lobby and veranda, questioning his guests. Disagreements and arguments broke out, until finally a consensus emerged of suspects in young Vansant's death: a giant tuna, a shark, but most likely a great sea turtle, which had the power, the fishermen said, to snap a man in half. The attending physician had a different opinion. He recorded the primary cause of death on Vansant's death certificate as "hemorrhage from femoral artery, left side," with the contributory cause being "bitten by a shark while bathing." It was the first time a shark bite had appeared as an official cause of death in U.S. history. Seeking to reassure his guests, Engle stood and declared bathers had nothing to worry about—the next morning, the hotel would erect a netting around the beach strong enough to block German U-boats. Swimming in the clear, paradisal waters of the Engleside would go on as usual.

But a somber mood pervaded the Engleside that evening as one by the one the hundreds of room lights that cast out over the shore winked out. A new and nameless fear had seized the guests, a fear of the unknown as well as a fear of the sea. Even those who watched the attack had little notion of what they had witnessed, except to agree, as W. K. Barklie told whoever would listen, "Mr. Vansant's death was the most horrible I ever saw."

PART TWO

A Reign of Terror

Screams for Rescue

⤛⤜

All morning the waves came in murmuring softly and occasionally rising out of line and falling in a muffled boom. But the swells were low where the Atlantic City beach canted gently toward the sea, and the bathers breached them easily. The sun was high as Gertrude Schuyler stepped into the surf and splashed seawater on her bathing costume. She glanced back at her husband and eight-year-old daughter on the beach, and then she was in, a cool shock in the beginning, but presently she was accustomed to it. A typist employed in an office in

Manhattan, her skin was porcelain white, city skin, and she glanced longingly at the warm, sun-bright sky, for a "ruddy sunburn" was coming into vogue. Sunburn took a harsh toll on the day-trippers, one of many hazards at the beach in those days. But it is not likely she worried about such things, for she was young and knew little about the sea beyond the excitement of being there. She'd had little experience swimming.

The view out to sea was splendid if a bit overwhelming for a city girl, the sea without end until Europe. Curling at the edges of her vision were the sandy wastes of Absecon Island. The island, she knew, was one hundred miles south of New York, not far north of Cape May. If Gertrude was aware that north across Little Egg Inlet lay Long Beach Island, and that on the island was a small village with a few hotels, she did not know that a shark had killed a man there the day before, or that the shark was now stalking the coast. The story had yet to make the papers. There were no notices on the boardwalk or in the hotels and no warning had been issued by the surfmen (the term for lifeguards then). In a world without radio or television, much of the news that summer traveled with traditional unhurried ease, by post and spoken word in local quarters.

In Beach Haven, Dr. Vansant made arrangements for his son's funeral, and the tragedy shadowed the bright July Fourth festivities at the Engleside Hotel. At the beach in front of the hotel, hundreds of heretofore carefree swimmers were afraid to go back in the water, and none but skillful and daring swimmers entered the breakers. Beach Haven officials, perhaps to protect the tourist trade, cabled no alarm of the attack beyond the hotel. All along the 127-mile Atlantic coast of New Jersey that Sunday, the first documented case in American history of a man taken as shark prey was attended by silence. From Cape May north to Atlantic Highlands, thousands of swimmers blissfully took to the beaches, unaware they shared the water with a rogue shark that had taken human flesh.

When Gertrude Schuyler had boarded the shore train from New York City that morning, the papers were preoccupied with a different undersea predator—the *Deutschland*, the enormous German U-boat menacingly docked in Baltimore Harbor. While the U-boat haunted Americans with the memory of the *Lusitania*, the *Times* reported with some distaste that women were mistakenly for peace at all cost in the European War because of "mother-love." The women's pages, meanwhile, were taken up with the importance of watering peonies during the summer months and baking custard in individual glass dishes, as well as the efficiency of the new electric candles for nurseries. There were significant sales in silk motoring hats and chiffon veils to keep out the dust for comfortable automobiling; modern bathing suits in mohair, satin, taffeta, and poplin could be had for $2.75.

Gertrude was grateful that the sartorial authorities of modern times allowed a woman to don practical bathing suits and sport attire in linen and *crepe de Chines* without the burdens of frivolous charms of fluff and frills of the past. She had been surprised to learn that in Atlantic City that morning, the director of safety had handed down the latest "canons of modesty at the bathing beach." The new law in Atlantic City decreed that on the land side of the boardwalk, "conventionalism shall reign" and men and women would be required to "seek covering for their bathing suits," evincing a "mighty modesty." Seaward of the boardwalk, "where mermaids sport," there may continue to be a "veritable Eden in the innocence of garb . . . nature and loveliness unadorned."

Gertrude Schuyler had demurely uncovered her bathing costume after crossing the boardwalk. Now, after a series of ablutions, she began to stroke along the coast, enjoying the freedom of a swim in shallow water, taking pleasure in the play of cool water over her torso and limbs as she and the water worked together to pull her beyond the crowds.

The new rules heightened the forbidden pleasure of swimming freely. To the first tremulous moderns, the shifting tides and supple boundaries of time and space at the seashore served as a release from the straitjackets of routine and repression. Nowhere was the release more potent than in Atlantic City, with its utopian architecture and great crowds of the new leisurely middle class sharing and affirming the sybaritic pleasures of bathing. Atlantic City at the turn of the century, wrote the Irish playwright James Hannay, was "all the seaside pleasure cities of the world rolled into one, then raised to the third power." There was saltwater taffy and the rambling pleasure of choosing from more restaurants than a reasonable person could count. A stroll on the world's first boardwalk allowed one the pleasure of being at the shore without tracking sand into the trains and hotels. From the boardwalk one could see fully attired "surf dancers"— men in suits and women in fancy dress, dancing in the shallows—and young women in scandalously short swimsuits, chased by the beach police armed with tape measures. Looming over the boardwalk stood a skyline that seemed inspired by Lyman Frank Baum's turn-of-the-century children's book, *The Wonderful Wizard of Oz*.

Gertrude Schuyler planned to join her husband and daughter in the afternoon for a visit to the great hotels designed by William Lightfoot Price, who introduced the modern style to Atlantic City a decade before it reached Paris, declaring, "This is America, and art is the utterance of the living and not the dead."

Rising over the ocean was Price's Marlborough Hotel, an immense Victorian hostelry of gables and turrets, circa 1902, with a tiny extra window conspicuously positioned on the side of each room. Price's public boast was that the Marlborough possessed the luxury, unheard-of then, of a private bath in every guest room. Connected by a bridge to the Victorian hotel was the Blenheim, a sultan's palace with Moorish domes. The fifteen-story tower of the Blenheim was the world's largest cement building built on sand, and people feared it would fall down. Beyond the Marlborough-Blenheim loomed the still-grander Traymore, nicknamed the sandcastle, an enormous beige pile of domed turrets that rose over the ocean.

The Traymore was an Edwardian wonder. Thomas Edison had developed the cement used in its huge art deco towers, and N. C. Wyeth painted the children's playroom with characters from *Treasure Island.* In the hotel restaurant, the Submarine Grill, Wyeth created a mural of mermaids, flying fish, and mermen rising to a ceiling that was a glass-bottomed aquarium-skylight through which sunlight streamed to the diner at the "bottom of the sea." In the music room, framed by classical columns, stood a fountain, in the center of which floated a hollow crystal globe. Tiny goldfish passing through the globe were magnified to monstrous size.

But the ultimate pleasure, increasingly rare in the big cities, was the joy of separating from the crowds. As Gertrude Schuyler swam farther out, the swirls of light reflected by the sand dulled and the water deepened to an opaque blue-green. Under the surface, small, silvery fish flickered. Above, steamers edged along the horizon, traced by swooping gulls, and as the bather traversed the border between sea and sky, it was said habit dissolves and one's sense of wonder is renewed.

The surfmen stood on the beach, coolly eyeing the horizon and sea and crowds as if by standing still they could somehow take it all in, eyes alert for unusual movement. The surfmen were assisted by athletic young volunteers who strutted about with spools on their belts containing five yards of stout rope to toss to distressed swimmers. The surfmen had their hands full that day: There were thousands of people in the water now, a number that would grow, by day's end, to fifty thousand. The director of safety of Atlantic City, in addition to protecting innocent bystanders from the shudders and chance bewilderment of spying a swimsuit worn by one of the freaks of fashion in all its filmy brevity, also boasted the coast's largest and best-trained rescue platoon. On the beach stood long, stout poles to which rescuers tied their ropes to tow upset swimmers to shore, ropes pulled by chains of men opposing the sea in a kind of tug-of-war.

Thousands of men, and women too, draped the boardwalk rails, surveying the panorama of shore and sea like swells departing on the *France* or the *Rotterdam;* for the masses it was the nearest experience to being aboard an ocean liner. Men in hats leaning elbow to elbow, women carrying embroidered sun umbrellas pushed along in Shill's wicker rolling chairs.

In the random arithmetic of crowds, someone would have noticed Gertrude Schuyler in trouble before the surfmen. At a distance, her hands waved soundlessly in the warm air, and around her a patch of sea frothed white. There were so many people in the water, it would have taken great concentration, or luck, for the surfmen to hear the screams.

Gertrude Schuyler had been swimming, when suddenly without warning an overpowering force pulled her under. She was in the grip of something unimaginably strong, against which struggle was useless.

In an instant she was gone. She flailed her arms before they disappeared. Resurfacing for a moment, she made one panicked shout for help, and then all one could hear were the frightful screams of men and women whose worst nightmare of the beach was realized.

One of the surfmen must have seen her, because swiftly several surfmen and rescue volunteers rushed to the point where the water had whitened, their lifeboat splitting the waves. The trick was to keep one's head above the waves and break sideways out of the grip of the thing. Whether luck or divine assistance came to Gertrude Schuyler is not known, but momentarily she was free and in the arms of rescuers. Long minutes later she was back on the beach, coughing up seawater and accepting comfort from her husband and concerned strangers. Exciting plans for touring Atlantic City's amusements had given way to the gratitude of being alive. It was a stunning if unflattering story for Gertrude Schuyler to take back on the train: She had nearly drowned.

The pattern was disturbingly familiar to Atlantic City's surfmen. Eleven times that Sunday they heard screams for rescue; eleven times the surfmen and volunteers rushed into the water with ropes and pulled men and women to safety. Drownings were common at the time before learning to swim was a childhood rite of passage. "A burst of panic, a few quick minutes of struggle, a few scattered bubbles, and another casualty was added to the list," according to beach historians Bosker and Lencek. Undertow was the terrifying shadow on the sun-bright days at the Jersey shore. Bathing expert Dr. John H. Packard, surgeon at the Episcopal Hospital of Philadelphia, believed day-trippers were in particular danger. They "know nothing of the beaches and venture far more than those who do. Often they cannot swim, and are helpless when in danger," he wrote.

That evening on the train, as Gertrude Schuyler returned with her husband and daughter to New York with hundreds of others, bearing the "badges of pleasure and leisure"—sunburn,

windburn, a few hands and faces swollen from jellyfish stings—
conversations turned inevitably to the dangerous sea, yet with no
reference to a shark, for there was no known shark to fear.

Not until the next day, Monday, July third, was the existence
of a dangerous sea creature on the shore publicly known. Readers had to turn deep inside the *Philadelphia Evening Bulletin*
to learn of the death of the son of a prominent Philadelphia
family two days earlier in a mysterious attack at sea. Charles
Vansant's death was overshadowed by the news that a Philadelphia society woman, Mrs. Florence Burling, had been granted a
divorce from the notable Mr. Arthur Burling. It was a scandal
beyond the pale as Mr. Burling had rushed about the immigra-
tion detention house, waving a gun, threatening to shoot
officials who refused to turn over his intended second wife,
whereupon Mr. Burling's would-be second wife was deported as
an undesirable and Mr. Burling was sent to jail. Quite apart
from its scandalous aspects, the story was worrisome to
Philadelphians, for the Burling divorce was one of seventy-two
granted recently in the city. Divorce, unthinkable to the Victorians, was now becoming the American mode.

The same day, *The New York Times*, then reaching its first
greatness under the great editor Carr V. Van Anda, devoted
prominent headlines to local heroes at the shore over the holiday
weekend—the men who'd rescued five passengers from a sinking pleasure boat off Manhattan Beach, and the surfmen who
prevented eleven drownings in Atlantic City. On the last page of
the *Times*, at the bottom of the page, was a small headline over
a brief, four-paragraph story, "Dies After Attack by Fish."

Van Anda's genius was to turn his "death ray" gaze, as his
staffers called it, on the news, penetrating the reality underly-
ing any myth. Four years earlier, while others widely accepted
that the *Titanic* was unsinkable, Van Anda's rapid calls at 1:20

in the morning on April 15, 1912, to *Times* correspondents and agents of the White Star Line had allowed him to deduce, before any newspaperman in America, that the *Titanic* had gone down. During World War I, he correctly dispatched correspondents to the scene of battles yet to occur. Covering the 1922 discovery of the tomb of the Egyptian pharaoh Tutankhamen, Van Anda, who read hieroglyphics, detected in a photograph a 3,500-year-old forgery and duly reported it.

On July 3, 1916, however, Van Anda's prescience failed him. The two-day-old story portrayed the death at sea as a freak accident. The *Times* did not report the speculation of local baymen that a sea turtle or shark had killed the young swimmer, for the facts were murky and such attacks were unheard of. What fish was capable of tearing a man to pieces the *Times* story did not say.

Fears Only Thinly Veiled

❦

Along the bottom of the night sea, the shark moved in cold thirty-foot indigo depths unilluminated by the light of the moon. Careful to avoid big predators, it dipped low in the water column while hugging the shore, the home of living things. The shark had killed and failed to feed, and discipline and wariness ruled its every movement. The spoiled attack on a large mammal, the noisome counterattack by many other mammals, deepened its preternatural caution.

As the shark swam, tiny organs, distributed all along its body, constantly "tasted" the chemical composition and salinity of the ocean water. These sensors possessed cells analogous to the taste cells on a human tongue and sensed, now, lower salinity in the coastal waters. The shark was reading the dilution of coastal waters caused by the rains of June 1916, so torrential the *Ledger* lamented, "There cannot be much more rain left in Heaven." Water had coursed from the mountains in the state's northwest, through central and southern farmlands, into lakes and underground streams and finally to the sea. With the swollen freshwater runs came masses of organic matter, myriad fish flowing into the channels and bays. For eons, lower salinity had pointed the shark and its ancestors toward new hunting grounds, and so the big fish moved now without thought toward prey. Fish sat at the head of the inlets, snaring other smaller fish that came from the creeks and bays. Just north of Little Egg Inlet, the great white had found prey fish from Great Bay and Little Bay. And it had also stumbled upon Charles Vansant.

Along with the shark's gifts of detection and concealment was the quality of anonymity, the gift of being unknown to man. By 1916, hundreds of men in the deep ocean and on the wastes and fringes of continents and in the prehistoric backwater of time had been devoured by sharks. But sharks attacked far from cities and civilization. Shark attack was an otherworldly story swapped by sailors and fishermen, a tale seldom reaching beyond cabin or dock or the range of a man's last desperate cries. It was a story, when filtered to a city, that was scarcely believed.

The Edwardians believed God had given them dominion over the fish of the sea and science had given them evolutionary supremacy over the earth. "In the course of evolution man became supreme and mastered all the other animals," said a letter to the editor of the *Philadelphia Inquirer* early in the summer of 1916. "Those he could not use he exterminated."

But there had always been a fish that man could not master, that at will exterminated *him.* After the long silence of prehistory, a story of anonymous human prey, Herodotus, the first great historian of the Greeks, wrote of a "marine monster" seizing a helpless man at sea in 492 B.C. Documentation is scattered over centuries. Seven hundred years before Christ, a potter working on the Italian island of Ischia, at the entrance to the future Bay of Naples, carved a vase with a representation of a man being seized by a giant fish—the first evidence, in art, of a shark attack. The word for the fish didn't enter the English language until 1569, when Captain John Hawkins towed to London a ferocious specimen his crew exhibited as a "shark," the term evidently derived from the German *schurk* or *schurke*, meaning scoundrel or villain. But with the first use of the word in English came denial of the creature's existence. Thus in 1778, the citizens of London were horrified anew to learn there was such a thing as a man-eating shark, this one in a painting by John Singleton Copley, "Watson and the Shark." Watson was the lord mayor of London, and he had hired Copley, considered the finest artist in colonial America, to portray the moment in 1749 when he had lost his leg as a boy, when he fell overboard from a ship in Havana harbor and was attacked by a shark. The painting caused a sensation at the Royal Academy, "exposing a previously ignorant segment of the population to the terrors of sharks."

Denial was a sensible response to the emergence of the shark, according to H. David Baldridge, the U.S. Navy officer-scientist who helped the navy research shark attacks after the death and dismemberment of navy personnel during World War II, and "a significant morale problem among fliers and survivors of ship sinkings." Baldridge continued:

> What could possibly equal being eaten alive by a monster fish?
> With very few exceptions, man has emerged the master in his
> relatively short period of competition with the beasts of this

earth. Yet, the tidelands of the sea clearly mark the boundary of his supremacy. Beyond that lies an unknown that still conjures up in most of us emotions and fears only thinly veiled by the gossamer of civilization . . . There is no conflict more fundamental in nature, more one-sided in conduct, or more predetermined in outcome than the attack upon a live human being by a shark. In an instant of time, the sophistication of modern man is stripped away and he becomes again what he must have been many times in the beginning—the relatively helpless prey of a wild animal.

Following the inlets, the shark moved along the thin sandy coast of Long Beach Island, keeping to open ocean along the narrow wastes of Island Beach for many miles. In several days the shark swept north past the whole of Barnegat Bay, the sedge islands, Metedeconk Neck, the river past the Mantolokings, and Bay Head to the Manasquan Inlet, where the barrier islands ended. There it began to hug the mainland for the first time.

Little is known about the migratory habits of great whites. A rare scientific measurement of a great white's travels occurred in 1979 off the east end of Long Island, when a Woods Hole biologist used a harpoon to implant a transmitter in a great white while it was feeding on a whale. In the next three and a half days, the shark averaged only two miles an hour but showed incredible endurance, swimming 168 miles, from Montauk to the Hudson River submarine canyon off New York City, until the boat trailing the shark broke down.

So in July 1916, the juvenile great white covered a third of the Jersey coast, approximately forty-five miles, in five days. The shark followed huge offshore sand ridges. The shadows of the ridges and the inlets on the coast sang with life, with normal prey. But the juvenile great white was not behaving normally. Day and night, the water thrummed with mammals, a new and different quarry in unusual abundance. Along the beaches of the Jersey shore that summer was perhaps the largest number in the world, perhaps in any era to date, of human beings in the water. Where a normal great white shark goes, and when or why or what it hunts would remain, for much of the century to follow, a puzzle, a mystery to which the shark of 1916 would add little but enigmas and riddles.

Ahead past Sea Girt, just south of Long Branch and Woodrow Wilson's summer White House, lay the wealthy Victorian seaside resort of Spring Lake, named for a lovely oblong spring-fed lake, three blocks from the ocean, whose banks had recently contributed fresh spring water to the edge of the sea.

Independence Day

❧

The New Essex and Sussex, a grand hotel opened in 1914 with colossal white entrance columns that faced the Atlantic Ocean, spread out to occupy an entire seaside block of Spring Lake, forty-five miles up the coast from Beach Haven. Old Glory fluttered high from four turrets above the soaring portico. In the first week of July 1916, uniformed porters attended the parade of chauffeured Pierce Arrows arriving from New York, Texas, the South, and the Midwest to join the summer colony. The sea with its high gull calls and soothing motion seemed a lovely complement to the hotel. By setting and architecture, the New Essex and Sussex had announced itself a capital of the new American empire, an enclave of wealth and power in a bright and optimistic new century. And this, in fact, it was.

Later that summer, President Woodrow Wilson and Mrs. Edith Galt Wilson, the newlywed First Lady, arrived to inhabit the summer White House in nearby Long Branch. The President was joined on the shore for the summer by his daughters, his Cabinet, and the entire White House staff, which occupied the top floor of the Asbury Park Trust, a small five-story bank building in nearby Asbury Park. Philosophically opposed to campaigning from the White House—"the people's house," he called it—Wilson campaigned for the November election from the front porch of Shadow Lawn, the grandiose Victorian mansion the president insisted upon renting in Long Branch, refusing free lodging from a wealthy benefactor. He ran the country from an office in the bank building, where he transacted the business of the presidency, including press conferences.

The gentlemen of the press were assigned a room in the bank, from which they dispatched wires datelined Asbury Park, Long Branch, or Spring Lake. The *Asbury Park Evening Press* claimed to be chronicling "the most important year in the history of the nation, perhaps of the world, for many decades." Mindful that the President would be mulling the Great War and the election, the *Philadelphia Bulletin* was likewise impressed. "New Jersey will have cause this summer to feel more important than ever, for its name will be blazoned all over the world daily, and that without allusion to its mosquitoes . . . [New Jersey's] shore resorts are more or less famous throughout the civilized world, as it stands now, but this summer will be the 'red letter year,' for President Wilson has . . . decided to establish his summer capital at . . . Shadow Lawn."

The President's arrival signaled that the New Essex and Sussex Hotel would become the center of the nation's social life. On Saturday, July 1, New Jersey Governor James F. Fielder, a Wilson Progressive who succeeded Wilson when he went to the White House, launched the social season by hosting the Governor's Ball in the grand ballroom of the "E & S," as it was fondly known. The "glittering throng" sent the newspapers into paroxysms of nostalgia over the Gilded Age when presidents Ulysses S. Grant and then James A. Garfield established New Jersey's "Gold Coast" as the summer capital; when the British actress Lillie Langtry, one of the most beautiful women in the world, frequented the coast as a respite from touring with *She Stoops to Conquer* or *As You Like It*; and when singer and actress Lillian Russell was escorted by the flamboyant and enormous gustatorial tycoon James Buchanan "Diamond Jim" Brady.

Three days after the Governor's Ball, as if to affirm the return of distant glory, a gleaming roadster cruised along the seacoast, turned off Ocean Drive at the New Essex and Sussex, and disgorged William Howard Taft, the ex-President of the United States, all 332 pounds of him. Taft had been only the third American President to ride in an automobile, and thus he was known to make a small ceremony of disembarking, standing regally in the backseat of the open roadster for the photographers, his great girth wrapped in a dark suit crossed at the chest by a gold chain, walrus mustache drooping in the middle distance between enormous jowls and soft, fair eyes. Politicians, socialites, and officials of the Essex and Sussex crowded around their guest of honor. The amiable ex-President was then a law professor at Yale University, greatly relieved to have surrendered the White House to Wilson in 1912. A confused hullabaloo attended Taft's visit to Spring Lake that day, but one fact is eminently clear: Taft was not glad to be there. He had been

summoned on July the Fourth, the nation's one hundred forti-
eth birthday, to make a speech. Giving speeches was something
Taft detested nearly as much as being President. He would
rather, he often said, be playing golf. More than likely, after a
long drive, he desired nothing so much as a good meal, or a nap,
which he often took in public.

Taft, famously good-natured, was a well-liked ex-President.
That afternoon, as he stood at the podium, magisterial in his dark
suit, looking out on the sea of faces in the ballroom of the Essex
and Sussex, murmurs of excitement swept the crowd. Emboldened by his enormous girth—a man so big, the pundits said,
there was no room for meanness—Taft enjoyed the symbolism of
rising and commanding a crowd. He had been the first President
to throw out the first pitch of the baseball season—at a Washington Senators–Philadelphia Athletics game on April 14, 1910.
Yet many of the summer colony, despite their wealth and position, had never heard Taft's voice. It was an extraordinary and
memorable event before radio for an American to hear the President speak.

As the baritone of the ex-President's voice filled the room,
however, the thrill quickly diminished. Taft spoke almost
mechanically of Americanism and patriotism in the style of an
earnest, careful lawyer with the soul of an honest bureaucrat,
a man who began his first inaugural address: "The office of
an inaugural address is to give a summary outline of the
main policies of the new administration, so far as they can be
anticipated."

To polite applause, William Howard Taft concluded his
speech, ending with an appeal to a shared faith in "Almighty
God," and the wealthy summer colonists spilled out of the hotel
onto the boardwalk to enjoy the remnants of daylight. The
sea was blue-gray and calm with a few swimmers in the water,

and roadsters whined along Ocean Drive behind them. It was at that moment that a crowd on the boardwalk—no doubt still discussing Taft's speech—spotted a large, dark fin in the ocean. Then there were many fins, rolling in a school parallel to the coast.

"Sharks!" someone in the crowd cried, and near hysteria rippled through the group. Local fishermen nearby attempted to calm the crowd by pointing out that the fins were not those of sharks but belonged to porpoises, which commonly moved in schools offshore. But to many in the summer colony who had read in the *Press* about the young man in Beach Haven who was attacked and killed the previous Saturday by a shark, sharks were a subject of worrisome gossip and speculation for days.

Still, the excitement subsided as longtime residents assured guests that sharks never attacked bathers on the Jersey coast. Some insisted that Vansant's death had been fabricated by the newspapers, or grossly misunderstood, as the youth must have simply drowned. Shortly, their confidence restored by knowing skepticism, the summer colonists returned to the hotel to prepare for a graceful evening of music and July Fourth dinner. "The first accident of its kind recorded in the annals of the Jersey coast created considerable excitement," the *Asbury Park Evening Press* reported, but "doubt as to the veracity of the dispatches from Beach Haven was frequently expressed."

The Distance Swimmers

⧯

That morning, the ocean was calm and smooth as blue fabric, and waves came spaced at long intervals like decorative fringes of lace.

A breakfast was served early with glimmering views of the ocean at the Essex and Sussex, the morning papers unfurled above clouds of steaming French coffee. The quiet on the western front was a small breather as the British and French prepared for more fighting at the Somme; Sir Edward Grey had been made an earl; Harry Vaughn, the "dry" candidate for New

Jersey governor, declared, "Prohibition is not a new breakfast food. It is a scientific fact. Science tells us alcohol is poison."

The presence of the First Family continued to titillate the social set. The President's daughter, Margaret Woodrow Wilson, had made her singing debut that week in Spring Lake, performing "My Old Kentucky Home." Society was especially atwitter over the arrival of the first divorced First Lady. A plainspoken woman, Edith Galt Wilson was said to be offended by the palatial ostentation of Shadow Lawn, particularly the "seventeen complete sets of porch furniture, all different" and "staircases grand enough to fit an entire army abreast."

As the First Family's every move was chronicled by the press that summer, Wilson became the first American president to achieve celebrity. Perhaps the most unsettling news was that forty-five miles north, in the tenements of New York City, twenty-four children in the past twenty-four hours had died of infantile paralysis. Spring Lake seemed, with its fresh and healthful sea breezes, the safest possible place.

Spring Lake was a haven designed for the wealthy to cavort amid the beauty of nature. The Reverend Alphonso A. Willits, the nineteenth-century "Apostle of Sunshine," had inspired the affluent of New York and Philadelphia to build around the lake-by-the-sea an Arcadian village.

Two days after ex-President Taft's speech, Spring Lake unwound in breezy summer reverie. Men in high-collared Oxfords and women in corseted skirts and parasols took their fresh-air strolls by the sea, a leisurely cadence softly echoed in the wooden timbre of the boardwalk. Rowers crossed the town's namesake lake, while boys and girls marveled over the porcelain swans and porcelain chicks in porcelain nests that rested on its grassy shores. Live black swans were imported for aesthetic reasons but failed to thrive and were removed. Nature was a classically refined, orderly element in Spring Lake, yet men and women by the lake, as all along the shore, were experiencing the out-of-doors, for the first time, as a balm for the ills of the industrial cities.

The shore was an idyll for the inhabitants of America's largest cities, all of which except Chicago were on the East Coast—New York, Boston, Baltimore, and Philadelphia. "We are crowded and hustled and irritated to the point of physical desperation in our thoroughfares and markets, our tenements and tiny apartments, our shops and street cars," *The Craftsman* magazine cried in 1907. "Give us more air and sun and ground under foot and we will give you fewer instances of unfortunate morality, knavery, greed and despair."

James A. Garfield, while campaigning for President in 1880, had outlined the challenge for America's emerging leisure classes. "We may divide the whole struggle of the human race into two chapters," he said. "First, the fight to get leisure; and then the second fight of civilization—what shall we do with our leisure when we get it." The solution for hundreds of thousands was the beach. By 1885, a contemporary noted that the whole East Coast, from Mount Desert, Maine, to Cape May, New Jersey, "presents an almost continual chain of hotels and summer cottages."

The back-to-nature impulse at the beach, however, did not extend to the bathing costumes. By the proper mores of Spring Lake, women's bodies were draped in dark wool, and men covered up in black, two-piece bathing costumes—mid-thigh trunks and a long, sleeveless jersey covering both groin and chest. The male chest in 1916 was a scandalous zone prohibited from public view. Not until the 1930s, freed by the new glamour of Hollywood, would the male torso be exposed in swimsuits. The California style of the 1930s also inspired the

Technicolor explosion of swimming wear, but in 1916, the palate, on man at least, was limited to black. Almost a century later, in the first worldwide study of great white attacks— covering one hundred and seventy-nine cases—nine of ten human victims wore bathing suits or wet suits, gear or clothing that was dark—74 percent were clad in black, 15 percent in blue. Thus, as they entered the waves in dark bathing costumes that July, swimmers were unknowingly true to the back-to-nature spirit of the shore, appearing underwater in harmony with the natural world, in the dark coloration exhibited by many marine animals—the great white's chosen prey.

On July 6, the newspapers declared it a fine beach day, made more precious by the rain predicted to arrive over the weekend from the South and Midwest. As the sun climbed that morning, bathers made their pilgrimage to the sea. On the broad, sandy beach, knots of children built sand castles, a beach activity being popularized by Lorenzo Harris, the one-armed sculptor from Philadelphia, who was molding "Neptune's Court" nearby. Wispy clouds decorated a china-blue sky, the air was warm and brilliant with light.

If young women on beach and boardwalk were demurely watching young men in their swimming sports, the glances that morning turned frank and blatant, for as the sun tipped toward afternoon, a young man suddenly demanded unseemly attention. Robert W. Dowling, nineteen years old, stood on the beach and declared he was going to swim four miles straight out into the Atlantic, sharks be damned. Long-distance swimming being an amateur sport of the Edwardian wealthy, men and women would have taken the measure of the young man in a glance, then turned toward the horizon, bidding their children do the same. It would be an impressive sight from shore, a story for a postcard or a letter home, something to witness. The quick feet of gossip deepened the anticipation. Robert W. Dowling was the well-known son of Robert E. Dowling, president of the City Investment Company in New York. The boy had made head- lines the previous summer, making a forty-mile swim around Manhattan Island. This new feat should not tax him, and the presence of a shark was not a true concern. And so Dowling swaggered to the line of the surf and plunged in. Soon he was as an arrow splitting the blue.

Not far south on the beach, Leonard Hill attracted no such attention. He was a wholesale druggist from New York City, treating his wife to a stay at the Essex and Sussex. That a hard- working American businessman could mingle with the social queens and princes said something about democracy then that William Jennings Bryan would have cheered. More ambitious, perhaps, was Hill's planned swim. He intended to swim straight out a quarter mile from the coast, then stroke five miles due south. If there were rogue waves about that day, Hill would be more likely to find them, but he was a strong swimmer and unafraid. He was unconcerned, too, about the reported shark attack down the coast, in the direction he was heading. Few people saw Leonard Hill as he gracefully turned in the water some distance from shore, and, powerfully windmilling his arms, struck out in the direction of Beach Haven.

Both swimmers grew smaller on the horizon, dissolving finally in distant trails of white.

To Find Prey

❦

Off the coast, a tall fin divided the sea into precise segments, signaling the path of the huge fish to the unbounded emptiness, to a few gulls and smaller fish that scattered. The fish appeared gray and white and moved with the precision and trajectory of an enormous bullet, a shot somehow fired in slow motion through the medium of the sea, moving with a purity and suppleness that were eerily beautiful. It is a principle of aircraft design that "a good plane is a plane that is nice to look at." The great white swam on the surface of the deep like an airship given the lift of a summer sky.

Yet the shark's design was sophisticated beyond the flying machines of Langley or Wright or Curtiss, beyond human understanding in 1916, for it swam and hunted with the inborn perfection of thoughtlessness and genetic memory. It kept a steady keel that afternoon, and its fins wobbled slightly to one side or the other. Invisible lateral lines running down the length of its body recorded changing water pressure. They signaled its brain to adjust its fins, and the shark righted itself, adjusting to smooth cruising mode. As it moved, it read the earth's magnetic field— or the electricity generated by ocean currents moving about the field—like an electromagnetic compass. What use it made of this information is not known, but as it traveled undersea it rode swells of water and magnetism and electricity like a sailor courses the wind.

The shark could see colors. It could see several feet out of the water, could have seen people in a small boat looking down at it were a vessel circling over it, and now it noticed the salmon-yellow light in the sky changing and slightly darkening like the water. The fish had traveled some fifty miles along the coast in five days, and it was hungry. It is not known how often it came near shore during those five days, explored bays and harbors or straddled inlets, fed or failed to feed. But judging by its actions, its need to consume prey had become acute.

Nature had equipped the shark more splendidly than anything that lived to find prey. The shark possessed eight organs like complex interrelated systems for detection, stalking, and identification, systems that worked at all hours and in total darkness, supported by numerous backup systems in case of failure. Shark researcher Xavier Maniguet has compared the approach of a shark to that of a modern torpedo "whose various electronic means of reaching the target make 'contact' almost inescapable." As the shark detected the lower salinity and the mass of organic debris in the coastal waters that after-noon, its genetic memory was triggered, drawing it inexorably toward shore. Toward the coast town of Spring Lake.

As the shark neared Spring Lake, sound ratcheted curiosity up toward urgency. The noises were deep, low-frequency sounds, bass notes beyond human perception: The noise emitted by a speared fish, thrashing about, or by a human being splashing in the water. Or by a swimmer, more than a mile away.

Dowling and Hill were far into the Atlantic by then, miles apart and miles from shore, unaware they had entered the tracking range of a great white.

The shark now turned its head slowly, side to side, letting water wash into its nostrils, widely spaced below the mouth, and out again. The horizontal balancing movement of the head allowed the shark to test a wide corridor of smell. Its nose was "thinking," and, turning its head reflexively in the direction of the nostril that received the strongest smell, the fish proceeded that way. Like a hunting dog, the shark's nasal cavity contained numerous folds to increase the surface area and number of olfactory sensors, but this nose was spectacularly more sensitive than a hunting dog's. Sharks can detect one part of blood in one million parts of water, yet the olfactory ability of the great white that day may have been far stronger. A shark is even capa-ble of responding to concentrations of fish extract of one part in ten billion. To survive as a great white shark was extraordinar-ily difficult, so nature had supplied it extraordinary weapons.

A quarter mile distant, the great white could smell its prey. It had entered an "odor corridor," a wide swath of scent in the rough shape of a crude Stone Age arrow, broad at the base and tapering to a point. The shark simply needed to follow the nar-rowing scent to its source.

The shark was in the water with them.

The thought would soon come to both Dowling and Hill. Yet it is perhaps not surprising that both men were unaware and also unafraid of the potential presence of a shark relatively near shore. The Edwardians were the first generation for whom the ocean had lost its terrors; the sea was a haven of leisure and entertainment, an illusion maintained a century later. "We've forgotten what the ocean is," says ichthyologist George Burgess. "The ocean is a wilderness. We would never enter a forest wilderness without being aware of its dangers, its predators. Yet we think of the ocean as our giant backyard swimming pool."

On the Atlantic Coast, sharks are constantly near shore, hunting and scavenging. Fly over Florida beaches in a helicopter or a small plane, Burgess says, and invariably you'll see them between the line of swimmers and the shore. The big shadows passing silently in four, six, nine feet of water, spying swimmers and moving on.

The great white in 1916 moved inexorably forward in its investigation of potential prey. Robert E. Dowling was four miles out to sea now, laboring to turn around, his strokes growing fatigued and sloppy, matching the profile of a fish in distress.

For its prey there would be no escape at this point. The shark's systems were designed to guarantee its death. Were the shark's eyes damaged or its hearing impaired, lateral lines beneath its skin would detect vibrations from any movement in the water—a frightened fish, a ship's propeller, a diver's flippers—and the shark would attempt to hunt down its quarry without hearing or seeing it. Given such faculties, Xavier Maniguet writes, "It is easier to understand how it is impossible for man to escape any determined investigation by a shark in the neighborhood."

In the daylight hours of July 6, 1916, the shark's sonarlike capabilities were not necessary. At sixty feet, the shark could see a man in the water long before the man could see the shark. Using its ampulla of Lorenzini, a small organ under its nose, the shark could detect the man's faint electric field. At the last moment, when the great white unhinged its jaw and rolled its eye backward for protection, its ampulla of Lorenzini would locate the prey's beating heart.

Robert W. Dowling swam unaware of the crude yet brilliant appraisal of him as potential prey, the silent, unanswerable judgment by judge-jury-executioner. His movements were erratic, like a wounded fish's, yet the ocean was gentle and accommodating as he stroked four miles to shore and soon climbed out of the sea to handshakes and applause. Farther south, Leonard Hill returned too, from the direction of the shark—to land, to safety, and to kudos of his own.

Neither man had a clue, until later, that they had swum through the territory of a stalking, man-eating shark. Perhaps these long-distance swimmers were judged unpalatable, or too large to attack. It is not known why the shark bypassed either man or precisely why it kept hunting humans, only that it did.

When Dowling and Hill received the news later how close they had come to a man-eater, the endorphin euphoria of a long swim dissolved in chilled sweat. It is on record that both men immediately made new vacation plans. Separately, they vowed to abandon their careers as long-distance swimmers. Leonard Hill, the wholesale druggist from New York, swore he'd never swim beyond the lifelines again. Dowling, the flamboyant New York scion and celebrity swimmer, was more emphatic. Of the two men, he had swum closer to the path of the shark, quite near it, there seemed no doubt. He swore he would never swim in the ocean again.

"Never again," he repeated. "At least, not here."

The Red Canoe

The sun crossed the coast road that afternoon in a declining arc, laying planks of shade under the entrance of the Essex and Sussex. From Ocean Drive, men in hats climbed stairs toward the columns and disappeared, small figures swallowed by the portico, leaving women on the porch in wicker-backed Morris chairs, glancing now and again from books propped on their knees out over the railing to the sea. The women angled the chairs in patches of sun, and occasionally the scrape of a wooden chair fled the nibbling shade. Across Ocean Drive, men and women were returning from the beach for the afternoon siesta, and beneath the hum of roadsters along the coast road came the hissing and sighing of the waves as if calling them back. Slowly, the hotel descended into afternoon slumber. Like clockwork, the hotel received the retreating bathers, porters and bellboys directing them to changing rooms near the elevators. The bathing costumes, smartly cleaned and ironed, would be returned to guests' rooms for tomorrow's swim. Meanwhile, no sandaled feet traversed the cavernous lobby, no seawater dripped across the endless Oriental rugs. Guests with little to do but wait for evening conversed unperturbed in the field of Queen Anne chairs amid a forest of square fluted columns.

Strolling through the lobby with the swagger of an athlete was a young man, blond and muscular and twenty-eight years old, striking beyond the sameness of his hotel uniform. Charles Bruder, the bell captain, a former soldier in the Swiss Army, ran his staff with crisp precision, creating the illusion that the hotel was a smoothly oiled machine, or a luxury liner that sailed through the days on its own power. Bruder's leadership, mature for his years, allowed the hotel to provide the "highest class of summer season hospitality" to meet the standards of the original Essex and Sussex, a beloved Victorian landmark that had burned to the ground a few years earlier, while also "sounding a modern note," with such amenities as bathrooms equipped with "both hot and cold seawater service." Yet Bruder was young; running the bell staff could not absorb all his energy. So it was that during the somnolent hours of a Thursday afternoon, after a holiday, the bell captain saw a moment to escape from his duties for a brief swim.

As he strolled through the lobby, Bruder was a familiar and welcome face to the swells at the Essex and Sussex. After a year working in a hotel in California, he had returned to Spring

Lake, just in time for the new season at the E & S. Bruder said it was a dream come true to run the bell staff in his adopted hometown. Dutifully, he sent his tips home to his mother in Switzerland.

Under his gaze, the hotel moved in expected and reassuring rhythms. Children played in the courtyard pool behind the hotel. Boys and girls, under the watchful eye of nannies, danced beneath a pergola spilling roses while mothers napped upstairs, taking beauty rests for evening. Men who would be sorely disappointed by Prohibition descended to the rustic nautical bar to sip Manhattans and Planter's Punches under the captain's wheel. Others, smelling of starch and cigars, stood in twos and threes in an open loggia above the courtyard, wisps of smoke and conversation lost in the coloring sky.

As Bruder crossed the vast marble floor of the lobby, the last of the bathers were returning with windblown hair and reddening skin and tales of sand castles lost to the tides. Bruder heard such conversations with a certain possessiveness, given his reputation as the strongest and most fearless swimmer on the beach. As the Essex and Sussex transformed from ocean resort to Edwardian parlor, the sea ceased to exist for the rich and mighty. It was the bell captain's now, for a quarter of an hour.

As he headed down to the ocean, Bruder convinced Henry Nolan, the elevator runner, to break for a swim, and granted several bellhops time off to join them. Bruder, brawny and not quite six feet tall, moved with a confidence that inspired followers. The bellhops were somewhat in awe of his long-distance swims. Bruder had wowed his charges with stories of his adventures swimming the previous summer in the Pacific Ocean. With his natural ability and competitive instincts, there was no telling how far their boss could swim.

The bell captain swam every day now in the Atlantic with his coworkers, but on July 6 he was especially eager for witnesses. Two other men had stolen his glory that same afternoon. Robert Downing and Leonard Hill were the talk of the hotel after their marathon swims, and Bruder was eager to reclaim his place as the beach's star. He also was eager to back up his boasts that he had swum many times with large sharks off the coast of California and was unafraid of them. That morning the bellhops had been discussing the death of Charles Vansant, recently reported in the *Asbury Park Press*. After Vansant's grisly death, there was talk about whether it was wise to swim in the ocean. Bruder, with characteristic cockiness, mocked the newspaper accounts and insisted Vansant could not have been killed by a shark. According to Bruder, sharks were large and scary-looking, but entirely harmless.

Bruder's experience with sharks reflected the untamed sprawl of America in 1916, before a global media shrank the country and world. What the bell captain knew he knew firsthand. In those days knowledge was local.

Bruder had worked the previous year at a hotel near Los Angeles, and on days off had gone swimming off Catalina Island, twenty miles off the coast.

Catalina Island was a dream for a young man who loved the sea. It was a major fishery in 1915, with huge takes of tuna and swordfish. Killer whales and mako and blue sharks crossed the ship channel, and the new activity of sportfishing was already fabled for black sea bass. Bruder loved swimming offshore amid the dolphins and giant sea kelp. He gravitated naturally to Big Fisherman's Cove, where a young man brave enough could swim with sharks. Diving in the popular swimming areas near the island, Bruder may have encountered docile angel sharks, and small species such as swell and horn sharks. But in Fisherman's Cove were schools of five-foot leopard sharks with dark saddle markings, often mistaken for the dangerous tiger shark, a formidable man-eater. With his characteristic bravado, Bruder swam among them unafraid and emerged, to the admiration of onlookers, unscathed.

But Bruder could not have known that the leopard is considered sluggish for a shark, and is quite harmless to humans, preferring fish, fish eggs, crustaceans, and worms. Or that later in the twentieth century it would be a compliant resident of public aquariums. On Catalina Island, Bruder had swum unknowingly in waters inhabited by great whites. The leopard sharks with which Bruder swam are an easy snack for a great white, often swallowed whole.

With dispatch that afternoon in Spring Lake, Bruder hustled to the bathhouses. He would not have time to match Dowling's four-mile trek, but he planned a fast, powerful swim, and a quick return to the hotel to serve the demands of twilight. Briskly, Bruder, Nolan, and the bellhops changed into standard black two-piece bathing costumes, and hurried down to the beach. While the crowds had left the water to rest for evening, dozens of people remained on the sands, and the Swiss bell captain approaching the edge of the sea at the South End bathing pavilion drew attention. Bruder's reputation was established: He put on a good show in the water.

Before he entered the water, Bruder stopped to talk with Captain George White and Christopher Anderson, of the lifesaving station, about the Philadelphia man who had supposedly been killed by a shark. Bruder repeated that "he was not afraid of sharks," according to *The New York Herald,* "that off Catalina Island, California, he had seen many and they always fled from bathers."

Perhaps the bellhops, given their discussions about Vansant, hesitated at the lip of the sea, but as Bruder charged in, they, too, entered the surf with a burst of noisy camaraderie. Bruder was one of the first swimmers in the water. With a slow, powerful crawl, Charles Bruder swam straight out from shore—the same direction the younger Dowling had swum earlier that afternoon. White and Anderson, the surfmen at the South End, didn't budge as Bruder dipped his head under the safety ropes and kept swimming. Anyone else would have been called back, but Bruder was a strong swimmer and often swam beyond the lifelines. With surprising speed, Bruder was soon a thousand feet from shore, drawing murmurs and comments from observers on the beach. At a thousand feet he was still going as if racing a clock. Soon Bruder was a diminishing figure on the eastern horizon, his arms slicing through the waves.

The water was remarkably shallow with the tide receding, the wind light, and the waves softening as the recent storms moved out into the Atlantic. A gentle sun, draped by passing clouds, glinted here and there on the surface of the sea. The waves swelled past Bruder in a comforting rhythm as he stroked evenly toward the horizon. It was the kind of day that recalled the majesty of California, and Charles Bruder kept swimming farther and farther out.

As graceful as Bruder appeared from shore, his movements were sprawling, rough, almost obscenely graceless for a creature of the sea, his limbs thudding flat and hard on the surface like a board, radiating erratic and insistent waves of sound. It was only natural that the shark, patrolling nearby, aroused by Robert Dowling's earlier swim, would decide to investigate. Through the murk of the darkening sea, the great white sped, trailing sonic waves, until it was close enough, within fifteen feet, to see plainly, with its small, emotionless black eyes, the source of the sounds.

Bruder, unaware he was no longer alone as he swam, was twelve hundred feet from shore. The water was over his head, but less than ten feet deep in the low tide. Had he turned around, the view toward shore would have been glorious. Almost a quarter mile back on land, the turrets of the E & S seemed to scrape the clouds. More impressive even was the domed immensity of the New Monmouth Hotel. So small were the distant figures on the beach, he barely made out the figures of the bellhops, frolicking in the surf near shore. The surfmen hadn't moved from their post, which flushed Bruder with pride. Most anyone else would require a boat to travel out this far.

As self-conscious as Bruder was of his gracefulness and form as seen from shore, he gave no thought to the strange and complex beauty he presented below. Below, in the water column, the long outline of his body was compressed and bizarrely distorted in a dark bluish-gray world dusted with sunlight. Yet in the murk was a pleasing form too, a loveliness to the proper observer: a whirling dance of light. As the pale bottoms of Bruder's feet turned this way and that, they emitted a faint light in the gloom—a light that shone more brightly in contrast to the tanned top of his foot. His palms were small points of light, too, as he stroked his arms in a crawl, tiny flares wriggling up, down, and around, darting to the surface and plunging down. The darkened flesh on the outside of Bruder's hand and on his wrist brightened the contrast of the pale palm. The whirl of light was imperceptibly dim to human eyes, but the shark's rod-rich, cone-poor retina gave it heightened ability to distinguish an object from a contrasting background. No more than a dozen feet away, the shark's brain processed the flickering light as the movement of a fish.

Moving closer, beneath its prey, the shark had seen its quarry in full silhouette, etched by sunlight—outlined, in a glimpse that triggered both excitement and wariness, as not a school of fish but a mammal. After its struggle with Vansant and his rescuers, the shark had good reason to fear the large, slow coastal mammals. Yet perhaps Bruder's shape suggested seal, and the shark considered an investigatory bite. The evidence suggests that the juvenile great white, driven by necessity or insanity, was deliberately stalking undesirable prey for which competition was scarce: human flesh. No sharks in history have been known to travel so far to locate and consume so much human flesh.

Something else about Bruder greatly appealed to the shark. He was alone—no one within hundreds of yards—a prerequisite to the vast majority of shark attacks on humans. A lone swimmer is particularly defenseless. Unlike the shark, for whom every movement is calculated for advantage in the struggle of life and death, the man swam with no protection, no attempt at concealment, no sense of urgency. Charles Bruder swam as if he were alone in the sea, as if he were invincible.

Bruder never saw it coming. The great white's surprise attack was launched with overpowering force from behind. Such drama eludes other man-eaters. The ferocious bull shark angles in slowly with little force compared to the white. In Florida shark attacks, in which white sharks have not been implicated, more than half of initial attacks are reported occurring "with minimum turmoil," George Burgess reports. More than 92 percent of white shark attacks on humans, however, have been reported to be "sudden and violent."

As the shark moved, its dark top reflected virtually no light. The denticles on its skin muted the whoosh of its movements as the shark rose, driven by the power of the great tail sweeping from side to side, like a scythe. The fish exploded upward.

Charles Bruder felt a slight vacuum tug in the motion of the sea, noted it as a passing current, the pull of a wave, the tickle of undertow. He could not have heard the faint sucking rush of water not far beneath him. He couldn't have seen or heard what was hurtling from the murk at astonishing speed, jaws unhinging, widening, for the enormous first bite. It was the classic attack that no other creature in nature could make— a bomb from the depths.

Concealed in grim privacy beneath the surface, white attacks are often not visible from shore. As the films of A. Peter Klimley show, the surface of the water tells the story. Klimley made films of 129 great white attacks on the aquatic carnivorous mammals (such as the seal or walrus) known as pinnipeds in California's South Farallon Islands. A sudden pooling of red was a great white attacking an elephant seal. In attacks on sea lions, the water simply erupted, rising in an explosive spray nine to fifteen feet high, indicating the force with which the white struck its prey.

History did not record Charles Bruder's thoughts or feelings as he experienced a surprise great white attack. Instead, the sea told his story.

Guests on the beach in front of the Essex and Sussex suddenly saw a massive spray of water rising out of the ocean, a quarter mile out. As the plunging wall of water descended, a woman on the beach cried out, "The man in the red canoe is upset!" The surfmen White and Anderson shoved their small rescue rowboat into the water and began to row frantically east, while panicked shouts rang from the boardwalk and beach. As White and Anderson pulled closer, they saw that the "red canoe" was blood, spreading now in a wide circle. Rushing toward the red stain, eyes straining the surface of the water for Bruder, they were suddenly greeted by the unimaginable sight of the bell captain—or what was left of him—pinwheeling above the surface of the sea with incredible force.

As the surfmen drew closer, the huge fish struck Bruder again and again. "Swimming away and darting forward like an aeroplane attacking a Zeppelin, the shark made another lunge, cutting a deep gash in Bruder's abdomen," the *Philadelphia Inquirer* later reported. Finally, Bruder was pulled completely under. As White and Anderson's rescue boat entered the sea of blood, the bell captain somehow managed to lift his head above water once more and to gasp, "A shark bit me." The surfmen lowered an oar, and Bruder, with tremendous effort, lifted himself onto the gunwales, then collapsed, clinging helplessly to the side of the boat, sliding slowly back toward the ocean. Quickly, White and Anderson grabbed Bruder under the arms, and pulsing with adrenaline, hoisted him into the lifeboat. The surfmen, their strength fueled by urgency, were surprised how easy it was to lift the husky bell captain to safety. Laying him carefully on the bottom of the boat, the reason was immediately evident: There was little of Bruder left to lift. In a glance, White and Anderson noted "the loss of both of his feet." The surfmen were covered with blood.

While one surfman pulled the oars of the boat, the other tried desperately to stop the bleeding from both Bruder's legs by ripping off his shirt to cobble together makeshift tourniquets. Blood continued to pump copiously, soaking the boat. There was little time, but Bruder was still conscious.

According to the *New York Herald*, Bruder described the attack to the surfmen in the boat. "He was a big gray fellow, and as rough as sandpaper. I didn't see him until after he struck me the first time. He cut me here in the side, and his belly was so rough it bruised my face and arms. That was when I yelled the first time. I thought he had gone on, but he only turned and shot back at me [and] . . . snipped my left leg off . . . He yanked me clear under before he let go . . . he came back at me again . . . and he shook me like a terrier shakes a rat. But he let go while I was calling, then suddenly . . . took off the other leg. He's a big fellow and awful hungry."

Perhaps the story was embellished by the *Herald*, but whatever Bruder said, White and Anderson listened wide-eyed as they rowed their wounded friend to shore, trying to hurry yet make him as comfortable as possible. As the lifeboat surged through the waves, Charles Bruder closed his eyes and lost consciousness.

The Grande Dame

❦

Mrs. George W. Childs of Philadelphia, the former Emma
Peterson, was ensconced in a high and lovely suite at the Essex
and Sussex, with fine views of the ocean. The space was small
and spartan compared to the Childs mansion on Walnut Street in
Philadelphia, where Emma and her late husband, publisher of
the *Philadelphia Public Ledger,* hosted Whitman, Twain, and
their good friend Ulysses S. Grant in the Gilded Age's most
glittering salon. Nor could any hotel suite match the comfort
of Wootton, her "splendid country seat" on Philadelphia's Main

Line, or the seaside cottage in nearby Long Branch, where Emma and George summered alongside President Grant and their closest friend, the Philadelphia banker, J. Anthony Drexel, who introduced them to his young and promising New York partner, John Pierpont Morgan. Those grand days were past, yet at the age of seventy-four, Mrs. Childs remained an imperial presence in Philadelphia society, a generous philanthropist, and a doting aunt. An ardent nature lover, Mrs. Childs had donated great tracts of open space to the state of Pennsylvania, and it was still a pleasure to breathe the wide sea airs at the Jersey shore. At the Essex and Sussex that summer, she planned to enjoy the ocean and society just a few miles from the old seaside cottage, and not far from the town of Deal, where her beloved niece, the child she never had, summered.

At 2:30 that afternoon, the grande dame had settled into her room for a respite before the social requirements of evening, when she heard, with a keen acuity for her age, disturbing noises floating through the windows over the sea. Her curiosity aroused, Mrs. Childs called to her maid to bring the field glasses, and stepped out on her private balcony, where she raised her glasses to the panorama of the sea. Far below and to the south was a scene of great confusion. Men and women were running toward the hotel in panic, their voices carried upward by the wind. Scanning south of the hotel, Mrs. Childs saw a small boat had breached the shore. Two men—in the bathing costumes of surfmen—lifted a man out of the boat and set him down on the sands. A small crowd had gathered at water's edge. Mrs. Childs's view was partially obscured by the shifting crowd, but presently she saw, to her astonishment, that the man lying on the beach was covered with blood.

Although born to wealth and security, Mrs. Childs was not unfamiliar with the idea that life could present not only disap-

pointment and tragedy but horror—her husband had owned
the original manuscript of *The Murders in the Rue Morgue* by
Edgar Allan Poe, a writer who certainly chilled her. In her Victorian salon the intellectuals discussed the sublime thrill, then
in vogue, of observing nature's terrifying displays from a posture of safety: a stirring view of mountainous waves from the
cozy warmth of one's seaside cottage, for instance. Yet it is not
likely Mrs. Childs had ever had an encounter quite equal to the
feeling that swept through her as the field glasses revealed that
the man's legs were missing. Mrs. Childs was a strong woman
in crisis, and by then perspiration on her temples and her own
beating heart sharpened her determination to learn what was
happening. On either side of the fallen man, mothers hurried
children out of the water as if it were boiling. On the sands,
women in long dresses swooned. Men rushed to assist them.
From her distant balcony the grande dame heard as if from the
wind and sea itself faint but unmistakable cries of "Shark!"
She had seen all she needed, and heard quite enough.

Putting down the field glasses, Mrs. Childs rushed for the
telephone and dialed the hotel office. F. T. Keating, assistant
manager of the hotel, picked up. Keating, alarmed, went straight
to the hotel manager, David B. Plumer, who—without time to
consider the uniqueness of the situation—put into motion the
first coastwide shark alarm in the history of the United States.
Plumer instructed Keating to call every physician booked in the
hotel, or anywhere in Spring Lake. Moving urgently to the E & S
switchboard, he ordered the operators to notify every "central"
operator on the north and central coast. The first central switchboard operators had been men, but they fought constantly and
were unruly with customers, so they were replaced by women.
So it was women who sounded the alert that the shore was in
chaos. Within minutes, the E & S operators reached every major

hotel on New Jersey's Gold Coast, from Atlantic Highlands, sixteen miles north, to Point Pleasant, six miles south.

For the first time in memory along the East Coast of the United States, a tranquil beach day was interrupted by surfmen running to the edge of the sea to frantically wave swimmers out of the water; by bathers thrashing and stumbling madly to shore for reasons that were urgent if not clear. Within half an hour, thousands of bathers fled more than thirty miles of beaches in a shark panic without precedent.

Perhaps it is not surprising that the first appearance of the great white shark as twentieth-century man-eater harkened back to apocryphal stories such as St. George and the dragon and foretold all appearances, in fact and fiction, of the great white to come. Men and women fled the water for sound and practical reasons, and they also fled their nightmares, long quiescent, of a creature buried so long in myth and rumor and repressed fear that when released expanded beyond any known and reasonable bounds. A simple act of nature in a few square feet of ocean sent a cloud of fear along vast stretches of coastal water and far inland. The crowds fled a sea monster, with its weight of evil, threat, and retribution.

Moments after dialing the assistant hotel manager, Mrs. Childs ordered her servants to bring around her automobile. She had tried to ring her niece on the telephone, but there was no answer. Within minutes, Mrs. Childs was speeding to Deal Beach, seven miles to the north, to personally stop her niece from entering the water for her afternoon swim.

Just north of the New Essex and Sussex on the Spring Lake oceanfront, the switchboard jangled urgently at the New Monmouth Hotel. The enormous New Monmouth boasted a central Palladian dome flanked by polygonal towers from which unfolded vast wings that embraced the sea. Within minutes, the sumptuous ritual of afternoon tea at the New Monmouth was sundered as Drs. William W. Trout and A. Cornell, the house physicians, sprinted through the lobby, carrying their heavy black bags.

Rushing south on Ocean Drive and down to the beach, the doctors pressed through the small crowd that had gathered around the body in the wet sand. "A morbid crowd had gathered, intent on seeing the remains," the *Asbury Park Evening Press* reported. The bell captain, or what was left of him, lay on his back in a welter of blood that was already crusting and drying on his bathing costume and diffusing on the sand. Trout and Cornell, the first physicians to reach Bruder, summoned their full professional composure, but jellyfish stings, crab pinches, and sunburn were the usual toll of the beach. In their combined years, the physicians had not seen such wounds from an animal attack. Bruder's left leg was bitten off clear above the knee; his right leg, just below the knee, was gone. A huge gouge was ripped from his torso, the wound edged with large teeth marks. The bell captain was already dead from massive blood loss. There was nothing to do but arrange for the body to be taken to autopsy and to calm the crowd.

Eyes full of questions turned to Trout and Cornell as they examined the remains, as though a doctor could explain what had happened, or promise it would not happen again. Facing gasps and muffled sobs, women shooing away the wide eyes of children, men sputtering anger that was the flip side of the coin of fear, Trout and Cornell were relieved to see the large, loose-limbed figure of Dr. William G. Schauffler, the governor's staff physician and surgeon of the New Jersey National Guard, ambling across the sands.

At the tender age of twenty-five, Schauffler was something of a local wunderkind—the highest-ranking medical doctor in the state. Tall and broad-boned, rugged yet affable in a small-town way, Dr. Schauffler was a born leader of men, trailed often by a group of youths "who were ready for anything, and afraid of nothing," a family friend remembered. Within a year, in World War I, Schauffler became an American hero, a captain commanding the legendary 90th Aero Squadron under Brigadier General Billy Mitchell. In the 1930s, he organized men into a pioneering sea and air fire rescue squad that responded to the fiery wreck of the *Hindenburg* in Lakehurst, New Jersey.

Now, as Colonel Schauffler kneeled to inspect Bruder's corpse, a troubled expression creased his youthful features. It was fifteen minutes after the attack and blood still oozed from the bell captain's tattered limbs. Schauffler's appraisal was that of a doctor who was also a skilled fisherman. He was a part-time charter captain who took his boat out of nearby Point Pleasant. A compulsive student of fish and their habits, he designed and sold his own line of rods for deep-sea fishing, and was credited for innovating a fighting chair where a man could strap in to battle big fish like marlin and tuna. Now, studying Bruder's partially devoured torso, the legs that ended in torn and bloodied nubs, Schauffler reached what he considered the gravest possible conclusion. The wounds were without a doubt the work of a large shark. Later, Schauffler filed the first detailed medical report of a shark attack victim in the United States. "The left foot was missing as well as the lower end of the tibia and fibula," he wrote. "The leg bone was denuded of flesh from a point halfway below the knee. There was a deep gash above the left knee, which penetrated to the bone. On the right side of the abdomen low down a piece of flesh as big as a man's fist was missing. There is not the slightest doubt that a man-eating shark inflicted the injuries."

Schauffler's report anticipated the classic study of shark attack victims by South African doctors Davies and Campbell half a century later. In the later terminology of Davies and Campbell, Bruder suffered the severest shark-inflicted injury possible, a grade-one. Grade one injuries involve major damage to the femoral artery in the area of the femoral triangle, or multiple artery severing. Had Bruder suffered the same attack in the early twenty-first century, he still would have died, even with instant and advanced medical response. In a grade-one shark injury, wrote Davies and Campbell, "the victim usually dies within minutes after the attack."

As Schauffler rose from beside Bruder's body, he was convinced of what had to be done. He was already forming plans to organize a patrol, armed men and a fleet of boats, to protect bathers and capture and kill the shark. The shark, he believed, was a confirmed man-eater, a large and deranged animal that would continue to threaten swimmers until it was destroyed.

Word preceded Dr. Schauffler to the lobby of the Essex and Sussex that the bell captain had been torn to pieces by a shark. Panic, like a billowing ether, occupied the grand room. Troubled guests had gathered in knots of conversation, and manager David Plumer found himself dealing with the matter of Bruder's body and comforting the stricken. "The news that the man had been killed by a shark spread rapidly through the resort, and many persons were so overcome by the horror of Bruder's death that they had to be assisted to their rooms," *The New York Times* reported. "Swimmers hurried out of the water and couldn't be induced to return." With the coming of twilight, local residents were drawn irresistibly to the hotel to make sense of the tragedy, but sense dissolved in a babel of opinion. Old-time fishermen insisted a shark attack was too farfetched to believe, that swordfish, giant sea turtles, and big mackerel were more likely man-killers than a shark. No one could recall a shark attack in Spring Lake since the pioneers built homes on the beach in the 1880s. Townfolk recalled, with knotted stomachs, the shark caught by a Spring Lake fisherman in 1913. In the fish's stomach was the foot of an unidentified woman, the foot still encased in a fashionable tan shoe. But it was concluded then that the shark had scavenged the body of a drowned woman. Sharks were considered too timid to threaten a live human being.

That evening, as dark waves brushed the beach and moist winds blew through the high windows of the lobby, Mrs. Childs moved with a quiet dignity under the cottony shadows thrown by electric chandeliers, collecting donations from the summer colonists for Charles Bruder's mother in Switzerland. Mrs. Bruder had only one other son to support her, Mrs. Childs explained. In addition, the Philadelphia grande dame hoped to raise money to send the young man's remains home to his mother, across the Atlantic, to be buried.

The Scientist

❧

Late on the afternoon Charles Bruder died, a balding man with a bemused professorial air, thin and ruddy as a stalk of rhubarb, strolled through the lobby of the Essex and Sussex in a crisp blue serge suit with three buttons, his ever-present pipe on his lips or not far distant. The suit was identical to the size and style he had worn a decade earlier at his Harvard graduation and would remain his trademark for another thirty years.

John Treadwell Nichols was impressively tall, with a stooped frame and preternaturally long head and wry manner that made him appear older than his thirty-three years. There was about his wide-set eyes and cheekbones a certain fishlike quality that seemed entirely appropriate, as he was one of the most distinguished ichthyologists of the day. Dr. Nichols had been rousted from his specimen-crowded basement office at the American Museum of Natural History in New York City, where he was the assistant curator of the Department of Recent Fishes (those in the sea, rather than fossils), by the director, Frederic Augustus Lucas. Dr. Lucas had instructed the younger man to commence what would be the first scientific investigation of a man killed by a fish in American history. Dr. Nichols, along with his young colleague, the ornithologist Robert Cushman Murphy of the Brooklyn Museum, were two of the more respected "shark men" in the country, but both utterly deferred to their aged mentor, Dr. Lucas.

Three months earlier, in April 1916, Nichols and Murphy had collaborated on a major journal article for the *Brooklyn Museum Science Bulletin,* "Long Island Fauna. IV. The Sharks (Order Selachii)," in which they used thirty-three pages to portray nineteen different species of sharks. After describing tiger sharks, blue sharks, thresher and dusky sharks, hammerhead sharks, and ten other species, the authors took the unusual step of removing themselves from their own article when they reached species number sixteen, "great white shark: man-eater." Nichols and Murphy yielded the next five pages to Dr. Lucas, who had "very kindly written for this bulletin the subjoined account relating to the status of sharks as man-eaters." Dr. Lucas's "long experience, coupled with his repeated critical investigations of 'shark stories' that arise perennially along our seacoast, eminently fit him to write with finality upon a subject so generally misapprehended."

Now, appearing in Spring Lake to investigate Bruder's death, Dr. Nichols, like Dr. Lucas, was not inclined to think of it as a shark-attack inquiry. Such attacks on man were rare, if not nonexistent.

Nichols had examined the torn and badly bitten body of Charles Bruder that afternoon, shortly after Dr. Schauffler's examination. Crouching over the body, he was likely appalled, perhaps sickened or angered, yet eerily fascinated by nature in its rawest form. He restrained his sympathy for the young man, to objectively consider the wounds as the quite natural acts of a fish or mammal species. But which one?

John T. Nichols would not have found it difficult to push aside distraction and plunge into the question, for he shared with his Victorian mentors a deeply romantic love of nature in all its variety. In 1890, when he was seven years old, Nichols had taken a steamship voyage across the Atlantic, and was so moved by the sight of an iceberg, he could not fall asleep that night aboard ship. "There was," he wrote, "a first tangible, permanent picture etched in memory, to which others were to be added, and spell the beauty and romance of the vast, impersonal, omnipotent, ever-changing, but eternal sea." After returning from a voyage around Cape Horn many years later, Nichols observed: "Once more in from the deep sea, the same old sea, deep blue out there beyond the reefs, difficult and fascinating as ever, guarding its mysteries. Back into the world, but days, weeks, months must go by before this world would seem altogether real again. . . . No, it did not seem real, some day one must wake again to contend with a world of sails and winds and rolling seas." But Dr. Nichols was more than a quixotic dreamer; he was a modern man with a Victorian passion to learn everything.

"J. T. Nichols was a self-taught ichthyologist of the old, old school," a colleague remembered. "He was enthusiastic about many different aspects of natural history, not just fish."

To illustrate the life of an ichthyologist of the old school, Dr. Nichols liked to tell the story of a gentleman who, in 1907, boarded a Long Island Rail Road train with a small box containing a turtle. When the conductor came to collect the fare, he inquired what was in the box. That brought up the question of extra fare, and after a brief discussion with the passenger the conductor rendered this historic decision: "Cats and dogs is animals—but turtles is insects. Insects ride free." That ruling was right in line with the American Museum of Natural History when Professor Nichols went to work there in 1908, fresh from Harvard. Fish were part of the Department of Insects. It wasn't until 1910 that fish won a department of their own, and Nichols became assistant curator of the Department of Recent Fishes.

Dr. Nichols spent most of his time in his large, cluttered office at the museum, bent over his rolltop desk, pipe in his teeth, pulling fish out of hundreds of jars of alcohol to measure their length and count their scales under a magnifying glass. (The alcohol, he noted, sank mysteriously low during Prohibition and was apparently sipped from.) "As I recall it through a small child's eyes," his grandson, novelist John Nichols, remembered, "my grandfather's office at the Museum was a magical and chaotic place featuring stacks of books and papers, messy ashtrays full of burnt pipe tobacco, and countless bottles and jars of pickled fish . . . as Grandpa . . . revealed to me the secrets and mysteries of the natural world."

By 1916, Nichols was emerging as one of the nation's most distinguished ichthyologists. Three years earlier he had founded the journal *Copeia*, named after the nineteenth-century scientist Edward Drinker Cope, which would survive into the twenty-first century as a prestigious ichthyologic journal. That year he was busy founding what later became the American Society of

Ichthyologists and Herpetologists (ASIH) with famed New Jersey fish scholars Henry W. Fowler and Dwight Franklin. It was the first group dedicated to the scientific study of fishes, amphibians, and reptiles, their conservation, and their role in the environment. Nichols was obsessed with box turtles, which he marked with his initials on his Long Island estate for thirty years in a private habitat study. He was a respected ornithologist, an expert in weasels and bats. He banded birds, wrote the important *Freshwater Fishes of China*, and was an ardent fan and student of flying fish. But he was awed by and frightened by the big sharks. If he had ever seen the rare great white shark in his life, he knew little about it except its reputation as being the ferocious man-eater of the ancients.

After examining Bruder's body, Nichols held a small conference with reporters in Spring Lake to discuss his findings. To the surprise of the newspapermen, the ichthyologist declared it was not a shark that had killed the young man. Dr. Nichols's leading suspect was *Orcinus orca*, the killer whale. Bruder's legs had been torn off in dull, jagged cuts, wounds that recalled to Nichols the enormous blunt conical teeth with which the orca rips the lips and tongues from the great whales.

Nichols's choice in 1916 was not surprising. Since antiquity, the killer whale had been reputed to be a man-eater, a voracious, merciless predator that killed everything that lived in the sea. Spanish whalers in the eighteenth century christened the species "killer whale" after witnessing schools of orca descending upon and killing other whales, like a pack of wolves. It was only in the 1960s and '70s, after killer whales were trained to perform at Sea World, that scientists began to appreciate the orca as the smartest member of the dolphin family, and to accept the fact that there are no documented cases of an orca ever killing a man.

The killer whale, Nichols told reporters in Spring Lake, was called orca and was "commonly 30 feet long" with "short, stumpy teeth which are very efficacious in dragging things under the surface"—which explained why Bruder was repeatedly pulled beneath the waves. The orca kills the giant blue whale, the largest creature on earth, Dr. Nichols pointed out, and could easily destroy a man if it chose. "It is not settled that the killer whale attacks humans," concluded *The New York Times*, "but Mr. Nichols thought there was as much reason to suppose it was a killer whale as to suppose it was a shark."

Arrival of a Man-Eater

F ar from shore the great white moved into deeper waters. In the literature of shark attacks, men often describe man-eaters as enraged, snapping at anything near: small fish, fishing lines, buoys. But the white shark now was likely doing what it always did: swimming steadily forward, dorsal fin high, searching for the next meal. All of Charles Bruder would certainly have sated the shark, but the legs left it hungry, imparted slightly more urgency to the search that never ended. If the attack on Bruder taught it anything—it was capable of crude learning, and attack was its only subject—it was that the mammals of the coast were vulnerable but not easy prey.

The great white had been frightened off by White and Anderson's lifeboat, which it perceived as a bigger predator, or it was simply spooked by a large foreign object, which sharks hastily avoid. Had the fish been mature, eighteen feet and three tons, neither boats nor men, oars, bullets, nor a larger shark would have stopped the feeding. Had the surfmen not rescued Bruder, the shark may have soared almost completely out of the water and plunged down, jaw agape, on the young man, taking him deep in the water. According to A. Peter Klimley's research in the 1990s of *Carcharodon carcharias* attacks on pinnipeds, white sharks carry struggling prey as far as three quarters of a mile away from the point of attack to allow the prey to bleed out. Then the shark can feed without distraction.

Now the great white moved off the coast of Spring Lake, deeply irritated, electric with hunger. Yet the shark had entered the only region of the world where a white shark population existed without the abundance of seals and sea lions, its favorite foods, to sustain it. To a great white, a man is a bony, unpalatable, low-fat choice, distressingly muscular. Enormous quantities of fat, scientists believe, fuel the great white's energy needs. The preference is striking: Whites feeding on a whale carcass have been witnessed carefully stripping away the blubbery layers.

Survival for a young white in the mid-Atlantic bight was precarious. Absent the fatty prey available on the West Coast—sea lions, elephant seals—the shark subsisted mostly on large fish such as rake and cod and red drum. As it grew larger than ten feet, the mid-Atlantic offered porpoises, sea turtles, and harbor seals, still extant off New Jersey in the first part of the century. But big, blubbery prey was scarce. Even if it were lucky enough to find a whale carcass, the juvenile great white would likely have been driven off by larger sharks.

Denied its usual diet, the great white would have turned to the lesser prey items it consumes as the need arises. Exactly what the great white eats in an emergency is a mystery ichthyologists solved by the late twentieth century after decades of investigation: whatever it wishes. The giant fish devours the living and the dead and the inanimate. Bottles, tin cans, cuckoo clocks, truck tires, a whole sheep, an intact Newfoundland dog with its collar on, have all been taken from the stomach of white. In the days when animal carcasses were thrown in the ocean, boars, pigs, the head of a horse, a whole horse, and the entire skin of a buffalo found their way into the stomachs of great white sharks. Almost anything is within the reach of a mouth that takes fifty pounds in a single bite. One white was found with five hundred pounds of bull elephant seal in its stomach, taken, no doubt, in a single battle—a grown bull elephant seal weighs fifteen hundred pounds. The white wears the mantle of the "natural undertaker." Without sharks the ocean would be littered with decomposing carcasses.

The white shark's preference for pinnipeds, fish, and other sea creatures over human flesh is documented. Burgess's worldwide study of white attacks shows that in the majority of the 179 attacks—56.8 percent of the cases—human victims received only a single bite and were "spit out." Some shark biologists believe humans resemble seals and, when proven to be imposters, are spit out; others insist humans are rejected as insufficiently fatty. Burgess disagrees. In a third of the attacks in the worldwide study, the great white bit its human victim repeatedly, clearly intending to feed. In such cases, "multiple bites occurred, including many instances in which victims were wholly consumed," Burgess says, indicating that "humans are not uniformly unpalatable."

Burgess interprets the shark's "bite and spit" behavior differently. The white shark's attacks on humans parallels its attacks on sea creatures—after the first strike it circles around, giving the prey time to bleed out.

According to George Burgess, the shark bit and spit not because its human victim was unplatable, but because it simply ceased its attack:

> It wasn't given an opportunity for a second bite. We have enough deaths and consumptions in the Attack File to know a white shark will happily consume a human being if it wants to. But because of our brain and social structure, a person grabbed by a white shark has a very good chance of getting to a boat, getting on a surfboard, having a swimming buddy help him escape the water. The poor sea lion doesn't have those assets. If humans were unpalatable we wouldn't have bodies disappearing and consumed.

In gray light the tide came in, covering the sands, and the globes of the streetlamps ensnared the brightness of dawn. In the early hours of Friday, July 7, before the hotels began serving coffee and distributing the morning newspaper, gentlemen made briskly to the boardwalk for their constitutionals, gentlemen in boaters and blue blazers, chins set to the breeze, who would not permit themselves to be thrown off balance. Later, intrepid young men, fewer in number, declared it a fine beach day, too lovely to waste, with the rain coming Saturday, and as the sun heated the shallows and the roadsters started down the coast road, they went into the sea.

Yet, as the sun rounded over the ocean at Spring Lake, a small squadron of boats split the shallows, gunning loud motorboat engines and trailing diluted crimson pools of animal blood. On the prows of the boats stood groups of men, faces hard and pointed down toward the water, long rifles and harpoons angled high against the delicate blue sky. Roped to the boats were chunks of lamb slaughtered by the butcher that morning, bait for the man-eater. Dr. Schauffler had organized the patrol to catch and kill the shark, and also to protect bathers, so those who wished could swim with peace of mind. Yet before long, as the sun tipped toward the hotel, young men, one at a time, left the water, returning to the hotel, or the pool at the Bath and Tennis Club, fed by the sea it faced. Shortly, the line of blue-green breakers rolled in uninterrupted, gulls swooped and called to a high and empty sky, and the beach at Spring Lake was bereft, for the first summer day in many years, of human presence—except for the men with the guns, and the sharp metallic smells of gasoline and lamb's blood.

In the lobby of the Essex and Sussex that morning, the white-haired figure of Mrs. George W. Childs moved through the crowds, emboldened by purpose, spreading news of the bell captain's funeral. Her plan to ship the young man home across the Atlantic had been refused by the Swiss counsel as too dangerous during wartime, with U-boats prowling the shipping channels. The bell captain would be buried the next morning in nearby Manasquan, and the management of the E & S vowed to cover all expenses, as if by doing the right thing—and doing it quickly—the hotel and its guests could put the tragedy behind them. But David Plumer, the manager, found himself patrolling the lobby that morning, calming nerves, and coaxing people to stay as the roar of motorboats drifted from the sea. Small lines of summer colonists stood at the front desk, shortening their vacations, making plans for the mountains. Word had reached the hotel that Asbury Park and towns up and down the coast were barricading their beaches from a man-eating shark. Yet the history of shark attack is footnoted by denial, and Spring Lake, perhaps inevitably, was opposed to such an alarming view.

Oliver Hush Brown, the mayor of Spring Lake and president of the First National Bank, possessed numerous public and private reasons to pray all talk of a shark would simply disappear. As mayor for thirty-two years, Brown was the town's prime mover; he led Spring Lake's comeback from the great fire of 1900, which destroyed whole blocks of businesses, and nurtured it as a tourist resort that would "cater to people of refinement and culture." His O. H. Brown variety store, filled with tasteful fineries from the mayor's buying trips to Europe, provided furnishings, floor coverings, china, and *objets* to the wealthy summer cottagers and hotels. The lobby of the E & S that morning was filled with O. H. Brown furnishings. In 1914, in fact, when the New E & S opened, the mayor had become a stockholder.

By midmorning, a commotion swept the lobby of the E & S as colonists crowded around copies of the day's *New York Times*, smudging their fingers with ink as they passed around the broadsheet pages. "Shark Kills Bather Off New Jersey Beach," the front page blared. "Bites Off Both Legs of a Young Swimmer. Guards Find Him Dying. Women Are Panic-stricken As Mutilated Body Is Brought Ashore." Even the habitually restrained *Times* could not report the arrival of a man-eating shark without sensation. There was no other way to tell the story. Men and women studied the newspaper with audible gasps. Dispatches by *Times* correspondents from the Battle of the Somme and the Russian front and the British sinking of twenty-one German ships seemed somehow tame and distant in comparison. With its headlines and stories of July 7, 1916, the *Times* introduced the great white shark to American culture as a source for general fear, the twentieth-century sea monster. As guests folded back the front page, the previous night's bold assertions that a shark could not have killed Bruder evaporated in the daylight. Some guests locked themselves in their rooms, others simply packed to leave. It was as if the horrors of the previous day, stamped in newsprint, could no longer be denied.

Some Spring Lake residents and fishermen stubbornly continued to claim that there were far more likely man-killers than sharks. They swapped stories of giant mackerels and huge, swift swordfish that could run a man through with their long, steel-hard blades. Whatever was out there concealed by the waves, for the first time in American history people en masse were afraid to enter the water. The four hundred to five hundred bathers who swam in the waters off the South Pavilion on Thursday dwindled on Friday to half a dozen brave souls drifting in and out of the surf. Finally, the surf emptied for good.

That afternoon, guests at the Essex and Sussex who elected to stay must have had second thoughts. The sounds of distant muffled gunshots reached the hotel, followed by an anxious account from the surfmen at the South Pavilion, on the water's edge. A large shark had been spotted perilously close to the beach. The armed men of the shark patrol had raised their rifles and opened fire across the waves, shooting at a large fin. The fish eluded the spray of bullets and, apparently frightened, disappeared out to sea. No swimmers were injured by the rifle fire; none were in the water. The pool at the Bath and Tennis Club grew uncomfortably overcrowded that afternoon. There were so many people in the pool, it would have to be emptied and refilled several additional times, in the days ahead, for sanitary reasons. Eventually, the club would petition the township for permission to lay a larger pipe to fill the pool. Nobody would go back into the ocean.

Myths of Antiquity

❧

Forty-five miles north of Spring Lake, New York City was a sea of buildings Henry James called "extravagant pins in a cushion already overplanted." Looming over Broadway was the tallest building in the world, the fifty-eight-story Woolworth Building, the new cathedral of commerce that symbolized New York's spirited modern ascension over Paris, trailing only London as the world's largest city. Everything in New York seemed new and modern in 1916—revolutionary words blowing through the city then. Penn Station and Grand Central,

Gimbel's and Ebbets Field, were all new to the feverish teens. At the Biograph Theater, D. W. Griffith launched the motion picture industry; Picasso, Matisse, and Picabia introduced modern art at the Armory Show; Emma Goldman and John Reed, anarchists, and New Women in Greenwich Village, swept away Victorian sexual prudery in a tide of free speech and free love. In 1916, Margaret Sanger opened the first birth control clinic in New York, after going to jail for writing about the subject. The *Lusitania* never returned to New York harbor, and the *Titanic* never arrived. The triumphal voyages of the ocean liners nonetheless extended the spell of the modern and new.

Rising over the Upper West Side like a castle, the American Museum of Natural History was another icon of the new, for under its ten-acre roof the museum had mounted the most painstaking effort in the modern world to illuminate the shadowy myths of the past with the lamp of scientific investigation: to acquire and transmit, for the first time in history, scientifically documented information about the animals, plants, and minerals of the earth's surface.

Late that July afternoon, a group of newspapermen presented itself at the grand entrance of the museum on Central Park West with a characteristic urgency. Hurrying past a gallery of marble busts—Benjamin Franklin, Alexander von Humboldt, Louis Agassiz, John James Audubon, Edward Drinker Cope, Robert E. Peary—the gentlemen of the press were dispatched to the office of the director of the museum and head of the scientific staff, Dr. Frederic Augustus Lucas.

Dr. Lucas was one of the preeminent scientists and "museum men" in the world, an authority in the fields of taxidermy, osteology (the study of bones), geology, and comparative anatomy. Once a lean New England sailor of clipper ships, Dr. Lucas at the age of sixty-four had attained a corpulence that to the late Victorians signified power. Thick white hair and a prominent walrus mustache set off by formal dark suits gave the director the bearing of a nineteenth-century financier. Preternaturally big, sad dark eyes in a drooping, jowly face revealed the humanist, one of the country's first great museum scientists, who delighted in bringing the "rational amusement" of science to the public.

The director was at the peak of his career. After twenty years as a curator at the Smithsonian in Washington, D.C., where he consulted frequently with Alexander Graham Bell, he had been appointed director of the American Museum in 1911 by the trustees, who included Theodore Roosevelt, Henry C. Frick, and J. P. Morgan. At Lucas's direction, the museum mounted the expeditions of many of the world's greatest botanists, anthropologists, and explorers. It dispatched Carl E. Akeley and Roosevelt to Africa and Peary to the North Pole. Dr. Lucas presided over major museums—the American, the Smithsonian, and the Brooklyn Museum—during the fifty years when museums grew from obscure collections scarcely open to the public to vast institutions of education and entertainment. It was he who mounted one of the world's most extensive efforts to reveal "natural" exhibits of animals and human tribes in their habitats within glass-enclosed cases.

With his professorial appearance, wit, and passion, Dr. Lucas was one of the great popularizers of science before television and radio, a Carl Sagan of an era of lantern-slide presentations and crowded lecture halls. He was an expert in demand by the great encyclopedias, including the *Encyclopedia Americana,* on all matters of natural history. He was most famous to a general readership for his short, best-selling book on fossils, *Animals of the Past: An Account of Some of the Creatures of the Ancient World,* in which he showed his gift for enlivening the driest science. Apologizing for using Latin scientific names, he wrote: "The reader may perhaps sympathize with the old lady who said that the discovery of all these strange animals did not surprise her so much as the fact that anyone should know their names when they were found." He steadfastly refused to report the ages of any fossil animals, since scientific estimates of the Jurassic period—"when the dinosaurs held carnival"—varied so widely, from six million to fifty million years ago. "It does seem as if it were hardly worth-while to name any figures . . . so the question of age will be left for the reader to settle to his or her satisfaction." The dinosaurs, then, were simply very old. Each chapter began with a poem by Lucas. In the "Rulers of the Ancient Seas" he wrote, "There rolling monsters armed in scaly pride/Flounce in the billows, and dash around the tide/There huge leviathan unwieldly moves/And through the waves a living island roves." His enter-taining survey of some of the recent discoveries of the fossil hunters—the mammoth, the mastodon, *Tyrannosaurus rex*—made him, in the public eye, one of the foremost scientists in the country.

But it was for a different reason the newspapermen requested an interview with Dr. Lucas. The director had stud-ied shark attacks for years, an endeavor that earned him the reputation of being the scientific community's reigning shark expert. It was Lucas who had dispatched John T. Nichols, one of his brightest assistants, to investigate the death of Charles Bruder in Spring Lake. But Nichols suspected a killer whale, while the newspapermen, and the public at large, were obsessed with the idea of a man-eating shark—a subject that, to the press's lament, no other men of science seemed to know much about. No less an authority than *The New York Times*—already the undisputed newspaper authority on matters of science—had declared Frederic Augustus Lucas "the greatest shark expert of this century" (leaving out the fact that Dr. Lucas was not an ichthyologist).

Frederic Augustus Lucas combined broad training in science with the Victorian naturalists' love of nature. Verging on childlike joy, he thrilled still to the gleam of enormous teeth appearing out of the shadows of vast halls, the gargantuan prehistoric forms reaching the uppermost ceilings. A brilliant popularizer of science in the new century, it was Lucas's unerring instinct to exhibit nature in its most spectacular and colossal forms. An eighty-foot blue whale swam silently behind a darkened glass window, the tentacles of a giant squid wrapped around its head. The Hall of Dinosaurs was the envy of the world, especially the tyrannosaurus skeleton—"mightiest of all animals that have walked the face of the earth," Dr. Lucas wrote, "for apparently nothing could have withstood the attack of this monster beast of prey."

Yet Dr. Lucas was uncharacteristically agitated as he strolled the cavernous stone hallways that afternoon. In his own estimation he had devoted far too much time to shining the cool lights of science and reason on the feverish public perception of sea monsters. The hullabaloo over a man supposedly killed by a shark in Spring Lake reminded him of the uproar over the "giant blob" that had washed ashore on Anastasia Island, Florida, in November 1896, causing an international sensation over the "Florida sea monster." Then, too, Dr. Lucas, at the time a curator at the Smithsonian Institution, was required to step in and disappoint the masses with scientific fact, identifying the "blob" as no more than decayed whale blubber. These hubbubs interfered with Dr. Lucas's real work, the careful, loving shaping of the museum, his research, writing, and scholarship, and the nurturing of young scientists.

He had been pressed into extra duty by the hullabaloo over the shark, and Dr. Lucas didn't tolerate work as he once did.

"The ideas do not come so quickly, nor the pen record them so readily as of yore," he lamented in the seventh edition of *Animals of the Past*. "Worst of all his brain has joined with the labor unions in demanding an eight hour day and refuses to work nights."

An avowed Victorian gentleman, Frederic Lucas was rankled by much of the modern world. A disciplined and orderly man, he grew weary that week as newspapermen interrupted him with queries about the young man in Spring Lake supposedly killed by a shark. What kind of shark was responsible? Are sharks man-eaters? Should swimmers be afraid? The names and faces of the men from the *Post* and *Times*, the *Herald* and *World*, the *Journal* and *Inquirer* and *Bulletin*, were different but the questions were endlessly the same. Dr. Lucas was in touch with his esteemed colleague Hugh M. Smith, director of the U.S. Bureau of Fisheries in Washington—the government's top fish scholar—about the so-called "shark attacks." Dr. Smith seemed equally perplexed by the Spring Lake incident, and shared Dr. Lucas's private sentiment that he wished the whole matter of the shark would simply go away.

A stickler for accuracy in educating the public, Lucas wasn't impressed with newspapermen's record in disseminating scientific knowledge. He ruefully recalled how the newspapers reported a colleague's discovery that the brain of the prehistoric creature was located near the posterior—dinosaurs were thinking with their pelvis! When Georgia newspapers had trumpeted the discovery of a "Giant Cliff Dweller Mummy," Dr. Lucas dispatched an investigator to Atlanta to see if it belonged in the museum. The mummy was sitting in the sheriff's office, made of paper skin and the teeth of a cow.

The director could imagine few myths as archaic and misguided as the myth of the sea monster, and particularly the weak-minded belief in a man-eating shark. The man-eating shark was a hysterical product of the myths of antiquity, but such a creature, as far as Dr. Lucas's thirty years of personal scientific investigations could determine, simply did not exist, or most certainly not in New York or New Jersey waters.

Asked by the New York press to comment on Bruder's death, Dr. Lucas declared: "No shark could skin a human leg like a carrot, for the jaws are not powerful enough to induce injuries like those described by Colonel Schauffler." The esteemed scientist was adamant to the point of "finality" that sharks were not capable of inflicting serious injury to man.

Dr. Lucas's authority on sharks was supported by a lifetime of scientific study. Frederic Augustus Lucas was one of the last of the old-time Victorian naturalists who relied on love of nature and a keen mind in lieu of a university education. Armed with an introductory letter from his nineteenth-century sea-captain father—"Do you have any use for a boy who seems mostly interested in skinning snakes?"—he studied at the Natural Science Establishment in Rochester, New York, where he absorbed the broad training of one of the last of the "all-around naturalists." Of all things modern, what rankled him most was scientific "specialization," which struck him as narrow and unmanly; he failed to understand how the new men of science could not clean skeletons, do taxidermy, and mount and build their own exhibits like carpenters, as he once did.

He was troubled by the lack of passion in young museum men: "Old-timers like Hornaday, Akeley and myself grieve over the helplessness of the modern preparator, his dread of working overtime . . . his readiness to make up for being late by quitting early. We worked a dozen hours a day and then went home to work for ourselves or took our best girl to the theatre. We heard nothing in those days of the artistic temperament— we heard more of laziness or general cussedness."

Dr. Lucas's knowledge spanned the whole of the animal kingdom. During his fifty-year career, he wrote 365 scientific journal articles—many in longhand, before the typewriter was invented—ranging "in the old-fashioned way from insects to dinosaurs through the whole gamut of fishes, amphibians, reptiles, birds, and mammals."

He had been first fascinated with sharks while sailing around the world with his father. By the time he was eighteen, Lucas had sailed to Europe and Asia and around the Cape of Good Hope. The persistent myth of the man-eating shark fired his skepticism, for nowhere in the world could he find documented evidence of such a fish. As was said of William Beebe, the "father of oceanography," whom Lucas employed as a young man and who later went down in the first bathysphere: "He was not prepared to take anyone's word for anything. He had to see for himself." And so in the 1880s, when he joined the United States Museum (later the Smithsonian), the Brooklyn Museum, and finally the American Museum, he continued his inquiries firsthand on the Atlantic Coast.

Again and again, his investigations of reported man-eating sharks on the East Coast turned up fabricated stories of large but harmless species. While Lucas allowed that "two really dangerous species, the white shark and the blue shark," wander up from the tropics, he maintained that "there is no record of any fully grown individual ever having been taken within hundreds of miles of New York." Furthermore, "ordinarily a shark is a very cautious animal, and it is difficult to get a big one to take a bait to which he is not accustomed." Thus, the danger of being attacked by a shark on the Atlantic Coast was "infinitely less than that of being struck by lightning."

As a recognized authority, Lucas was often called to set the record straight. He had watched from a distance the previous summer the ongoing shark debate in *The New York Times*. The director was dismayed when a spate of local "shark scares" revealed that an unreasoning fear of attack still existed, and later cheered when *The New York Times* published its August 2, 1915, editorial, "Let Us Do Justice to Sharks," declaring that Hermann Oelrichs had been right and "that sharks can properly be called dangerous, in this part of the world, is apparently untrue." But when a subsequent rash of letters to the editor of the *Times* purported to describe dozens of gruesome man-eating shark attacks around the world, Dr. Lucas could not let pass what he regarded as unscientific, unsubstantiated anecdote or rumor. Dr. Lucas had not changed his opinion since 1905, when, as editor of *Young Folks Cyclopaedia of Natural History*, he classified the great white shark, *Carcharodon carcharias*, under its popular name "the man-eater shark." "This, the most voracious of sharks, does not hesitate, it is said, to attack a man, but practically few or no authentic cases are on record of such a thing having taken place."

So the director was understandably disturbed when J. T. Du Bois, an American diplomat, began the broadside of evidence on August 15, 1915, with a grisly letter to the *Times*, "The Man-eating Shark." Even carefree New York and New Jersey swimmers must have shuddered as they read the report of the diplomat, then consul general in Singapore, British Malaya, of the collision and sinking of French and British passenger steamers in the Straits of Rhio in November 1907. "The panic stricken passengers threw themselves into the water and were instantly attacked by some man-eating sharks, and the waters were reddened by the slaughter. About ninety people lost their lives. When the news of this disaster reached the United States, I received several letters asking if it were true that such a thing existed as a man-eating shark."

Intrigued, Du Bois immediately dispatched fifty letters to

diplomats around the world, from the Philippines to the Red Sea, "asking for verified incidents of the work of the man-eating shark." The response astonished him: "I received sixteen affidavits from American Consuls, Philippine officials, and one Indian official, reciting interesting incidents of the man-eating sharks attacking and wounding or killing and eating human beings." He was sent a photograph of a Tomali boy, coin-diving on the Gulf of Aden, being "seized by a man-eating shark and dragged back into the waters, never to return."

Eight days after the diplomat's letter, another letter in the *Times*, signed cryptically "N.S.W.," denoting the Australian state of New South Wales, gave convincing and gruesome details of three cases of sharks devouring humans, adding that "any one who doubts that sharks in temperate waters do attack human beings will visit Sydney, N.S.W. . . . and . . . his doubts will be speedily resolved." The letter reported the case of a boy dangling his legs off a wharf at Ryde, on the Parramatta River, which feeds the harbor, when "a shark came up, seized a foot, and disappeared with the boy, whose body was never seen again." The very next day, Herbert MacKenzie, a native of Sydney, Australia, capital of New South Wales, published in the *Times* a letter confirming to the last detail his memory of the three cases reported by "N.S.W." "As a native of that beautiful city, I can with authority corroborate the statements . . . and know of others where lives and limbs have been lost as a result of these sea monsters in the beautiful waters of the harbor." In the late 1880s, MacKenzie reported: "I distinctly remember a young man losing first an arm, then, just as rescue was at hand, the entire body disappeared, leaving only a blood path in the water. This happened in Rushcutters Bay."

If readers of the *Times* were unsettled by these accounts, they must have found reassuring the rebuttal from Dr. Lucas, the famed expert who had investigated alleged shark attacks on the East Coast for forty years and verified none as authentic. In his letter to the editor, "The Shark Slander," Dr. Lucas announced he knew of only "two fairly reliable references to such cases" in the world—one in Bombay, where a man lost his leg, another in the Hawaiian Islands, where a human victim was surely mistaken for offal dumped in the water.

Those who believed a shark had killed Charles Bruder, Lucas declared, had made one of the commonest errors in such cases, "that the shark bit off the man's leg as though it were a carrot." Such a feat was not possible, Lucas said, and the mere statement "shows that the maker or writer of it had little idea of the strength of the apparatus needed to perform such an amputation." In his contribution to Nichols's and Murphy's journal article for the *Brooklyn Museum Science Bulletin*, published three months before Bruder's death, Lucas described the common sense behind his theory. "The next time the reader carves a leg of lamb, let him speculate on the power required to sever this at one stroke—and the bones of a sheep are much lighter than those of a man. Moreover, a shark, popular belief to the contrary notwithstanding, is not particularly strong in the jaws."

As evidence, Dr. Lucas noted that his protégé, Robert Cushman Murphy, during an expedition to South Georgia Island, witnessed "the difficulty of sharks in tearing meat from the carcass of a whale." And Lucas recalled his own "disappointment at witnessing the efforts of a twelve-foot shark to cut a chunk out of a sea lion. The sea lion had been dead a week and was supposedly tender, but the shark tugged and thrashed and made a great to-do over each mouthful."

Given the weakness of even the largest sharks' jaws, Lucas reasoned, a man would lose a leg only "if a shark thirty feet or more in length happened to catch a man fairly on the knee joint where no severing of the bone was necessary." A shark was not capable of biting cleanly through the bone and therefore could not have been the animal that bit off Charles Bruder's legs below the knee. What animal was capable of the attack, Dr. Lucas couldn't say, but "certainly no shark recorded as having been taken in these waters could possibly perform such an act." According to Lucas, the best scientific data concerning the question of the East Coast shark attack remained the uncollected wager Hermann Oelrichs made in 1891. Twenty-five years had substantiated the tycoon's position, Lucas concluded, that there is "practically no danger of an attack . . . about our coasts."

A Long-Range Cruising Rogue

⚛

As the motorboats rumbled and bloodied the waters of Spring Lake, not far offshore the great white swam with growing urgency. Never straying more than a half mile from shore, it swept north and south, fronting the coast, stalking the two-mile-long beach of Spring Lake and the coastline a few miles north toward Asbury Park. The shark moved with increasing expectancy, for it had hunted with success, and prey was very close now, abundant prey; it could sense it with numerous electrical, sonic, and olfactory systems. Wary of boats and oars, the shark safely tracked its prey from a distance, with no need to approach the shore. Its lateral lines tingled with the distant vibration of motorboat engines. Gasoline engines for boats were a new invention, and men then could not have known the acoustic chorus they sang over time and space for sharks. The shark detected the sonic pulses of swimmers under and beyond the blockade of the boats like a submersible receiving coded signals beneath an antiquated navy. Molecules of blood in the water, carried on currents from miles away, moved in and out of the shark's flapped nostrils, firing its cerebellum to adjust its fins for a new direction. As the shark haunted the coast that afternoon, the men of New Jersey were growing edgy enough to shoot at anything that swam. It is likely the rogue great white was among the targets that the Spring Lake patrol fired at, for there is compelling evidence that it remained in the area after killing Bruder. The shark, like its pursuers, was growing increasingly edgy, attacking oars and boats and anything that moved.

There is scant science on the matter of a rogue shark, a deliberate man-eater, while skepticism persists that such a creature exists. As people are not a regular prey for sharks, a purposeful hunter of humans like a rogue lion or elephant must be injured, crazed, aberrant. Furthermore an oceanic "serial killer" is nearly impossible to catch and convict, its work concealed, the evidence eradicated by the enclosing sea. But the late Dr. Sir Victor Coppleson, a distinguished Australian surgeon knighted by the queen, tracked the global movements of rogues across the twentieth century, beginning in 1922, when he began treating shark bites as a young doctor at St. Vincent's Hospital in Sydney. In 1933, Coppleson coined the term "rogue shark" in the *Medical Journal of Australia*. "A rogue shark," he wrote, "if the theory is correct, and evidence appears to prove it to the hilt—like the man-eating tiger, is a killer which, having experienced the deadly sport of killing or mauling a human, goes in search of similar game. The theory is supported by the pattern and frequency of many attacks."

Rogue attacks began, Coppleson believed, with the rising popularity of beaches for recreational use at the turn of the century. Coppleson's ground zero for investigation was Sydney, where rogue attacks were unknown until the sport of surfing arrived in 1919. Then, on February 4, 1922, Milton Coughlan, a surfman, was "cracking a few waves" on Coogee Beach when a large shark "struck with such terrific force that he was lifted from the water," whereupon a crowd watched a large pair of jaws snap off Coughlan's arm. He died shortly afterward at a local hospital. Coppleson suspected a pattern when, less than a month later, twenty-one-year-old Mervyn Gannon was struck and killed at the same beach. During the next three years, Nita Derritt, a saleswoman, lost both legs in a shark attack, and Jack Dagworthy, sixteen, lost a leg when a shark leapt out of the water at him, mouth agape. The work of a single deranged shark, Coppleson concluded in such cases, was the only logical explanation. It seemed to him far-fetched to believe that a beach swimming area, free from shark attack for decades, would suddenly be invaded by groups of man-eating sharks, then, just as suddenly, be free of attack for years to come. Often, the "rogue series"—a reign of terror lasting several days or years—ended when a single man-eater was captured.

In a pattern eerily similar to that of great whites in California observed hunting sea lions on or near anniversary days, the rogue sharks in Australia often took human victims in the same area near the one-year anniversary of an earlier killing. What Coppleson considered "the most spine-chilling . . . attack known in Sydney waters" was part of an "anniversary" pattern. Zita Steadman, twenty-eight, was swimming with friends near

Bantry Bay in January 1942, standing in waist-deep water, when a friend named Burns warned her not to go too far. Zita had just turned to go back, when she suddenly shrieked, and a huge shark was clearly visible to her friends, mauling the young woman. Burns grabbed an oar from their rowboat and began smashing at the attacker, but to no avail. Burns then rammed the shark, which shrugged off the boat and kept attacking. The shark struck Steadman "with such ferocity that it was throwing itself into the air" and began to draw its prey into deeper water. In desperation, Burns pulled Zita Steadman away from the shark by grabbing her long, dark hair; Steadman had been bitten in two. Less than a year later, while standing in the same waters, fifteen-year-old Denise Burch was torn apart by the same shark that killed Zita Steadman, Coppleson believed.

In twenty-five years, Coppleson discovered the work of rogue sharks all over the world. In December 1957, in Durban, South Africa, during the three weeks known as "Black December," three swimmers were killed, one was severely mauled, and another lost a leg. In San Juan, Puerto Rico, in the 1920s, he investigated five attacks on the same beach during three years, including that of an American schoolteacher who died almost instantly as a shark removed most of her hip, thigh, and related bones in a single bite, and that of a Professor Winslow, found with both arms and legs almost severed from his body, his hands gone. In Africa and Australia in the 1950s, Coppleson's theory was useful to people seeking an understanding of shark attacks, and led to the erection of shark nets to combat rogues. Only in the United States, where "writers for many years . . . have labeled most stories of shark attacks on humans as 'fish yarns,' were scientists skeptical," Coppleson found. Such skepticism was ironic, since in Coppleson's research, the United States trailed only Australia and Africa in shark attacks and "one of the most remarkable series of shark attacks in world history" occurred on its Atlantic coast, in New Jersey, in 1916. The New Jersey case was one of a number that supported Coppleson's contention, "as fantastic as it may seem," that a rogue shark can strike at distances of sixty to eighty miles apart over several days or weeks. In fact, the Jersey shark was "the classic example of . . . a long-range cruising rogue."

Coppleson believed that he was so expert in profiling the tendencies of rogue sharks that he was able to predict days in advance when a man-eater would strike. When a shark attacking dogs near Botany Bay was mentioned in the *Sydney Morning Herald* in early January 1940, Coppleson later regretted not writing a letter to the editor that it fit the profile of a rogue. A large shark that appeared near a beach or harbor deeply agitated, "acting savagely, snapping fish from lines, tearing nets, and attacking dogs," charging boats or attacking anything in sight, was an incipient man-eater. On January 23, a thirteen-year-old boy, Maxwell Farrin, was killed by a shark near Botany Bay. The next day, Coppleson published his letter, advising capture of the shark and warning swimmers to be cautious, for "on the rogue shark theory it would strike again." John William Eke, fifty-five, didn't heed the warning, and eleven days later, four hundred yards from the Farrin attack, he lost his life to a shark.

Scientists in 1916 were ignorant of Coppleson's theory (it was not published for another forty years). By the twenty-first century, Coppleson's theory was widely dismissed by scientists. Yet the rogue theory gave shark-stricken coasts in the mid–twentieth century some grasp, some understanding, of the apex predator. Cluster attacks can now sometimes be explained by coastal water-temperature changes that draw sharks to beach areas when swimmers are in the water. In 1916, there was no such awareness. As the shark moved off the coast of Spring Lake and Asbury Park on July 7, 1916, there was no clue that it was escalating toward a series of attacks unprecedented in two thousand years of shark attacks on man. Many years later, Coppleson, in his exhaustive if anecdotal survey, concluded with some surprise that none of the fabled, huge "white pointers" of Australia had ever traveled as widely to kill as many human beings, nor had any "ever shown the ferocity of the 'mad shark' of New Jersey in July 1916."

A Great Many Bathers
Are Rather Scarce

⤬

His broad back to the sun, Benjamin Everingham dipped the oars of a small rowboat into the listless gray sea and pulled. The boat glided a few feet, slapping against the grain of the waves, and slowed, and he exhaled and pulled again. He was fifty feet beyond the ropes at the Asbury Avenue beach, moving parallel to the coast. A line of salmon clouds floated on the horizon. As the boat coasted, he looked toward the horizon, squinting for a fin, and, seeing nothing, he put his head down and pulled again. It was after eleven in the morning and the mild weather was a surprise. Mindful of the gift of a clear day, the summer people in the hotels and boardinghouses crowded the beaches early that Saturday.

There were more than a hundred people in the water at Asbury Avenue, thronged behind the safety ropes. Hundreds more sat on the beach under muted green, blue, and siena umbrellas. The Fourth Avenue and Seventh Avenue beaches were crowded too. The *Asbury Park Press* sang with reassuring headlines: "Will Assure Absolute Safety to Bathers . . . Asbury Park Bathing Grounds All to Be Surrounded by Wire." A heavy, close-meshed wire netting, used for fishing but thought to be strong enough to keep out sharks, had been installed the day before at the Fourth Avenue beach from sea bottom to the high-tide level. Work hadn't started at Asbury Avenue yet. The beach was open to the sea, thus Everingham's assignment to row along the coast and keep an eye out for sharks.

Everingham was captain of the surfmen for the resort city, but by all accounts he was taking his assignment that day lightly. He was skeptical of reports that a shark had killed a man on Thursday in Spring Lake, four miles south. Fishermen in Asbury Park were saying it must have been a freak big mackerel or swordfish, and, in any case, as an old-time seaman had said in the *Press,* "Such an accident is not apt to happen again in a thousand years." Instructed to carry a rifle and ax on his shark patrol to protect the bathers, Everingham hadn't bothered.

Everingham's lapse in judgment would come as a surprise to officials of the beach town. Asbury Park was a fabled Gilded Age resort of broad Parisian-style boulevards and grand hotels and mansions, one of which was built by John D. Rockefeller. In 1916, Asbury Park was considered a "flossy" place, a new word then for "classy." A John Sousa band performed a summer concert series in the bandstand; a nationally famous parade of babies toddled down the boardwalk; an electrified trolley system, the second in America, ran down to the sea.

That Saturday, Mayor Laughlin Hetrick had announced a new theme for the baby parade of "demonstration of national preparedness from the standpoint of protection for mothers and babies." Strollers on the boardwalk, who came to Asbury Park for health, looked for bottled cures such as Lenox Water, which "Relieves Rheumatism, Nervous Exhaustion and Lassitude . . . restoring nerve force," although the Pure-Food Act had recently driven many such potions off the market. At the Asbury Avenue beach that morning, young women sported the new colorful swimsuits with bold checks and stripes, no doubt relieved at the removal of the bathhouse sign: "Modesty of apparel is as becoming to a lady in a bathing suit as it is to a lady dressed in silk and satin. A word to the wise is sufficient."

At a quarter to noon, as Benjamin Everingham rowed parallel to the coast, perhaps he was distracted by the flashy new bathing costumes. Perhaps he was wearied from staring at the endless ocean and thought his eyes were playing tricks on him. But when he turned toward the horizon, he saw a type of gray fin cutting the low waves. In an instant he recognized it as a large shark. It seemed to be fully eight feet long, and it was bearing directly for his boat. Everingham must have regretted for a fleeting moment that he had neglected to bring a rifle or ax. Just as the shark was about to strike his boat, the surfman stood and "lifted one of the oars from its lock and struck viciously at the slimy sea monster." Stricken, the creature turned sideways as if to flee, whereupon Everingham swung the oar and struck the big fish again, "and with a swirling of the waters the shark turned and shot out to sea."

Crowds watching from the beach and a nearby fishing pier were puzzled as they saw Everingham standing up in his boat, striking the surface of the water with an oar. But the mystery was answered as the captain of the surfmen rowed frantically to shore, shouting that he'd seen a shark. Everingham's announcement, followed by an order to his colleagues to clear the surf, caused considerable excitement on the shore. In an uproar, more than a hundred men, women, and children ran shrieking from the Asbury Avenue beach. It did not require much urging of the guards to clear the water of the bathers.

The captain of the surfmen tried to calm the panic, telling all who would listen that "had he been armed with an axe or harpoon he might have succeeded in killing or wounding the shark." But as soon as Everingham reported the news to his superiors, Asbury Park officials closed the beach and ordered bathers out of the water at the Seventh Avenue bathing grounds as well. The Fourth Avenue beach, enclosed by protective steel nets, remained open that afternoon, but many bathers chose to leave the water. They sat huddled on the sands, watching armed patrol boats move up and down the coast outside the netting.

The shark aroused in men old angers and thrills and new possibilities of blood lust. That afternoon, Mayor Hetrick returned from a fishing trip on his luxury yacht, *Tuna*, to find Ben Everingham's battle with a shark the talk of Asbury Park. The mayor immediately ordered shark hooks fashioned for his boat and announced from then on the *Tuna* would be fishing for sharks to keep them away from the populace. The crew of the *Tuna* had its own reasons, he said. Earlier that day the *Tuna*'s passengers had been alarmed by the sight of blue sharks playing about a buoy about a mile from Asbury Park. The mayor had spied blue sharks like this before, far from shore, but the sight of the fins appearing and disappearing from the surface and vanishing south to points unknown upset and frightened his paying passengers. The captain of the *Tuna*, A. A.

Thompson, had experience with sharks in southern waters, the mayor said. As if to prove his readiness, Captain Thompson boasted that "should the monsters of the deep remain in this vicinity they are liable to find their ranks depleted."

That afternoon, Harold Phillips, a member of the Asbury Park Fishing Club, joined the mayor in spirit, declaring he would tow the carcasses of horses and cows to a remote area a quarter mile off Sandy Hook, "the idea being that the sharks would all be attracted to the spot and done away with." The idea caused an uproar in the club. There was no shortage of sportfishermen eager for a try. The carcasses would attract "the greatest roundup of sharks ever seen," Phillips promised, sketching it out right in front of them, and then the fellows from the Asbury Park Gun Club would train their rifles "for what would no doubt prove most exciting sport, shooting the big game of the seas."

But Asbury Park officials were not reassured by plans to eradicate all the man-eaters in the ocean. By the end of the day, they announced that both the Asbury Avenue and Seventh Avenue beaches would remain closed because of the "shark menace" until they could be surrounded by the steel-wire nets. In the hotels on Grand Avenue, and in trolley car 32 that ran from the train depot to the beach, the talk was of a killer shark. Whether the shark that attacked Everingham was the great white that killed Bruder didn't seem to matter; fear was growing general on the coast at the pace that hysteria outruns reason. One shark now represented all sharks, white or blue, near or far from shore. Two days after the death of Charles Bruder in Spring Lake, declared the *Asbury Park Press*, "The shark scare in Asbury Park has become a reality."

Late that evening, a newlywed woman spending her honeymoon in Asbury Park mailed a postcard to a friend in Ludlow, Massachusetts, titled "Bathing Scene, Asbury Park, N.J." The photograph of the beach showed crowds of people in the water behind rope lines, and a beach dotted with sunbathers and umbrellas. The woman, whose name was Mona, wrote on the back in small Palmer script compressed to fit: "This card is the picture of the beach where we go bathing. They have screened it in and it is patrolled by boats since the scare of a shark biting off the legs of a man a few beaches above here the other morning. The man died. Since then a great many bathers are rather scarce."

The news of Bruder's death flew that summer from Manasquan to Massachusetts to Virginia and across five hundred miles of coastline. The news held sway in billiard parlors and smoking rooms and on carriage rides until men and women looked out to sea and saw in the fins that had been there summer after summer new and alien shapes. Everyone along the shore was thinking about sharks during the summer of 1916: an Edwardian matron watching a child's first swim, a man folding back the front page—*both legs are bitten off just below the knees*—to find the sports, a traveling Victrola scratching out Irving Berlin's "When I Lost You" under the blowing sand of a beach picnic. Whether borne by word of mouth or by printing press, the story traveled the shortest distance to the frightened heart, for it was the oldest suspense story of all—man killed by monster. And if this once-truest tale was forgotten and denied or polished up by the sweet civilized shine of metaphor, the story stirred latent yet hot in the veins of the moderns, raw, antediluvian, real. "Killed by Shark," the *Press* said. "Boy, Legs Bitten Off by Shark," Pulitzer's *World* screamed, "Dies on Beach . . . Precautions to Safeguard Bathers."

Never had this aged yarn been borne so far so fast or been so thoroughly reinvented as new, by the *Times* of Adolph Ochs, William Randolph Hearst's *Journal*, Joseph Pulitzer and Frank Cobb's *World,* and by the "great octopus" that was "the most tremendous engine for Power which ever existed in this world," the Associated Press. The titans of the yellow press knew the shortcuts to the frightened heart. Cobb hired young college men conversant with the Ajax of Sophocles; Hearst went for the "gee-whiz" effect; Ochs knew the thrill of murder and shark attack like any man, but while "the yellows see such stories only as opportunities for sensationalism," he said, "when the *Times* gives a great amount of space to such stories it turns out authentic sociological documents." However the story was told, people already knew it by heart and knew without asking what the end was. On the eastern seaboard, men took hold of the fear and anger and made it their own.

In New York Bay, on Saturday, July 8, seven days after Vansant's death, two days after Bruder's death, the very day Ben Everingham clubbed an attacking shark at Asbury Park, a score of boys and girls were bathing near the Robbins Reef Yacht Club, in Bayonne, New Jersey, when several of the children saw a shark, a big one, some eight feet long, appear off the float that extended out from the clubhouse. The children saw something black approaching them and, becoming frightened, started for shore. Somebody yelled, "It's a shark!" and the children ran, screaming, for the bathhouses.

In the yard adjoining the bathhouses, Dennis Colohan, a police lieutenant, was working with Amos Harker, superintendent of the city water department, and two other policemen to place an engine in a motorboat owned by Harker, when they heard the screams. Looking out on the water, the men saw a shark lift its head only a short distance from where the children had been bathing.

Lieutenant Colohan had his revolver with him and, followed by the other men, ran to the end of the float. The shark was still coming, headed toward shore. Colohan waited until the big fish was twenty feet away. He saw that the fin alone was three feet high out of the water and he squeezed the trigger. Some of the shots lodged in the shark's head, and yet the shark kept coming and Colohan kept shooting, emptying the revolver. The shark "seemed stunned for a moment, and then, lashing its tail, it turned quickly about, headed toward the Robbins Reef Lighthouse and disappeared," Colohan said.

Word spread on the beach rapidly and "many bathers along the shore decided to quit," reported the *New York World*. The police issued a warning to all bathers not to venture far out in the bay. According to an old bay fisherman, "The shark was the first seen in New York Bay in many years and the first ever so close to shore." Lieutenant Colohan stood on the shore with the other men for half an hour after the shark disappeared by the lighthouse, waiting for it to return. The next day he was a hero, elevated by the *World* to the same pedestal as Everingham: "Two More Sharks Sighted and Sent to Sea A-grieving."

More than two hundred miles south, along the coasts of Maryland and Virginia, swimmers and boaters spied the ocean and the waters of Chesapeake Bay as something menacing and foreign. The *Washington Star* urged swimmers to beware of whatever had killed two men in New Jersey. Hundreds of thousands of people on the Atlantic coast were now afraid to go in the water, the *Star* noted, for good reason.

A warning came from silent film star and world-renowned beauty Annette Kellerman, who in 1914 starred in *Neptune's Daughter* and was then appearing as a mermaid in *A Daughter of the Gods*. "Whether . . . Bruder was killed by the dreaded shark or by some other species of large fish," Kellerman was moved to write in a major article in the *Washington Post*, "something in the water . . . attacked him and tore his limbs from the body, that we do know."

Kellerman's voice was an important one in educating America

about the terrors of sharks. The world's most famous female swimmer, later portrayed by Esther Williams in the 1952 movie *Million Dollar Mermaid*, Kellerman was arrested in 1907 for wearing a one-piece bathing suit, which pointed the suffragette movement toward androgynous bathing styles and freed women from the gloves, hats, stockings, and pumps that made it impossible to swim. Kellerman was an early prophet of swimming as a safe, democratic, and wholesome sport. Now, in July 1916, she urged Americans to accept a hidden danger inherent in swimming: to fear sharks and to raise their children to fear them, especially the white shark. Well known to Australians, the white was "the nearest to what we term man-eater," for it "will attack with terrific ferocity, and nothing will stop him from attaining his end . . . whatever his eyes see he will go for, and at one gulp swallow a man . . ." In Australia, "from the time a child is able to understand things the fear of the shark is forcibly impressed upon the mind. The shark to an Australian child occupies the same position as the bogey man does to American children."

She closed her essay with a prescient warning: "That shark that killed Bruder will hover about the spot and perhaps others will join him. Then we will be subjected to a reign of terror that will cause the public to shun the beaches and bring ruin to the bathing-house owners. Let a word in time suffice. We must have no more shocking cases on the order of the Spring Lake beach affair."

That same morning in Spring Lake, the soul of Charles Bruder was committed to eternal life at a funeral service at St. Andrew's Methodist Church, as employees of the Essex and Sussex, the New Monmouth, and other hotels filled the pews. Outside the windows, patrol boats buzzed along the coast through a steaming summer morning, and rowboats, packed with armed men, moored near the north and south bathing pavilions.

Despite the heat, the beaches were almost empty, particularly at the South End pavilion, where Bruder was attacked, "indicating the fear felt by members of the cottage colony," a local newspaper reported. Only a few ventured into the ocean and seemed to have no fear.

The fear had spread to nearby Manasquan, too. E. E. Sweeting, proprietor of Sweeting's bathing pavilion, tried to persuade bathers they had nothing to worry about. Sweeting had assigned Captain Charles Bentz of his surfmen to patrol the beach in a boat, "armed with a marlin spike, axe and other hardware that a shark might resent if he ventured too near." But bathers were reluctant, and attendance was sparse.

After the church service, the funeral procession wended to Atlantic View Cemetery in Manasquan to bury the bell captain, in a grave near the sea, with a brief ceremony to bring closure and peace. Yet it was as if burial confirmed the strangeness of Bruder's death, as if opening the ground for a man killed by a shark released feelings of alienness and threat. Shortly after interment, five miles almost directly off the coast, John Anderson, a respected Manasquan fisherman, had a frightening experience he would later tell everyone on the docks. He was cruising in his small boat, when he saw "a school of sharks and porpoises disporting in the briny" with "other sea denizens which might have been whales." Anderson had seen many sharks in his years at sea and worked among them, but now, fearful, he turned his boat toward shore, "loath to stay near the sea monsters."

Disporting in a Perfect Surf

⁓

The next morning, Sunday, July 9th, Asbury Park's summer people in the hotels and cottages sat by eastern windows, as the newspapers instructed, to catch the healthful light from the sea. Hotel guests had breakfast and headed to church, where they heard soloists sing "Eye Hath Not Seen." Afterward, gentlemen in straw hats and matrons in silk dresses strolled down the boulevards to the sea. Trolley car 32 was swollen with passengers bound for the beaches, for "visitors and hotel guests had fully regained their confidence," the *Asbury Park Press* reported.

There was talk of the jewel heist of a huge eighteen-hundred-dollar diamond, the St. Claire was advertising for "colored waitresses," the Surf House for "two experienced white chambermaids," and Asbury Park had regained its "normalcy," a word in use prior to its appropriation by Harding to restore the feeling of sultry days before the disillusionments of the Great War. Days like this one.

The beaches were thronged with crowds, the water aswarm with bathers who appeared to have forgotten the deaths of Charles Vansant and Charles Bruder with the denial that attended shark attacks. For if nothing could be more horrible than being swallowed by a monster fish, what could be more rewarding to forget?

Besides, sharks were nothing to worry about now. A day after hysteria swept Asbury Park, "the shark scare . . . is practically dead," the *Press* crowed, "albeit there are sharks somewhere in the ocean and whales, too, for that matter. But Asbury Park's bathing grounds are free from sharks for the very simple reason that no sharks can enter them." The beaches were all barricaded by steel wire that formed a U shape around the bathing grounds, and "timidity had given place to the pleasure of disporting in a perfect surf unmarred by the slightest evidence of danger."

Just north of Asbury Park, in the village of Ocean Grove, town manager Frank B. Smith announced that a contract had been awarded to erect a protective net around the beach, but it was hardly needed. Unaware that shark attacks were more likely in shallow water, Smith declared the Ocean Grove beach was not as deep near shore as those at Beach Haven and Spring Lake and this "difference in character" would "greatly lessen the danger of a visit from sharks." Even in Spring Lake, three days after Bruder's death, beach attendance was improving. While bathers were "loath to venture very far out," the *Press* reported, "it is possible early next week will again see bathing in vogue."

Bathers were reassured by the comments that week by Hugh Smith, director of the U.S. Bureau of Fisheries, that they ought "not be unduly alarmed or deterred from going in bathing" as "sharks are not vicious." Smith, fifty-one, one of the most respected fish scientists in the world, had directed the marine biological laboratory at Woods Hole, Massachusetts, at the turn of the century. From 1907 to 1910, he led the government's expedition on the steamer *Albatross* that collected four hundred thousand fish and aquatic animals, one of the largest and most diverse collections of marine life ever assembled. Aboard the *Albatross* he had befriended an international roster of renowned scientists, including Frederic Lucas. Like Dr. Lucas, Hugh Smith had studied sharks for years and shared his opinion that a shark had not killed Bruder or Vansant.

The commissioner believed the likeliest culprit in both men's deaths was the broadbill swordfish *Xiphias gladius*, whose tall dorsal fin would explain the fins sited during both attacks. The swordfish possesses great speed and enormous size—up to fifteen feet long and a thousand pounds—and there were reports, the commissioner said, of men run cleanly through by its long, flat sword.

"When we consider that there are hundreds of thousands of bathers on our eastern coasts every year and that for as long as anyone can remember no one has been bitten until these two recent cases, I think it is a word in favor of the sharks," Smith said. "Our domestic animals, horses, dogs and others, have not anything like this record."

PART THREE

TO DESTROY NO MORE

Toward the World of Men

As the sun slid into the sea along the darkening coast, the shark descended with it, plunging thirty, forty feet to the bottom, where it righted and cruised on the pebbly landscape of the ocean floor. The night sea floor was scattered with fish seeking shelter, making themselves less of a target to predators. The shark blended imperceptibly with the ocean floor as its huge tail propelled it in the gloom.

The black eyes of the shark absorbed light, and out of the dusk swam the huge rusted boilers and engines of the steamer wrecks. Schools of big blackfish and hordes of cunners moved in and out of the wrecks maddeningly, somehow beyond reach. Through an eerie world of dead forms the shark swam past shipwrecks scattered like a behemoth's graveyard—such as the bones of the *Western World*, a clipper ship that sank sixty years earlier with three hundred passengers, and the *Malta*, a 244-foot steamer that went down in 1885. The shark surveyed the bottom for the living and the dead, for things that couldn't flee. Deadeyes and bolts and deck lights, blue glass bottles and mustard jars, riding spurs and whiskey flasks, inkwells and school bells from the last century, were all there on the coastal bottom as the shark moved north. Pewter cups of a last supper, ginger ale bottles still full, gentlemen's pipes and ladies' perfumes from the 1870s, a load of Civil War rifles moldering in their cases.

And so the young shark darted falteringly toward great clouds of weakfish and black bass, red hake, monkfish, and menhaden. It was hapless to feed as it was accustomed. The fish of the mid-Atlantic were well organized in classes of predator and prey, a natural structure from which the shark had somehow removed itself or been removed through illness or failure. In the brute and unsparing choreography of nature, it no longer held a proper part. The waters of the deep were murkier than those it knew in the tropics, dulled by pale northern light and cloudy with masses of fish more numerous, if less diverse, than in southern waters, fleeing clouds of life that were mute witness to his enfeebled efforts to survive.

On the coast of southern and central New Jersey, old time fishermen were now speculating that the man-eater, whatever it was, would drift north in coastal currents—and this conclusion, among the many confounding puzzles of its behavior, would prove to be right. The pounding blows of an oar off Asbury Park, the gunshots splitting the waves of Spring Lake, were like larger predators frightening it north with the currents into a world that no longer sustained it. Its hunger or its madness were reaching an urgent point.

Yet the shark was adapted to handle the crisis of hunger in ways human beings did not know in 1916, and struggled decades later to understand. As the shark swam, there is evidence the legs and bones of Charles Bruder cut off below the knee and pieces of the bell captain's torso remained preserved in the fish's stomach for later consumption, in the manner of a camel. Gleaming specimens of dolphins and mackerel, fresh as if iced in the fishmonger's window, have been pulled from the stomachs of sharks, as well as still-legible paper documents. But the most compelling proof of the shark's camel-like ability in crisis occurred on April 17, 1935, when Albert Hobston caught a thirteen-foot tiger shark off a Sydney, Australia, beach and towed it alive to the Coogee Aquarium. Eight days later, dying in captivity, the shark regurgitated a bird, a rat, and, eerily visible in a cloud of muck, a human arm—a thick, muscular arm, so well preserved that the forearm was clearly marked with a tattoo of two boxers. On the basis of a photograph of the tattoo, published in a Sydney newspaper, a man identified his brother, James Smith, forty-five. The arm was preserved so well, it was accepted as evidence that led to the arrest of a man for murdering, dismembering, and dumping Smith at sea.

While myths have arisen to explain a mysterious "storage" capacity in the shark, in July 1916 there was no mystery. In the cooler coastal waters that week, the great white's body temperature lowered and its rate of digestion slowed. Gradually, the shark digested the flesh from a pair of human legs, gaining nutrition. The bones were indigestible, and the shark would later expel them with turtle shells and porpoise bones—like a dog retching up chicken bones.

But Charles Bruder's remains wouldn't sustain the shark for

long. It may be difficult to understand that a young great white shark could falter in its native environment, that in the ocean wild animals make mistakes unprovoked by man, get themselves into situations they cannot get out of. The great white, in particular, has an image of perfection—invincible, unconquerable, free. Man is faulty, but evolution worked overtime at something and got it right.

At dawn the shark rose from the deep, quickly leaving the vulnerable middle depths to cruise on the surface, where its white underbelly glittered alongside the camouflage of the sun. As the fish swam, the day's sunlight penetrated the sea and was refracted and scattered, breaking and muting the spectrum to better conceal it. Twenty-five feet down, the long rays of red light were absorbed by the sea, disappeared, and the shark swam in an ether of dull brown little more apparent than the outline of a current. The fish was superbly concealed from its prey in the ocean and perfectly equipped to thrive. Lost, hungry, the ocean's foremost predator was still formidable. Yet, out of its habitat, it was an alien creature, headed toward the world of men.

The Beloved Heart of the Town

⮞⮜

Seventeen miles inland from Asbury Park, on the banks of Matawan Creek, was a typical early twentieth century American small town. Main Street rolled through its center, paralleling the creek, where flat-bottom boats set out with loads of tomatoes from the farm country. The tallest structures were the white church spires, which rose up over the shops and the fine houses that marched down the length of Main under elms and sycamores before thinning to barns and long gray fences that angled over brown fields and the vegetable rows beyond.

Matawan had long been a crossroads of the north-central New Jersey colonial breadbasket. The air was still clear and quiet but for the smoke from the beehive tile kilns along the creek and the percussive rhythm of the train making for New York City with tiles for the Eighth Avenue subway. More of the outside world was coming and going through towns in the new century, but little of it stayed or altered the people of Matawan, Scotch-Irish families of farmers and merchants and old self-reliant blood. These were the years small towns dug in against change and began to die slowly and with a long, sweet wistfulness, the years that spawned Norman Rockwell, then twenty years old and producing his first *Saturday Evening Post* cover, and Thornton Wilder, nineteen and gestating the bittersweet American fate of *Our Town*. If any change was most profound, it was that the goods and people and ideas now came by locomotive and motorcar and wire, and the town had stopped producing generations of rugged sea captains and fishermen. It was losing its old umbilical link, by the creek to Raritan Bay to the Lower New York Bay, to the sea, the blue Atlantic, fifteen miles distant. The town's mercantile heart had shifted from the Atlantic Ocean to Main Street.

Not all were happy with the transformation. Old-timers thought it a shame that Captain Watson Fisher's son—the only boy of the distinguished retired commander of the Savannah Steamship Line—had chosen, at twenty-four, to be a tailor. It seemed a waste to see the brawny W. Stanley Fisher—at six foot one, two hundred and ten pounds, the town's best athlete, tow-headed and handsome, a giant of a man for the time—in his Cecil suit and Arrow collar, soft eyes behind wire-rimmed glasses, bent over needle and thread. But Stanley Fisher was a new kind of American youth, the first generation of the automobile and mass production, a lad with the freedom to do anything, go anywhere, to forsake the small town of his birth. To his father's dismay, Stanley had left Matawan as a young man to make his way in Minnesota, where his sister lived. But Captain Fisher's heart was soothed when Stanley returned home and, after apprenticing as a steamer and presser, opened a tailor's shop on Main Street. The strongest young man in town was no prodigal son. The boy took out large advertisements in the weekly *Matawan Journal* to announce his presence as a merchant, and was swept up in the new community-minded small-town life—joining clubs, hauling buckets with the volunteer hook and ladder brigade, reclaiming his birthright as the star athlete on town teams, singing every Sunday morning in the church choir. As soon as Stanley Fisher met the right girl, he'd be settling down and having children. If it seemed a close, small existence to the men who'd spent their lives at sea, there were compensations that dazzled the older generation—motorcars, fancy clothes, telephones, the bounty of things available with seeming ease. Such bounty would soon be called the American Dream.

The older folks were somewhat taken aback, however, by young Stanley Fisher's aggressive *Matawan Journal* advertisements. Advertising had been an unseemly or unnecessary thing in the last century when each man had his place and advertisements were little more than listings; not to merely publish relevant information but to sell was unheard of. But now with competition in town, Stanley Fisher's advertisements displayed drawings of a gentleman in the tailor's newest suit, the Cecil, costing $16 to $38, a sophisticated "New York" look, "the ultra nifty style" he would custom-tailor "for *you* . . . to your *absolute* satisfaction from any of the hundred splendid fabrics in my store."

The tailor's shingle was also a newfangled thing: Stanley Fisher was not a man hanging out his own name but working under the sign "The Royal Tailors, Chicago–New York." The sign evoked the glamorous style of wealth and leisure associated then with the British Empire—twin columns framing an elegant Indian tiger, fangs bared—but was vaguely unsettling to old-timers who'd never gotten used to the new combinations of wealth. Stanley was not merely a tailor but an "authorized resident dealer."

With the overeagerness of youth trying to assert his place, his advertisements declared, "We are doing a *splendid* business, and the best of it is that old customers are coming in for new orders—a splendid recommendation." In fact, it was known in town that Stanley was struggling to establish his customer base like any new merchant. The previous week, he'd sold his skills in barter, and when his friends heard about it, they laughed incredulously, for Stanley Fisher, young and vigorous, had exchanged a custom-made new suit for a ten-thousand-dollar life insurance policy. The old sea captains wagged their heads over the timidity and caution of the new generation. Stanley's young friends were astounded. "A life insurance policy!" one said, suggesting his friend should concentrate on enjoying this life, and hardly be thinking or worrying about the next one. "What are you, crazy? You're twenty-four years old." The big, good-natured tailor just smiled.

On Tuesday morning, July 11, as Main Street awakened for business, Stanley Fisher opened the Royal Tailors early and, while his shop assistant tended to customers, sized a new suit. Old Dobbin, the big brown draft horse, clopped down Main, pulling the wagon of the Springdale Dairy, delivering Wooley's Aerated Milk in glass bottles. Main was still a wood-plank road with lots of dirt, and Old Dobbin wore netting to keep off the horseflies, whose bite could send the big workhorse into a runaway, which was dangerous with all the new traffic. Noisy, hand-cranked Model-Ts rattled behind the dust clouds of horse-and-wagon teams bringing crops to the train station. The smell of horse manure wafted over the street, mingled with gasoline vapors, yet gentlemen and ladies in Edwardian finery strolled the three blocks of Main Street with no fuss, for these were not fussy people. Rather they were hearty and resourceful.

It was unusual for a man like Stanley Fisher to have the luxury of a single profession. Martin Weber was a tailor, but there wasn't a living in the old days in fifty cents for a custom suit, so he opened the Weber Grocery Store right in his house, 263 Main. Weber sold flour and whatnot in bulk, scooping and packaging orders for women for miles around. John Wright, the bartender at the Aberdeen Inn across from the railroad depot, alternated mixing drinks with running the town telephone switchboard, which was behind the bar. Harvey Johnson operated the Farmer's and Merchant's Bank on one side of a house on Main and lived on the other side with his wife and children. And John Mulsoff, the Main Street barber, doubled as the constable. If a small town strangled a man with small-mindedness and familiarity, an idea Sinclair Lewis would soon introduce into the American consciousness with his best-sellers *Main Street* and *Babbitt*, these men felt the benefits of being known and needed.

Despite the town's traditional ways, many of the citizens of Matawan considered themselves modern and sophisticated, for they had time—freed at last from plowing and planting— for leisure. Matawan happily shared the new American craze for sports and clubs and entertainment. It would be thirteen years before the Rivoli Theater dominated entertainment by showing talkies. For now the domino tournament was the talk of the town. On the Fourth of July, men played the ladies' baseball team wearing long Victorian dresses and women's broad-brimmed hats festooned with flowers—all except the mayor, who dressed like Uncle Sam. People were proud of the town library, which boasted more than three thousand volumes. If a man wasn't interested in James Joyce's new *Dubliners* or the new poem by Joyce Kilmer, "Trees," there were dime novels and westerns, and the new magazine, *Detective Story*, and the pulps *Argosy* and *All-Story*, whose editors vowed to "give the ordinary guy what he wants, that is . . . action, excitement, blood, love, a little humor, a taste of sex, a pepper of passion, a lot of escape." "Tarzan of the Apes" was a new adventure in *All-Story*.

Yet the industries that gave men and women the money and time for leisure in Matawan—the town made not just tiles but matches, candy, pianos, baskets and bottles, waxes, asphalt, and copper castings—crowded portions of the creek and the land beyond Main with factories and tainted the air. By 1916, the creek was dotted here and there with manufacturers but still wound through vast tranquil prairies of spartina grass and sky. And so it was that by July of that year Matawan Creek flowed as an increasingly sentimental link to the rural and Romantic past, a place where "overcivilized man," as Roosevelt called the urbanizing masses, could retreat to the quieter stretches. A woman could be courted in a natural setting, and a man could seize his last chance to be a boy or at least remember what it was like. Behind Main Street, sixty feet down a muddy embankment, was a place where boys went fishing and snared turtles for soup. The *Matawan Journal* was filled with poems and odes and remembrances of Matawan Creek—the gentle waters where friends picnicked on the banks, where lovers idled in moonlit canoes. The creek was the beloved heart of the town.

That afternoon of July 11, a hot summer day, Rensselaer "Renny" Cartan Jr., a dark-haired boy unusually athletic and broad-shouldered for fourteen, left the Cartan Lumber and Coal Company, his father's business, and walked down the street to find his cousin, Johnson Cartan. Johnson, a smaller, quieter boy of thirteen, stocked shelves at Cartan's Department Store at 92 Main, owned by Renny's uncle, A. J. Cartan. The Cartans were one of the most prominent families in town. A. J. Cartan had started as a telegraph operator before opening A. J. Cartan Furniture, Dry Goods, Shoes, Groceries, Hats, Western Union Telegraph Service, where folks got almost everything they needed. In recent years he'd dropped the telegraph service and put in one of the new telephones for the whole town to use.

Renny and his cousin Johnson cut down a bank to the creek, winding through tall grasses toward the swimming hole. Skinny-dipping in the old swimming hole was a Matawan tradition going back generations, and all the businessmen along Main let their sons and hired boys go to cool off for a few minutes every afternoon. Back behind the houses on Main was a barn, and beyond it the old brick limeworks stood on the bank of the creek. The limeworks, which crushed oyster shells into lime, had closed recently, as industry along New York's lower bays killed the oysters and the oysterman's trade. Yet the old warehouse shaded a lovely wide bend in the creek. Sheltered by the limeworks and a thicket of trees was a natural cove, the most popular swimming hole in town, framed at one end by the old Wyckoff propeller dock.

The boys scrambled onto the pier and pilings and threw off their clothes, laughing and shouting, the beginning of a daily ritual of roughhousing boys enjoyed like a natural entitlement. Renny Cartan was standing naked on a dock piling, joking with his cousin and friends, when he began to lose his balance. The creek was only thirty feet wide and shallow, but the water was darker than usual with the turbulence of recent rains and

Renny couldn't see the bottom, couldn't see what he'd be hitting as he fell. But a naked boy at the lip of a swimming hole in the middle of the placid farm country during the last summer of peace had little to worry about.

Renny Cartan gave in to gravity and the joy of the moment and let himself go, laughing, into the creek.

Alien World

◈

Barely two years old, the young shark was at the beginning of an epic growth spurt. At nearly eight feet and four hundred pounds, it was a seed of what it would become. How large white sharks grow is unknown, but the largest documented was almost twenty feet and several tons. Numerous reports of larger whites—as big as twenty-nine feet, five tons—have been debunked, but some shark biologists believe the goliaths are out there, at twenty-five, even thirty feet, so big no man-made gear or boat could land them. The young shark would simply grow as long as it lived, and no human knew what gigantism it could attain. Its life would be lengthy, half a century or more, and remarkably hardy. It would be free of cancer, infections, circulatory diseases, competition. Its wounds would heal themselves with a speed people associate with science fiction. If the law of nature was competition, it would operate above the law. But there were limits to the great white's power, and in July 1916, the young white moved like a creature raging against those limits.

After days of swimming north along the shore, it came to the northernmost tip of the Jersey coast, the Sandy Hook peninsula. Sandy Hook—with the Rockaways and Coney Island six miles north across the lower New York bays—framed the ocean's door to New York Harbor.

The shark rounded False Channel at the tip of the peninsula. To the east was the open ocean bounded by the fertile southern coast of Long Island, where—unknown to men at the time—dwelled some of the largest great white sharks in the world, and plenty of prey to nourish them. Passenger steamers plied up the Narrows to Ellis Island, passing the Statue of Liberty and its beacon torch, lit by electricity for the first time in 1916. Following its instinct to hug the coast, the shark cruised around the tip of Sandy Hook and left the ocean for good, curling into Sandy Hook Bay. From the deep clean currents of the Atlantic, the big fish now wallowed in five and six and eight feet of bay water. The great white was on a path away from the ocean, toward a coast lined with brackish waterways.

Of the more than four hundred species of sharks, only a few can pass from salt- to freshwater, and only one is a large predator, the bull shark, *Carcharhinus leucas*. The bull, along with the tiger shark and great white, is part of the "unholy trinity" of proven man-eaters. In the 980 shark attacks on humans and boats recorded by the International Shark Attack File between the year 1580 and October 2000, more than half of the attacks were attributed to only three species of shark: great white (348), tiger (116), and bull (82). The bull shark possesses a unique ability to cross into rivers and lakes. It has been recorded 1,750 miles up the Mississippi River in Alton, Illinois, and 2,500 miles up the Amazon in Peru. It devours the dead laid to rest in the Ganges River in India. The great white could survive in brackish water, but only temporarily. This is one of the few limits of the apex predator, a niche filled by another species. In brackish water a great white loses the salt balance between its body and the water. To restore the equilibrium, the shark's flesh loses salt to the water, and slowly its basic physiological functions shut down. For a short time only, the shark's huge mass would protect it from feeling the deadly effects.

The young white meandered west, winding around the mouths of creeks and rivers and harbors, hugging the tortuous shore, traveling farther from the life-giving sea. Familiar prey was gone, and the shark became further weakened. Sluggishness heightened its urgency to feed. Confusion or sluggishness was certain death.

The shark was neither the first nor last sea creature to become disoriented on the labyrinthine shore of Sandy Hook Bay. Seventy-eight summers later, in 1994, a pod of dolphins left the Atlantic side of Sandy Hook just as the shark had done, and, rounding into Sandy Hook Bay, instinctively following the coast, swam up the Shrewsbury River. All summer they frolicked and fed in the shallow waters of the river, but come January, as temperatures dropped to freezing on the Shrewsbury, three of the dolphins were trapped, desperately hurtling their gleaming gray bodies through the ice to make breathing holes. At last a Coast Guard vessel enticed them to swim to within two miles of the mouth of the river that led to the bay and then to the freedom of the sea. But the dolphins circled in confusion and, instinctively heading south, turned back up the ice-choked river, where they perished.

The great white swam west, instinctively trying to find its way back to the sea but traveling ever more distant from it. It passed the Shrewsbury River, the dolphin's downfall, and then Ware Creek and Belford Harbor and Pewes Creek as it sluiced from the marsh. The coast was swampy and quiet and strung with the small towns of Atlantic Highlands, Port Monmouth, and Keansburg. Two hundred feet above sea level, at Atlantic Highlands, shone the double lights of the Twin Light of Navesink, the country's most powerful lighthouse, beaming twenty miles across the bay.

Around the promontory of Point Comfort, the shark dropped south into a broad natural harbor of windswept marshland, climbed northerly out of the harbor past tiny Flat Creek and East Creek, and swam around another promontory, Conaskonk Point, into Raritan Bay. Conaskonk Point opened wide to Keyport Harbor approximately half a mile across, and the shark followed the line of the harbor south, past the town of Keyport, following the coast. But the coastline of Keyport Harbor did not sweep around seamlessly back to Raritan Bay. Keyport Harbor funneled into a cut some seven hundred and fifty feet wide, narrowing again to the mouth of Matawan Creek, a wide tidal creek, two hundred feet across. Matawan Creek was wide enough for a fish inclined to follow the coast to mistake it for the shoreline, and so on that morning, the great white shark hewed to the coast and turned into the creek, surely unaware it had left Raritan Bay.

The shark swept into the creek on the high tide, surging in on currents of saltwater. Yet not far from the mouth of the creek, the inland waterway dramatically narrowed like an inverted telescope, tapering down from two hundred feet across to a hundred to fifty to barely twenty. Within a few sweeps of its powerful tail the shark entered a diminishing world, murky and sluicing with fresh water, and it grew unsettled.

The big fish was forced to swim in the deeper middle of the creek, a narrow navigable channel, a tighter trap. The creek was only eight feet deep at high tide and sank to one foot at low tide, when the local farmers and fishermen went clamming. This was a situation it had never encountered before. The world it was born into had no walls or edges. The sea was forever. There were only two corners, two boundaries: the beach and the bottom. In brackish water, with the bottom and sides closing in, the shark may have experienced a kind of claustrophobia, shark biologists speculate. By the time the shark became aware of its mistake, it found it difficult to escape the small waterway. Perhaps it tried, and failed to return to the sea, redoubling its frustration. In alien environments, sharks become weakened, desperate, highly agitated.

South African researcher Campbell has suggested "petulance, possibly induced by environmental conditions" as a leading cause of shark attack. But Campbell's theory refers to a normal shark exposed to stress. The big fish that entered Matawan Creek was profoundly disturbed before it became trapped, already on a rare and fragile edge of violence, even for its species—"like a person," ichthyologist George Burgess says, "who goes off the deep end and starts shooting." Yet as it swam with slackening thrusts of its tail, the shark detected signals that washed about its lateral line through the brown and clouded water, signals of interest, thrumming with sonic and then olfactory cues and then explosions, signals of prey. A mile and a half ahead, as the creek wended in a lazy S shape through the sedge marshes, lay the town of Matawan.

The Creek

⌒

In the cool, shaded embrace of the swimming hole, the other boys leapt into the creek. The sun was high, and a breeze stirred the grasses on the opposite bank, rousing warm odors of decay. Their legs disappeared in darkness toward the bottom, mucky and cool between their toes. Silvery fish wriggled on the edge of the muck, and there was the small thrill, different from anything else, of being part of the creek. The light that speckled through the trees afforded privacy as the naked boys splashed and shouted echoes off the old limeworks. The noise of their play momentarily obscured the wailing pitch of a scream, a sound absorbed by the spartina grass on the opposite bank.

Moments after Rensselaer Cartan entered the water of Matawan Creek, it betrayed him. He was in almost up to his neck, and the pleasing sensation of a refreshing dip gave way to a searing warmth ripping across his chest. It was a strange sensation that fourteen years of experience couldn't process. He was bleeding and he didn't know what was in the water, what was tearing him, and in an instant the knowledge of what was happening turned to a long, high scream.

With a rush, unseen in the murky water, the shark came like a torpedo and hurtled past Cartan. The splashing in the swimming hole, barely a mile from the mouth of the creek, had drawn the great white shark to investigate. The creek teemed with life, but none of it large enough to sustain a great white shark. So when the shark spied the whirling porcelain limbs of the boy underwater, it grew excited and charged. In the view of some researchers, the shark's pass may have been investigative or even a form of play. There are numerous accounts of sharks bumping surfboards and surfers and not attacking, frolicking in a rather one-sided game only the apex predator understands. But the great white's true motive that afternoon was likely ominous. Its thick skin was so abrasive that shark hide, called shagreen, was once used by carpenters to smooth the hardest woods. Shark attacks on man are often preceded by a bump that causes gashing wounds. The purpose of the bump seems to be to determine size and strength of possible prey.

Renny Cartan had no idea he had been bumped and scraped by a great white shark. He knew only that it didn't hurt at first, then the pain was like hot needles, and larger than the pain was the loss of control and the unknowing. In that instant he saw something dark moving in the water, something larger than any fish he had ever seen. And then it was gone. The water was washing against his chest, sharpening the focus on the pain and the surprise.

Renny Cartan scrambled out of the creek, screaming. His chest was bloodied, as if raked by the tips of knives. The other boys, streaked with mud, crowded around, trying to calm him. Cartan would not be calmed. He said he had been hit and wounded by something in the creek, something huge. None of the other boys had seen it. Renny's wounds looked painful but not serious, as though he had scratched himself on a branch. His friends listened as long as boys do when play has been interrupted and awaits and is calling them back. Soon Renny's cousin Johnson and the other boys scurried onto the dock and leapt back into the creek.

As Renny Cartan left the creek to get his wounds bandaged, he shouted at his friends to get out of the water, but his warning fell on deaf ears. After Renny left the swimming hole, Johnson Cartan was swimming happily along the surface of the creek, his friends nearby. They shouted and splashed and jumped from the dock, unaware that sonic cues were now exploding along the narrow banks of the creek to a great white shark, a shark that had taken the measure of the noisy mammals and was slashing now through the brackish water, highly stimulated.

The next morning, Wednesday, July 12, as ketches and small craft moved slowly on the creek, Thomas V. Cottrell, a retired sea captain, set out from his house at the mouth of the creek for his customary walk.

Captain Cottrell strode the creek with a prodigious energy for his fifty-eight years, making a pace that was the envy of his contemporaries, the few still above sea level. But that morning he was a bit more excited than usual, and excitement wasn't good for him. The old captain was an incorrigible storyteller and jokester, a man of a hundred friends and a thousand tales, who never troubled his wife or his seven children with his heart disease. It was known he wasn't well, but the captain had plenty of years left, everyone figured, and he kept his health problems to himself. He had the redoubtable strength of a man who made friends easily and was an admired local citizen.

As the captain strolled along the creek that morning, the sun was high and water lapped softly on the banks, and he found himself staring at the brown water more intently than usual. The captain had heard of the boy who cried wolf the day before, about something in the creek that bit or scratched him—the boy's aunt was Sarah Cottrell Johnson—and he felt bad for the boy, and a bit curious over what manner of fish Renny Cartan had seen.

No one monitored the waterway like Captain Cottrell. He lived in Brown's Point at the mouth of the creek, in the handsome old port town of Keyport, whose Victorian homes overlooked the bay. His walks took him out of town and over hill and meadow and down dusty roads bordered with split-rail fences and views of silos and horses and cows. He strode as if people were too numerous and the world too small, as if, having spent the prime of life sailing the seven seas in clipper ships, he couldn't shake the urge to stretch his legs, whistling as he went his favorite song, "Beautiful Island of Somewhere":

Somewhere the day is longer,
Somewhere the task is done;
Somewhere the heart is stronger,
Somewhere the guardian won.

His walks always took him back to the creek. The captain had been born in Matawan in 1857, when it was still called

Middletown, named for its position on the creek, once plied by steamers and paddleboats. As a young man, he had moved to Brown's Point at the mouth of the creek, where the Cottrell clan had built the first boats on the bay. He was of a prideful, seafaring family, and if a drawback of a garrulous old sea captain was a want of fresh stories, Thomas Cottrell would presently have that problem solved. For as he took his constitutional on that morning, walking over the new trolley bridge spanning Matawan Creek, he saw something for which neither man nor God, tide nor typhoon, had prepared him.

Rippling up the muddy waters of the creek, toward the bridge, was a large dark-gray shape trailing a long, pointed dorsal fin. In the moment it took for shock and disbelief to subside, Captain Cottrell recognized it as a shark, a big one, no different from the many he'd spied in the Pacific and Atlantic and Indian Oceans, winding slowly up the tidal creek past fields of oat and barley, chickens and dairy cows.

As the shark swam closer to him, it loomed bigger still, a wide, gray-brown fish, possibly nine or ten feet long, until it passed directly under Cottrell and slipped under the bridge. He turned to watch the fin disappearing up the creek. Thomas Cottrell realized with an incredulous shudder that the shark was headed unswervingly toward town.

If the retired captain shook his head over the ribbing the Cartan boy had taken, the musing lasted only a moment, and he was on the move. The town of Matawan could not have placed a better sentinel for the approach of the shark than Thomas V. Cottrell. The captain had brine in his veins and was accustomed to thinking under pressure. He had taken note of the newspaper stories about two recent shark deaths on the Jersey coast, and wondered if it was the same shark. Captain Cottrell was of the lot of seafarers who took shark legends seriously. He'd seen what they could do to living things, if not men. Furthermore, the captain knew well, since his own boyhood after the Civil War, the delights of swimming on summer days in Matawan Creek. And so Captain Cottrell, pumping new life into his aging seaman's legs, turned around on the bridge and raced toward town, breathing hard and walking fast, hoping to reach town before the shark did.

In minutes he had climbed up from the creek onto Main Street, his eyes wild, his face reddening, pushing his blood pressure to perilous levels. As he hurried past motorcars and horse teams and old colonial houses, trying to balance the skittering of his heart with the urgency of the moment, he saw everywhere men he knew, but he saved his message for the man who counted. Next to the small post office at 129 Main—where the postman that morning carried his usual bag of letters with no street addresses—stood a small white house with a spinning red and white pole out front. When Thomas Cottrell pushed open the door of John Mulsoff's barbershop, the men gathered there fell silent, for the old sea captain was gasping for breath, his face animated with a crazed look.

The burly German-born Mulsoff, the barber who moonlighted as the town constable, was one of the most admired men in town, personable and humane yet a tough cop who commanded attention as he strode Main Street with authority, a longtime resident remembers. Mulsoff had to have been a formidable man to have earned such respect as a German-American in a small American town in 1916, in a country allied with England against the kaiser. Yet Mulsoff retained such high regard that in 1917, when young men from Matawan went to war against Germany, the doughboys wrote letters home in care of John Mulsoff on Main Street. As townsfolk gathered in the barbershop, Mulsoff in his German accent read the letters from the boys at the front in a way that gave hope to mothers and fathers, friends and wives.

Now the stout constable turned his competent, compassionate eye toward Cottrell. Yet the old sea captain's story about a shark from the ocean, headed up the creek toward town, sounded mad. John Mulsoff considered it for a moment, tipped back his head, and laughed incredulously. Disbelieving chuckles rounded the barbershop. Flushed with anger and embarrassment, Cottrell stumbled out of the shop and took his story urgently to the sidewalk, where a cluster of merchants met him with more skepticism and puzzled looks. A shark in the creek? Old Cottrell must have been in one too many nor'easters. With growing frustration, the sea captain pressed his case up and down Main Street, to men who'd known him for years and admired his sea stories, but "everywhere the captain was laughed at," *The New York Times* reported. This was not going over like a tale of plying thirty-foot seas at night. "How could a shark get ten miles away from the ocean, swim through Raritan Bay, and enter the shallow creek with only seventeen feet of water at its deepest spot and nowhere more than thirty-five feet wide?" the *Times* inquired. "So the townfolk asked one another, and grown-ups and children flocked to the creek as usual for their daily dip."

Thomas Cottrell had not survived forty years at sea by distrusting his own instincts. Ignoring his ragged breath, his quickening heart, he hurried down to the docks by the creek and climbed in his small motorboat, the *Skud.* Coaxing the motorboat to a hiccuping start, he gave it some gas. He was soon chugging up the creek, cruising the center channel, on the water, where he'd felt in command all his life, but perhaps never so out of control as now. Shielding the sun with his hand, he scanned the narrowing distance for a fin and the boyish heads of swimmers. As he motored, he shouted warnings of a shark, shouted out over the creek until he was hoarse. It was hot and humid and his collar was beading up in sweat. Soon there was only the sound of the old man's ragged breathing under the rumble of the engine, loud and trembling in the midday air.

Under a Full Moon

❦

A great dorsal fin sliced the middle of the brown creek as the shark swam along prairies of sedge grass and wound slowly past deserted banks, undetected by anyone. The air was warm and ripe with the sulfuric rot of the marsh. The water was rising under the shark, and it was attuning itself to new atmospheres. It passed easily through changing water temperatures, and the rising tide was protecting its salt balance.

Also unseen, in the bright afternoon sky, the moon's orbit was on a course that would put it in the earth's shadow two days

later. The coming lunar eclipse of July 14, 1916, held no interest for scientists then, but the phases of the moon were fundamental to the shark. The hidden moon was waxing, three days
from full, radiating near maximum gravitational pull, and the
great white was growing excited and vibrant in reaction to the
moon's surging power. Around the world, ocean tides were rising
and the tide was coming up Matawan Creek now, swelling the
banks and lifting the shark, bracing it with life-giving seawater.

The shark was moving upriver no faster than a walking
man, swaying its body from side to side, smelling the water and
processing information with great rapidity. As the fish swam,
its huge olfactory lobe was evaluating the smells and sounds in
the water for potential prey.

Streaming onward in the creek, the shark began to whip
powerfully, picking up speed until it was sending water rolling
toward the banks. No one saw the shark moving then, nor
would anyone have understood the pull of the hidden moon
like a trigger on the jaws of the shark, although a man may
have felt something different in his blood as well.

The citizens of Matawan in 1916 would not have laughed at
the idea that the full moon exerted a powerful effect on people,
plants, and animals. It was well known at the time that "lunacy"
gripped the residents of jails and mental hospitals during the
full moon. In the old German, French, and Scot folk cultures
brought to Matawan, evil preyed on human beings under a full
moon. If by 1916 lunar superstitions were the fodder of emerging modern entertainment (*Dracula* was a popular novel),
"moon farming," following the cycles of the moon when planting or harvesting crops, and other myths continued to flourish.
Moonlight is harmful to the health, the not-yet-old wives' tales
said; fleece will be lighter if sheared when the moon is waning;
pork from pigs killed in a new moon will shrink when cooked;

rail fences built in the light of an old moon will sink into the ground; wood cut in the waxing of the moon will be "sappy"; fish will bite more on the night of a full moon.

Scientists were dismayed by the persistence of popular myths. "Scientific men devote a deplorable amount of time felling Antaeus, in the shape of one or another of a host of irrepressible superstitions," Charles Fitzhugh Talman wrote in 1913 in *Scientific American.* "Whether the giant happens to be the equinoctial storm, or unlucky thirteen, or the climatically impotent Gulf Stream, or the super-moon, the Hercules has not yet arisen who shall crush him conclusively in mid-air."

The moon held little mystery for science in the early 1900s. Though study of the heavenly body continued, the work was quantitative—the distance from the earth, the strength of the reflected light, the size of the satellite. Scientists believed they understood the moon, and each experiment served only to further prove already established ideas. During the lunar eclipse of that July 14, thousands of New Yorkers would crowd rooftops and towers to watch with fascination the passage of the earth's shadow across the face of the moon, one of the clearest lunar eclipses seen in years. Yet Professor Harold Jacobi of the Astronomical Department at Columbia University declared "it was of no material interest to scientists because it could not possibly reveal anything that was not already a matter of positive knowledge."

Later, scientists would find evidence that sharks attack more frequently during very high tides, caused by the gravitational pull of the full moon. A preliminary study by researchers at the International Shark Attack File has found a worldwide correlation between "the phases of the moon, the height of tides and the frequency of shark attacks." Researchers are studying the phenomenon, according to George Burgess, "from a practical standpoint" to "cut down on the number of attacks by warning people of an increased risk." While there is yet no conclusive proof the white shark fits the pattern, "a study of white sharks near South Africa shows a peak in attacks at the highest of high tides."

There are several possible explanations for lunar-related shark attacks. The folklore about lunar effects on animals may be true. "There is no doubt that an animal could be more on edge or more active in looking for food due to the phases of the moon," Burgess says. Sharks could be reacting to the effect of the moon on other ocean species. The reproduction of coral and many types of fish coincides with the cycles of the moon. High tides also reduce beach space, drawing prey such as seals into the water and sharks nearer shore.

Whatever the reason, as the juvenile great white shark cruised through the murky waters of Matawan Creek under a weakening sun and a waxing moon, the waters of the creek were rising. It was nearly two o'clock on the afternoon of July 12, 1916, and the moon would soon be at its most luminous, the creek tides rising to the highest recorded levels of the month.

Like a Cat Shakes a Mouse

❧

In the low gloom of a factory by the railroad tracks, the hammer blurred as if trailing sparks, and in less than a minute the battered hands of William Stilwell held a delicate but sturdy round basket. Swiftly, Stilwell struck another basket into existence and stacked it with the others. The shouts of the line boss and the thudding of hammers wielded by men and boys along the bench filled the scorching, humid air. Bill Stilwell's chest and arms dripped with sweat, but the line boss paid fifty cents for a hundred baskets and Stilwell worked with the speed of a man who had a young wife and five young children to feed and could take home three dollars that day if he raced.

There were worse jobs along the creek than making baskets. Hauling tile and clay in the baking yards; breathing paints and varnishes or cooking scalding columns of flaked rice, which was invented in Matawan. The basket factory and its long, low line of wooden warehouses lettered ANDERSON'S BUILDING MATERIALS & BASKETS had its own sawmill, a huge and dangerous blade that sent rafts of logs to the Chesapeake. Basketwork was comparatively safe and paid well. Occasionally, Frank Anderson himself came through the basket factory, and the men were glad to see him, for Frank upped the pay to seventy cents for a hundred baskets at the peak of the summer market. Fashionable ladies preferred their summertime bouquets of flowers in lovely baskets, like Anderson's, and New Yorkers used them to carry home the season's Jersey peaches and tomatoes.

Bill Stilwell's work wasn't easy, but despite the labor struggles of the era, the good, honest workman was widely romanticized. "William Stilwell is of the sturdy type of American workman," the *New York Herald* wrote, "with a large and happy family, occupying their own cottage, surrounded by a pretty garden."

Now and then Stilwell watched his oldest son, Russell, getting the hang of it at age sixteen, and kept an eye down the line on Lester, his youngest boy. When he saw Lester, small and struggling, he could only hope the boy wouldn't get the shakes and hurt himself. Bill worried about Lester especially. His youngest boy did well in school and was ambitious, not only making peach baskets but selling a weekly magazine as a "subscription agent"—saving enough money to keep himself in clothes and books for a year. But the boy seemed weak and suffered from epileptic fits Doc Reynolds couldn't do much about. Stilwell also worried because President Wilson was talking about a child labor law setting a minimum work age of fourteen, and what would the Stilwell children do for extra money if they couldn't make baskets?

As the sun slanted over the creek and Bill Stilwell had passed a couple of hundred baskets, he saw the line boss give a nod, and the younger boys dropped their hammers and made for the door, Lester with them. Bill hated to lose the money, but Lester had already earned seventy-five cents making peach baskets that morning. Besides, it was brutally hot, and it was a tradition for the boys to sneak away to the creek on summer days. It was a break Bill Stilwell had enjoyed himself on many a lazy summer afternoon thirty years before. Lester dutifully ran up to his father to say good-bye, and Bill told him to be careful and stay near the dock in case the shakes came.

Shortly before two o'clock, Lester Stilwell, who wore knickers and suspenders to school and a cap over his Dutch boy, was running free on Main Street. Lester was one of the youngest and poorest boys who played in the creek, but soon all confinements and distinctions would disappear. In the waters of the creek, noted the *New York Herald*, Stilwell swam with boys who were "all of the same age and types of the best kind of American boys. They spend their school vacations working in a basket factory mornings and playing in the afternoons." Near the small library, Lester met Albert O'Hara, eleven, and Anthony Bublin, thirteen, whose older brothers also worked in the basket factory. Another thirteen-year-old, Charles E. Van Brunt Jr., joined the group.

On Main an older boy joined them—Frank Clowes, nineteen, taking time off from his work at his father's gas station, the first in the area. Frank was a mechanic and a carpenter and moved with a knowing swagger.

Young Johnson Cartan, from Cartan's Department Store,

trailed along, and the boys moved quickly now, since their fathers and bosses cut them only a few minutes. If Johnson was afraid of going in the water after what had happened the previous day, he didn't show it to the other boys. Everyone agreed that his cousin Renny was as crazy as old Captain Cottrell, whose story of a shark in the creek had made its way around town.

The six boys went down Main to Dock Road, cutting behind the barn to the creek. It was bright and hot and the boys threw their clothes on the banks and began diving off the dilapidated docks at the old Wyckoff steamboat landing. One by one, Clowes, the older boy, then Cartan and O'Hara and Stilwell, dived and stroked to the middle of the creek and swam back to the docks and dived again in a ragged chain.

Some two hours earlier, unknown to the boys, Captain Cottrell had sailed through Matawan warning of the shark he had seen. A few swimmers had been warned away. But that had been during the noon hour, when most people along the creek were at luncheon, and Captain Cottrell did not spread the alarm far enough. Convinced Matawan was safe, Cottrell had motored down the creek to warn others.

Now as boys took turns diving and swimming back to the docks, Albert O'Hara had taken the lead in the chain. He was swimming ahead of Johnson Cartan, Frank Clowes, and Lester Stilwell back to the dock to make another dive. O'Hara was about to climb out of the water when Lester Stilwell cried, "Watch me float, fellas!" Lester gingerly laid his body on the surface of the creek and achieved the small miracle of floating, a proud moment for him, for the boy was so weak that he usually had trouble staying afloat. In the next instant, Charlie Van Brunt saw what he called "the biggest, blackest fish he had ever seen," streaking underwater for Lester. Lester screamed, and Charlie saw the shark strike, twisting and rolling as it hit

Lester, exhibiting its stark white belly and gleaming teeth. To Johnson Cartan, the sight was something he found words for only later. Something huge, something that looked like "an old black weather-beaten board," rose up out of the water high over little Lester Stilwell. As the boys looked on in horror, they saw Lester's arm in the mouth of the shark and "Lester, being shaken, like a cat shakes a mouse, and then he went under, head first." Both Lester and the shark disappeared. As the shark jerked the boy underwater, it gave such a mighty swish through the water that its tail hit Albert O'Hara and knocked him against the pilings supporting the pier. Too shocked to feel the painful scrape, O'Hara stared at the reddening circle on the creek and cried, "Oh, Lester's gone!" For a horrific second, Lester Stilwell reappeared, rising out of the water screaming and waving his arms wildly. Then, in an instant, he was pulled back under and disappeared for good.

Small waves had upset the waters of the creek, but they were smoothing and the water was crimson where Lester had been. Suddenly, boys cried, "Oh my God, he's gone!" and swam and stumbled and scrambled out of the water and up on the muddy banks, crying, "Shark! Shark!" Rushing in a group past their heaped clothes, the five boys ran naked down Dock Road and turned right on Main. Frank Clowes was leading them, for he was the oldest, but they were all running dripping wet and wild-eyed into the heart of town, shouting that a shark had taken Lester Stilwell.

A Splendid Type of Young Manhood

In the languid middle of a Wednesday afternoon, Asher Wooley was busy under the striped canopy of his new hardware store at 116 Main Street, setting out watering cans, packs of seed, and flyswatters to tempt passersby. A few doors down, the white-smocked butchers of the new Bell Beef Company were visible behind the big plate-glass window at number 120. Down the block under the shaded awning of Cartan's Department Store, women were picking through the bushels of fruit and vegetables stacked in front, while inside the store—long and dimly lit by hanging lamps—half a dozen Cartans and associates pulled items from open shelves packed with bolts of fabric and shoes, teapots and enamel washbasins.

Abruptly, with a panic that would be remembered for years, Charlie Van Brunt, Johnson Cartan, Frank Clowes, Albert O'Hara, and Anthony Bublin came running down Main Street, naked and smeared with mud and grass and shouting wildly about a shark and Lester Stillwell. At "no time in recent years has there been so much continued excitement hereabouts as on Wednesday," the *Keyport Weekly* would report, noting that the hysterical boys had neglected to dress themselves before running into town.

The children hollered, "Shark! A shark got Lester!" to anyone who would listen. A crowd surrounded the boys, trying to calm them. Constable Mulsoff, hurrying to the commotion from the barbershop, had a crisis on his hands. Panic was quickly spreading. A crowd set off to look for a boat "to find the man-eater." Other friends of the Stilwells who had been nearby were already running frantically along the creek, shouting, "Lester! Lester!" Mulsoff thought it eerie that young Stilwell had disappeared shortly after Captain Cottrell's crazed warning of a shark, but the constable was a sturdy and rational man and the boys' claims were scarcely more believable. He was eager to restore a sense of order.

Moving quickly, the constable rounded up a group of men and marched them toward the creek to rescue the boy, or, more likely, to recover his drowned body. Poor Lester Stilwell must have suffered one of his epileptic fits, the constable feared, perhaps worsened by a sudden cramp, and gone under. The rescuers included men from the Cartan and Van Brunt families, relieved their sons were safe, and Bill Stilwell. Hurrying from the basket factory with Russell, his oldest boy, Bill found his wife, Luella, who he feared was near to collapsing with grief. But Luella proceeded with her husband to the creek, trailing young Mary, Anna, and Jennie, Lester's sisters.

Upset that no one believed their story of a shark, some of the boys continued on down Main to the door of the Royal Tailors, where Stanley Fisher was sewing a custom suit. Some town residents "thought the boys were playing a prank until finally they appealed to Stanley Fisher," the *New York Herald* reported. "They knew he was a powerful swimmer . . . and a friend of all the boys in town." With evident pride, the *Keyport Weekly* reported that Fisher was "a splendid type of young manhood with a host of friends."

Schooled by his sea-captain father in everything there was to know about the water, and comfortable—by virtue of his family's prominence, his size, and his athletic ability—with leadership, Fisher decided to assume command of the crisis. Putting his sewing off for later, promptly told his assistant to take the day off and closed the shop. But not before he slipped into the back room and put on a bathing costume.

Out on Main Street, the big tailor ran into his childhood friend, George Burlew. Burlew, twenty-three, was a driver in town who listed his occupation as a "schofer," but already showed yearnings for the sea. He got work when he could as a commercial fisherman. His dream was to be a big-game fisherman, taking out charters in his own vessel, and the idea of a shark excited him, although he, too, assumed it couldn't be true. When Stanley Fisher told him to put on a bathing costume, he felt a surge of adrenaline. Along with the possibility of seeing a shark, Burlew was anxious to make sure that young Charlie Van Brunt, his neighbor on Main Street, was okay.

A huge crowd of townspeople was already gathered along the dock and banks of Matawan Creek. Among shouts of "Lester," men in rowboats soberly patrolled the banks, poling the murky water. Bill and Luella Stilwell and their son and daughters stared in shock at the spot where Lester had vanished. The arrival of

Stanley Fisher sent a wave of anticipation through the crowd. The tailor was said to be the strongest man in town.

Fisher quickly took command. He and Burlew climbed into a rowboat and strung chicken wire weighted with stones in the shallower water downcreek, stretching a barrier twenty feet from bank to bank, "so the tide wouldn't take the body out," Burlew recalled. Fisher and Burlew joined the other boats poling for the body, but after an hour of working the creek with no success, people on the banks were stirring restlessly and Fisher and Burlew suddenly dove overboard.

Shouts and warnings to watch out for a shark sounded from the banks, but the men ignored them and swam to the middle of the creek, where they began to make dives to the deep center channel where the poling couldn't reach and where Fisher believed Stilwell's body had sunk.

The men plunged toward the creek bottom, disappearing for several moments then surfacing, gasping for air. The creek was so murky, Fisher and Burlew said they couldn't see anything, and the bottom of the channel was too deep to reach. After almost half an hour of exhausting dives, they surfaced and stroked to the opposite bank, where they paused to discuss what to do next. They concluded there was nothing more they or their fellow townsfolk could do except perhaps wait for low tide to find Lester Stilwell's body. Fisher and Burlew swam slowly back toward the bank, where the crowd had assembled.

In the center of the creek, Fisher abruptly decided to make one more dive for the bottom, and, upending his big body, plunged under the surface. But again he came up empty-handed. Ignoring pleas to call off the search, Fisher plunged once more toward the bottom. George Burlew was nearing the dock when he heard his friend break the surface and cry, "I've got it!" Shouts and cheers ringed the shore. Fisher had found Lester Stilwell!

Riding the enthusiasm of the crowd, two men rowed out quickly toward the center of the creek to help Fisher bring up the body. George Burlew swam out to help his friend, but the sensation of the water churning furiously caused him to stop. What he saw in the center of the creek would stay with him the rest of his life.

Stanley Fisher now called, "He's got me!" Screaming and fighting for his life, Fisher was caught in the jaws of a shark. Years later, when George Burlew became a world-renowned big-game fisherman, setting a world record for a marlin catch, he was better able to evaluate what he witnessed. "I never saw the entire fish," he recalled, "but from the tremendous upheaval of the huge tail that thrashed above the water it had to be a big one." Unknown to observers then, however, the "tremendous upheaval" and the suddenness and ferocity of the attack were a signature of a great white shark.

Burlew was astonished at Fisher's courage. "Stanley was a big man, and he fought back at the shark, striking it with his fists," Burlew recalled. "He was fighting desperately to break away, striking and kicking at it with all his might. Three or four times during the struggle the shark pulled him under, but each time he managed to get back to the surface. He seemed to be holding his own, but at best it was an uneven battle. The shark was at home in the water—and Stanley wasn't."

Fisher finally managed to get his head once again above water, but suddenly "he was jerked under again and the men in the boat saw the dirty white belly of the shark as he turned and went down. Then the water became crimson in a constantly widening area, and when Fisher came up he was so exhausted he could hardly call out."

Men and women stood frozen in awe and fear on the banks, and George Burlew, too, found himself unable to move to help his friend. Instead, he turned and swam frantically for the dock. He said later it wasn't an action he regretted, for terror, he explained, robbed him of conscious choice. "I don't know how I ever got to the shore, but I remember the awful fear that the shark was right behind me and had slated me for his next victim."

Battling the big fish alone, Fisher, incredibly, had fought himself free of the shark. With astonishing purpose, he swam toward the bank. The shocked crowd saw that Fisher had one arm around Lester Stilwell, or what remained of the boy. Three of Fisher's friends tried to rescue him, but their motorboat stalled in the creek and the men frantically paddled with their hands to reach Fisher. Other boatmen managed to row close to try to provide cover for him, slapping the water with oars to keep away the shark.

Fisher had nearly reached the bank of the creek, when witnesses heard him utter a terrible cry and saw him throw his arms in the air. Stilwell's body fell into the creek, and with another desperate shout Fisher was dragged in after it, disappearing completely underwater.

"The shark! The shark!" people screamed. The boatmen again raced to assist, but Fisher, with remarkable fortitude, struggled once again toward the bank. Stilwell's body had disappeared; the shark had apparently fled with it. Fisher was able to keep his head above water now, but as the rescuers reached him, the men in the boat saw that most of the flesh between the hip and the knee of the right leg had been taken off. Having risked his life in a heroic rescue attempt and fought off the monster, Stanley Fisher deserved cheers and welcoming arms as he climbed out of the water.

Instead, anguished cries and screams rent the afternoon air. "There was a crowd of 200 or 300 people present at the time," the *Matawan Journal* reported, "and the sight of Mr. Fisher being brought ashore was sickening, to state it mildly."

Not until Stanley Fisher attempted to climb up the bank of the creek did he realize what had happened. He lifted his leg to examine it, said, "Oh, my God," and dropped back into the water again. "Just about half of the thigh was missing," Burlew recalled, "That single bite from the knee to the hip was made by a huge pair of jaws. Several women fainted, and I just missed fainting myself." Amid the gagging of his fellow townspeople, several men laid Fisher down on the bank in a rapidly spreading pool of his own blood. A rope was wrapped around the hideously damaged leg near the hip, forming a tourniquet, and calls for a doctor resounded down Main Street.

As blood gushed from his tattered limb, Stanley Fisher began to groan with the increasing pain, but still he tried urgently to tell George Burlew something. Men and women ran from the docks up to town and along Main Street to Doc Jackson's big Victorian house at number 209, where he saw patients, but the doctor was out of town. Dr. George L. Reynolds, who owned the most notable house in town, the mansion at 94 Main, was also not at home. Next on the list was Dr. Straughn. But Dr. Straughn had left the day before for a physicians' meeting in Atlantic Highlands. With the makeshift tourniquet on his leg, Fisher lay by the creek for half an hour, until Dr. Reynolds was finally located and brought to the scene.

Reynolds had never seen such an injury. A wide, open wound, it stretched eighteen inches from below Fisher's hip to just above his knee. At the edges of what appeared to be a huge bite or a series of bites, the flesh was ragged, as if fistfuls of flesh had been extracted, Reynolds observed, by a set of "dull knives." The femur, while scratched, was not penetrated. But the femoral artery, bleeding profusely, was completely severed. Despite the severity of the wounds, Stanley Fisher was still conscious, and as Dr. Reynolds worked to bind the huge bite, Fisher described how he had seen the shark feeding on Lester Stilwell's body and how, when he tried to recover the boy's body, the shark had released it and attacked him.

The wound bound as well as possible, Dr. Reynolds ordered men to build a stretcher. Working quickly, they cobbled together wooden planks, and a group of them strained to lift the 210-pound Fisher and bear him up the hill and across to the center of town to the Matawan train station. The nearest hospital was Monmouth Memorial, ten miles east in Long Branch, and apparently the doctor didn't believe Fisher would survive the trip in an automobile. The men set Fisher's stretcher down on the train platform, and the doctor asked for a volunteer to make the trip with Fisher. The next train to Long Branch left Matawan at 5:06 P.M., and would arrive at 7:45 P.M.

Fisher had suffered what the shark attack injury specialists, Doctors Davies and Campbell, would in the 1960s describe as a grade-two shark attack—dire injuries that could be survived with prompt emergency medical treatment. That afternoon in 1916, however, the medical treatment Stanley Fisher required was two hours and thirty-nine minutes away. Dr. Reynolds surely recognized that Fisher's injuries were mortal. Like other doctors of the era, he feared the bite of the shark was poisonous. With the doctor beside him, and what must have seemed an eternity of pain stretching before him, Stanley Fisher lay on his makeshift stretcher, fighting to retain consciousness as he waited for the train.

Farther downcreek toward the bay, the vast and clear horizon over the sedge marshes was streaked by billowing tendrils of dark smoke. The smoke rose in columns and drifted lazily over the creek toward the bay from a compound of smokestacks and kilns, brickworks and tileworks that smoldered like ruins on the marsh in the afternoon air. The largest chimneys rose up around the factories and warehouses of the New Jersey Brick Company, a leading American producer of bricks. The creek bottom and the lands along the creek were veined with rich clay deposits, and so in those days Matawan produced the stoneware containers needed for a growing country: jugs, jars, churns, crocks, spittoons. Matawan boys learned counting and numbers with various sizes and colors of tile, skimmed tiles along the creek and ponds, and played hide-and-seek amid pallets of tile and brick. Yet another virtue of the brickyards was a dock that feathered out over the creek, and late on the afternoon of July 12, Joseph Dunn, twelve years old, his brother Michael, fourteen, and their friend Jerry Hollohan cut a trail through the brickyards to the dock over the creek.

Joseph and Michael Dunn, the sons of John Dunn of East 128th Street in New York City, were spending the summer with their mother at Cliffwood, a quarter of a mile below Matawan. Not only did Cliffwood represent an exciting summer at the shore, the creek itself tantalized boys with the legends of pirates and buried treasure. It was said Captain Kidd sailed on Raritan Bay and Blackbeard had come up the creek and attacked farmers and villagers.

That Wednesday afternoon, however, the boys were simply looking to cool off with a swim during the late hot part of the day, and Joseph Dunn, the youngest, raced to get in the water first. Neither Joseph Dunn nor his brother or friend knew that Lester Stilwell and Stanley Fisher had been attacked half an hour earlier, three quarters of a mile away. Had Joseph looked upcreek, he might have seen a large fin trailing toward the brick docks; "the shark, after feasting on the Stilwell boy and . . . Fisher's flesh, was on his way out to sea again and still was hungry," the *New York Herald* wrote. "Apparently the shark had finished his disturbed meal in the channel at Matawan and, knowing, as such creatures

do know, in some mysterious manner that the tide was running
out, had started back for the deeper water of the bay."

A quarter mile away, the small engine of the *Skud* beat the
turgid water to a froth as Captain Cottrell motored along bends in
the creek, shouting his warnings to people on the banks and to
any swimmers he could find. But the creek was wild and deserted
for long stretches; the work was slow, and the captain felt he was
racing the shark. After the attack on Lester Stilwell, a small
armada had joined Cottrell. At the mouth of the creek in Keyport,
a mile and a half from Matawan, A. A. Van Burskisk, borough
recorder of Keyport, and William O'Brien had gone up the creek
in a motorboat armed with pistols and a rifle, prepared to save
swimmers and "ready to shoot any shark showing himself." By
the time Stanley Fisher was attacked, half a dozen motor craft
were out on Matawan Creek, searching for the shark and spreading the warning.

"It would seem that few could miss such a warning," the
New York Herald later reported. But Joseph Dunn and his companions were among the few. Dunn looked into the brown surface of the water and saw nothing but his own reflection. And
so, at about four o'clock that afternoon, he jumped.

Dunn swam toward the middle of the creek. His brother
Michael was in next, and he, too, was swimming, and then Jerry
Hollohan joined them. Moments later, the warning finally
reached the boys at the brickyard docks. A man ran to the creek,
warning of a shark, and the boys swam quickly back toward the
docks. Hollohan and Michael Dunn climbed the ladder out of
the water and Joseph was swimming toward the ladder as fast as
he could, when something enormous and hard and "very rough"
struck him and scratched his skin, resulting in a painful cut.

"I was about ten feet from shore and looked down and saw
something dark . . . I did not see him the first time he hit me . . .

then he turned and came back and got my leg." The enormous jaws of the shark closed on Dunn's leg and began to pull him away toward deeper water. The shark was struggling in the shallow water to turn its great body around and flee with its prey. "Suddenly I felt a tug, like a big pair of scissors pulling at my leg and bringing me under . . . the teeth of the shark evidently clamped down on my leg quickly and I thought it was off. I felt as if my leg had gone." In fact, the shark's serrated teeth were grating and shredding Dunn's leg as it tried to pull the boy into deeper water, where it could attack and feed without distraction. Incredibly, Dunn felt very little pain. The screams came instead from a terrifying thought: "It seemed the fish was [trying] . . . to get my whole leg inside his mouth . . . I thought he would kill me . . . I thought it was going to swallow me."

A shark attack on a human being, like the crash of a modern airliner, evolves from an unlikely sequence of rare events, and rescue attempts, too, are governed by chains of extraordinary occurrence. So it was that Matawan lawyer and developer Jacob Lefferts, at thirty-four one of the most prominent men in town, was motoring downcreek in his boat, issuing shark warnings, when he witnessed the Dunn attack. And not far behind him, in the *Skud*, came Captain Cottrell.

Lefferts, fully clothed, dove into the creek toward the attacking shark, while at the same time Michael Dunn swam to his brother's aid. Man and boy grabbed Joseph Dunn and attempted to wrestle him from the mouth of the shark. The shark clamped its huge teeth, but somehow Joseph and his rescuers made it as far as the dock ladder. "As he drew himself up on the brick company's pier, with only his left leg trailing in the water, the shark struck at that," *The New York Times* reported. "Its teeth shut over the leg above and below the knee and much of the flesh was torn away."

At last the shark let go of Dunn, and his companions dragged him, yelling, up onto the pier. The boy's wounds appeared ghastly. After making hasty attempts to stop the bleeding with makeshift bandages, Lefferts, Captain Cottrell, and Michael Dunn lowered the stricken boy into Cottrell's motorboat.

As the *Skud* led the rescue party upcreek, Captain Cottrell noticed how far the tide had gone out. It was only the shallowness of the creek at the brickyard docks, he thought, that had prevented the shark from swiftly making off with Joseph Dunn in its jaws. It had been pure luck that he had reached the boy in time. In the old days, when the big boats went all the way up to Matawan, before the creek silted in, the shark would have had a deep and clear path to the bay. Racing back along the S curves of the creek, looking down at the tattered and bloodied limb of the small boy in his boat, Thomas Cottrell wondered if luck would matter.

Fleeing for Safety

❧

The shark had vanished from human view, camouflaged by the dark creek water, leaving no trace of its presence but the distant shouts of men and a small wake washing diluted blood to the banks. Releasing huge stores of energy summoned during its attacking frenzy, the shark was fleeing for safety. It did not know fear but responded to danger, and certainly there was threat from the men and boats on the creek.

The attacks on Stanley Fisher and Lester Stilwell had not sated the shark for long; more than ten pounds of human flesh was a small meal. The shark's life consisted of taking ten, twenty, forty pounds of fish in a single meal and moving ever onward for more, never knowing when the next meal would come. All that had changed was that the meals now included humans. The brackish water weakened the shark, and the confines of the creek were disorienting. So the big fish hurtled downcreek, seeking a return to that open world, the world of the sea.

Yet everywhere it traveled in this small space, driven by hunger, it sensed the lure of prey. Far ahead in the creek, pulses exploded underwater, sounds and scents that shortened the closing distance. Above in the deepening sky the moon was wheeling toward an eclipse, waxing and intensifying its brightness and its pull on tides and fish and the predatory instincts of sharks. The shark made a series of adjustments in the set of its pectoral fins and the thrust of its tail, hunting now in a frenetic state.

To See Its Body Drawn Up on the Shore

❧

At four-thirty the sky was tinted with hints of russet and gold yet still bright with the intensity of the longest summer days. Shadows lengthened along the creek, but the views of the surface were clear for the men with rifles standing in the tall grass. Matawan Constable Mulsoff had come down to the creek with a police detective from Keyport. With a nod from the constable, the group turned away from the old steamboat docks, climbed into town, and filed onto Main Street.

On the plank road that afternoon the sputter of motorcars and clop of horses marked a steadying pace under the sycamores and elms. Matrons and domestics tended to late shopping as merchants rolled their canopies. It was a typical hazy, humid summer afternoon, until the men from the creek surfaced in the late shadows. Their faces were hard and streaked with sweat and mud from thrashing through the creekside grasses high as a man's chest. The townspeople stood aside to let them pass. The shark hunters' trousers were wet and smelled of creek rot from poling the shallows as they moved like forms of unbidden memory past the shops and churches.

They had seen Stanley Fisher savaged by a shark and then spent two hours searching for Lester Stilwell's body, and as they pushed opened the door at 116 Main, Asher Wooley's store, they had no interest in Wooley's hardware. The store sold dynamite by the stick in the back, and the men bought up all of it.

As they headed back toward the creek with armfuls of explosives, the tranquility of a midsummer day was replaced by an urgent feeling that traveled in their wake and issued through town, a feeling of threat and reprisal as innate as the response of the shark to stimuli. After the death of Lester Stilwell and the mauling of Stanley Fisher, "The word spread that one or more man-eating sharks were in Matawan Creek feasting on the bathers," the *New York Herald* reported. Whereupon, "Residents of the town, including hundreds from the factories, hurried to the river."

Down Main Street, in house after house, and later, in the fields and farmhouses on the outskirts of town, men reached above the fireplace and in the corner of the barn for shotgun, rifle, and harpoon. Young men in fishing caps, dark trousers, and white Oxford shirts, sleeves rolled up, took the front rank; businessmen still in dark suits, striped shirts buttoned to the collar, and boater hats followed behind. Boys in suspenders and baseball caps peeked warily behind their hard-eyed fathers. Women in full-length summer dresses gathered on both banks up- and downcreek.

The word at the creek was that the shark was trapped. Wire nets had been stretched across the creek at narrow places near Keyport, where it emptied into the bay, to block the shark's escape. When A. B. Henderson, the acting mayor of Matawan, announced the borough would pay a one-hundred-dollar bounty "to the person who killed the shark, if one, or if more for each shark killed" an emotional torrent swept along the banks.

As five o'clock approached, the constable gave a signal to clear the creek of boats. Men with rifles and and jittery trigger fingers scanned the surface of the creek for movement. The slightest quivers of fish aroused shouts of "There! There!" But the gun men were ordered to hold fire while others on the banks carefully prepared the explosives. The work was slow and punctuated by more shouts. The citizens of Matawan knew nothing of the shark's weaknesses or habits, only that it was a man-eater, only that it possessed a power that required all the munitions in town to match. The destroyer could be met only by the sum of destruction.

Watching from the banks, Bill and Luella Stilwell prayed that if Lester was now dead, at least his body could be recovered for a proper Christian burial. But the unstated fear of the shark hunters was that the boy had been totally devoured by the shark. The men were convinced that dynamite offered the hope of killing the shark and of finding Lester's remains, if any. Fishermen had advised the county prosecutor that "the shock of the explosions will stun the shark or burst the gall inside its body and cause it to rise to the surface." (And the shark hunters thought that blasting the creek would also bring forth what was left of Lester's body.) They did not know that the great white shark possesses no such flotation gall. Heavier than water, it must keep swimming with powerful thrusts or succumb to gravity. Unlike whales and other fish, it sinks when it dies.

Just before the first charge was to be set off, a motorboat appeared downcreek and the noise of its engine grew louder as it came into view. Captain Cottrell stood at the wheel of the *Skud* with Jacob Lefferts. As the boat drew nearer, Lefferts announced, "A shark got him!" Lying on the bottom of the boat was Joseph Dunn, his leg encased in bloodied bandages. The men laid down their guns and went to the boat to carry the boy—a boy Lester Stilwell's age—onto the dock.

Dr. Herbert Cooley of Keyport had responded too late to the summons to help Lester Stilwell and Stanley Fisher, never suspecting yet another person would need emergency care for a shark attack within an hour. Like Dr. Reynolds, Dr. Cooley was reluctant to touch the ragged cut, fearing that sharks infected their victims with poisons. But the doctor persevered and cleansed the wound as the half-conscious boy cried out. "The calf muscle was severely lacerated," the doctor later reported, "and the front and side of the boy's lower left leg were cut into ribbons from knee to the ankle." If there was good news, it was that "the bones were not crushed and the main arteries in the calf of the leg were not cut." From the perspective of half a century later, in the modern parlance of Australian doctors Davies and Campbell, Dunn had suffered grade-three shark wounds, the most common and most minor arterial, abdominal, or limb damage. In such cases the victim is expected to survive if treated immediately.

Having wrapped the wound with clean bandages, Dr. Cooley instructed a bystander to rush the boy and him to the hospital, assuming he was treating a mortal injury. As the roadster throttled north toward New Brunswick and St. Peter's Hospital, some ten miles away, Dr. Cooley fought the certainty that the boy would soon die, overcome by toxins from a poisoned bite.

In the villages of Matawan and Keyport, whistles ended the day in the plants that had not already emptied and more men with guns as well as curious women and children streamed down through the grasses to the creek to join the mob.

Now the waterway once again was cleared of boats. At Constable Mulsoff's signal, the first gunshots flashed over the creek and the percussion of a dynamite blast sent a geyser of muddy water high over the crowd.

After eight o'clock, when darkness had settled on the creek, word reached the banks that Stanley Fisher was dead. At 5:06 that afternoon, Fisher, fully conscious after more than an hour's wait, had been carried aboard the train bound for Long Beach. Some two and a half hours later, Fisher reached the operating table at Monmoth Memorial, where, still conscious, he told his surgeons he had wrested Stilwell's corpse from the shark's mouth. After five minutes on the operating table, Stanley Fisher died from massive blood loss and hemorrhagic shock.

As news of Fisher's death reached Matawan, feelings of powerlessness and dread swept through the growing crowd, fears that something unknown, something alien and deadly, awaited men in the creek. "Tonight the whole town is stirred by a personal feeling," *The New York Times* reported, "a feeling which makes men regard the fish as they might a human being who had taken the lives of a boy and a youth and badly, perhaps mortally, injured another youngster."

More armed men left their homes and gathered at the creek. With no understanding of the shark, there was no place to put fear except into rage, and the feeling was general now. Crowded along the banks, men lifted rifles and bullets ripped into the water. Onlookers scurried for cover from dynamite blasts as the tranquil creek erupted as if a primal force had been loosed. Small fish eviscerated by the blasts floated on the surface.

Between dynamite blasts, men trolled the dark creek in boats, working in eerie ribbons of lantern light, dredging the creek bottom with oyster hoops, trolling the muck for Stilwell's body. During cease-fires, more than a hundred armed men in boats patrolled up and down the creek, scanning for ripples that signaled the man-eater. Reporters crowded closer to the townsfolk on the banks with their notebooks and visions of a village besieged by a sea monster. Despite the bright light of the waxing moon, there were no sharks in sight, but that hardly mattered as men shot and bombed everything that stirred. "The one purpose in which everybody shares," the *Times* reported, "is to get the shark, to kill it, and to see its body drawn up on the shore, where all may look and be assured it will destroy no more."

The Jersey roads were gravel and the roadster wheezed and shimmied as John Nichols crawled along at a frustrating pace. He had sped through New York at thirty miles an hour but couldn't exceed fifteen in the open Jersey countryside. Soothed by the sight of the widening bay on his left, he rattled along the coast road. In a while it began to rain.

The rain kept down the dust but slowed him further, and by the time he crossed a small bridge and followed the trolley into Keyport, it was six o'clock. Half a mile up was the main part of the village, and as he came up Front Street along the bay and turned onto Broad, the blocks of storefronts were dark.

In the shuddering halo of his headlights, Keyport appeared to be a ghost town, and that did not surprise him. The creature had struck in Matawan a mile and a half upcreek. But to understand what the creature was, John Nichols wanted to see the mouth of the creek where it first came up and where he might catch it leaving. He parked, stepped out of the roadster, and stood in his slicker, looking down from the rising steam of the rainy street toward the bay and the creek head.

The death of Lester Stilwell and mauling of Stanley Fisher twenty-two miles south of New York City had drawn the ichthyologist to the tidal creek the following day. If any man could solve the mystery of their attacks, John Nichols believed it was he, and he had vowed to "be present when the ravager was captured." Whatever it was coming up the coast, Nichols suspected its extraordinary appearance and behavior represented a possible breakthrough in the relatively new science of ichthyology. He also believed the creature was bound for the bays and beaches of New York City, for thousands of summer bathers, and needed to be stopped.

Nichols had been in his vaporous office, amid shelves of bottled fish, in the basement of the American Museum of Natural History when the telephone call interrupted the steady musings and jottings of a naturalist. According to Nichols's desk diaries, he had turned his sights away from the baffling deaths of Charles Bruder the previous week and Vansant the week before that, hoping as did his mentor, Dr. Frederic Lucas, that the sea had capably resolved the problem.

But the third and fourth attacks in two weeks along the coast had startled Nichols that morning. Under the patina of the scientist was a man who had written "I want to see the wisps of hail/go drifting through the morn/And meet my match mid broken men/that scorn the ocean's scorn." With long strides he had sought out Frederic Lucas. Dr. Lucas was glad to send his young protégé to Matawan to investigate the matter, for to Dr. Lucas the attacks were evolving from annoyance toward crisis, and the director, nearly seventy, hadn't the stomach for a crisis. Moreover, he was confident there was no finer man or wiser fish scholar for the job than John Nichols. Like Lucas, Nichols was highly skeptical that sharks were man-eaters, convinced the ocean attacks on Vansant and Bruder were not the work of a shark. Now the attacks on Stilwell and Fisher all but confirmed it. Sharks, as far as Nichols knew, did not go up tidal creeks, but his leading suspect was quite happy in a narrow inlet. John Nichols envisioned himself as a detective, and in Matawan Creek he expected to find the fingerprints of *Orcinus orca,* the killer whale.

Making his way in the darkening port town, as the rain pummeled his slicker and swelled the creek and the bay, the tall scientist met the mayor and town officials, who had taken lead roles in trying to capture what they could conceive only as a giant shark. Lucas insisted that a killer whale was quite possibly the man-eater, while a shark a far less likely candidate. Regardless of what the men thought they saw, Nichols insisted, there was no reliable record of such an unprovoked shark attack on man in history—no less three in one afternoon.

"It is a striking fact that the greatest expert on sharks in this country, Dr. Frederic A. Lucas . . . is also the greatest skeptic about them," Nichols told the Keyport officials. "He has been trying many years to obtain proof of genuine danger from ordinary sharks. Whether these sharks eat men or not is impossible to say. Personally, I wouldn't like to try it. Still there is no authentic record of such a shark ever having attacked a man except when cornered in a net."

Yet, as he made his way down to the mouth of Matawan Creek in the rain and authorities introduced him to fishermen in the small port village, the ichthyologist quietly assembled facts that challenged prevailing theory. Surveying the narrow creek at Keyport, Nichols could see plainly that an adult killer whale, thirty feet long and ten thousand pounds, would have trouble navigating the tidal cut, particularly when the tide went out and the creek was a foot deep. Witnesses also put to rest his killer whale theory—not only was the orca much larger, but no one had seen something Nichols expected to find: the characteristic spouting of the whale as it moved. To Nichols's surprise, a number of witnesses described the creature they had seen in the creek in some detail. Unlike the confused and uncertain witnesses at Spring Lake and Beach Haven, all swore it was a shark.

Several old-time fishermen Nichols interviewed insisted the attacker was not only a shark but more than one shark, "saying they never go singly"; but the majority of witnesses "believed there was but one big hungry fellow." Slowly, Nichols began to close in on the identity of the creature. Jerry Hollohan, the nineteen-year-old who was swimming with Joseph Dunn during the attack on the boy, had reported the fish was a big shark that appeared "about ten feet long and weighed probably 250 pounds, maybe more." George Burlew's memory of the shark that seized Stanley Fisher was a shark "nine or ten feet long" with a huge tail, almost exactly matching Captain Cottrell's report of the fish he'd seen moving upcreek toward town the day before. The men working on a drawbridge across the creek at Keyport had seen a "big dull white body" of a shark gliding upcreek—and the boys in the creek with Lester Stilwell saw a huge black fish that flashed "a shark's white belly, with gleaming teeth."

The eyewitnesses excited Nichols's scientific curiosity, although he was careful to temper his enthusiasm around men experiencing the trauma of a tragedy. Nichols presumed all the attacks were the work of a single creature. It defied logic that more than one marine animal was suddenly stalking human beings. For the first time, he seriously countenanced the possibility that the man-eater was a shark. As he climbed into his car for the trip upcreek to Matawan, the ichthyologist remained doubtful, however. He counted himself among the "many scientists who have doubted tales of their [sharks'] ferocity toward humans."

Curving right with the trolley and motoring up along the creek, Nichols thumped across the tracks at Matawan Station and proceeded down Main Street. The rain continued as he reached the old Matawan House Hotel. The three-story wooden building was ablaze with gaslights. Loud and agitated men crowded the long front porch under a painted sign: TREFZ FINE LAGER BEER. Men with guns and drinks in their hands held court with newspapermen and newsreel photographers, and Nichols heard wild talk of sea monsters. Bounty hunters with rifles drifted through the lobby along with fishermen, merchants, and friends and families of the victims. Knowledgeable men insisted the idea that sharks were in the creek "was a myth, pure and simple." That afternoon a U.S. Weather Bureau report caused an uproar: The man-eater had been captured five miles up the coast. A fisherman in Keansburg had caught an eleven-foot, three-hundred-pound shark with human remains in its stomach, the remains of Fisher and Stilwell. The report turned out to be a hoax.

On the front porch of the hotel, wind and rain stirred a set of empty rocking chairs as men took cover, and Nichols could see the storm building to a fury. Main Street was blanketed by black clouds that extended up the Jersey coast and across to Long Island. A storm was prowling the region with thunder and lightning that would fell trees that evening and set houses afire and strike and kill two horses and three men working on railroad tracks, miles away. Leaning into the wind, John Nichols hunkered through the darkness and the rain and the booming thunder toward the shouts at the creek. The muddy bank trembled with percussions of the thunder and dynamite. Nichols saw illuminated by lightning the shadowy figures of men along the creek with rifles and heard the shouts and the explosions that filled him with woe.

No shark had been spotted, but men continued to kill anything that stirred. Dynamite blasts rent the creek to cries of "Shark!" whereupon bubbles appeared that were mistaken for signs of the shark's presence, leading to more shouts of "Shark!" and more dynamite until "the excitement became intense" and "many believed they saw sharks moving after each blast," *The New York Times* reported. Patiently, Nichols moved among them, explaining that dynamite would never find the man-eater, and as for bullets, "a shark's thick, tough skin would hardly take an impression from buckshot and would probably turn the .32-caliber bullets fired off them." He also warned that the fish being killed in the creek could attract sharks. But men proceeded as if Nichols were a specter.

If John Nichols had hoped for better cooperation for his investigation as he trudged back toward town and a room at Matawan House, he received it later that evening as the creek made him a grisly prophet. Ralph Gall, one of the hunters riding a motorboat downcreek, claimed to have seen not one but four large sharks heading upcreek toward Matawan. Shouting wildly and firing warning shots into the air, Gall motored upcreek to give the alarm, but by the time he reached town, the sharks had vanished with the supple mockery of phantoms. Gall's alarm triggered panic up- and downcreek as everywhere people saw sharks or apparitions of sharks. Three big sharks were reported near the old steamboat docks. Men plunged heavy pig-wire into the water to trap them, and the firing began anew, hitting nothing now but currents and tides.

By five-thirty the next morning, the storm had blown over and the sun warmed the tranquil waters of Matawan Creek. The muddy banks dried and the tide came in clean, as if the rage from men and heavens was spent or had never happened. One by one, the dozens of shark hunters had gone home; William Stilwell had at last retired. Edward Craven was walking like a dead man along the creek, his rifle crooked in tired arms, about to turn in himself to get some sleep when he saw something large moving in the creek. It was right behind the old bag factory, and it must have just surfaced, for other shark hunters had recently passed behind the bag factory on their way home and seen nothing.

Craven gripped his rifle and hurried closer, charged with adrenaline. He was one of the last of the armed men who'd spent the night without having glimpsed one of the monsters, and he must have felt pressure now to be a hero. If it was the shark, Ed Craven wanted to blast it out of the water. But the thing in the creek was rocking listlessly with the lap of the tide. If it was a fish, it was a big one and already dead. If it was the shark, the village's worries were over and he would deliver the good news. Scrambling down the muddy bank to get a closer look at the floating mass, he realized with a lurch in his gut that the thing was a body.

Wary of touching the body himself, Craven ran to get Constable Mulsoff, who called the Monmouth County coroner in Freehold. Shortly thereafter the body was lifted easily onto the dilapidated dock from which Lester Stilwell had dived two days earlier. The small face was badly swollen but smooth and clearly belonged to Stillwell. The face was unmarked, but the rest of the boy was scarcely recognizable. The left side of the abdomen, the left shoulder, and the right breast had been eaten away. The left ankle had been chewed off. The flesh between the hip and the thigh had been mangled, and the stomach had been ripped open as if by giant claws. Authorities decided to bring the remains of the boy to Arrowsmith's Undertaking in Matawan. But first they carried Lester Stilwell to his home on Church Street to confirm his identity. Bill Stilwell must have been sleeping after his long nights at the creek, for his wife, Luella Stilwell, answered the door, and when she saw what the men had brought her, she screamed and collapsed. "The body had been horribly chewed by the sea wolf," the *Asbury Park Evening Press* reported. "When it was taken to the Stilwell home, the lad's mother swooned. She was revived only to relapse into unconsciousness."

As soon as Lester Stilwell's body reached Arrowsmith's that morning, the undertaker, alarmed by the "terrible" condition of the body, rushed to prepare the boy for burial, which took place that afternoon after a small service in the Stilwell home.

That same afternoon, most of the village gathered at Rose Hill Cemetery to pay their respects to W. Stanley Fisher. Standing by the open grave, the Reverend Chamberlain eulogized the tailor as a hero who had "immortalized himself." According to the *Shore Press*, "Scarcely an eye was undimmed by tears. The whole town was in mourning, for young Fisher was known and liked by nearly every man, woman and child in Matawan."

Numbed by grief, the shark hunters would return to the creek with their boats and guns and hooks that day and the next, trolling for the man-eater, but on the third day a carnival atmosphere prevailed. Extra-large charges were set to push white geysers dramatically high above the creek for the benefit of the newsreels. It was a fine, clear day for pictures, and with newspaper photographers lining the banks, the young shark hunters, cigarettes drooping from their lips, focused angry gazes at the camera lens instead of at the water. Women in day dresses posed grinning for photographers, while angling rifles toward their own toes instead of the creek. "It is to be hoped that she did not discharge this shotgun while holding it in this position," read one photo caption. The earnest shark hunters seemed a ragged and quixotic bunch to the crowds from miles around that now appeared on the banks, for the shark and the suffering of the small town had become a novelty. "Society turned to shark hunting as the latest wrinkle in summer pastimes," the *Philadelphia Inquirer* reported. "Almost 100 automobiles were packed along the bank of the creek today, and fashionably dressed women and girls from Jersey coast resorts tripped down to the water's edge to watch the shark hunters at work."

That afternoon, as Stilwell and Fisher were eulogized, a newspaperman from New York City rode a motorboat downcreek to the mouth at Raritan Bay and inspected the steel nets erected to contain the shark. Shortly afterward, he reported that Matawan had lost its battle with the sea monster. A large hole had been chewed in the steel nets, and the chunks of meat set as bait were gone.

Intense with Need

＊

The great white shark moved free in the wide curve of the bay between New Jersey and Staten Island. Matawan Creek was miles away.

Against considerable odds, the shark had survived battles with men, withstood and escaped the brackish, shallow creek, and sought the freedom of the sea. Yet the shark was weaker than it had been when it entered the creek, and hardly satisfied by five attacks on human beings. The bays below New York City were a great melting pot for the Atlantic seaboard, where freshwater and industrial flows from the city mixed with oceanic water from the continental shelf that curled down from Georges Bank around Cape Cod and Long Island. Raritan and Sandy Hook bays formed a rich estuary that generated marine life for the entire coast from the Gulf of Maine to Chesapeake Bay, hosting more than a hundred different species as diverse as dogfish sharks and moray eels.

But this womb of the sea was a hostile place as well—subject to extremes of temperature, salinity, and chemical degradation as profound as any estuary in the world. In this degraded environment, the great white somehow failed to capture the fish that abounded, its normal prey. With human flesh in its stomach, it continued on a strange and aberrant course.

Precisely because of that course, the lower bays of New York bristled with greater threat for all manner of sharks. Armed men were on the bay that day, killing sharks in unprecedented numbers. Bloodied hooks baited with meat and fish trailed boats, steel shark hooks dangling and glinting. In Raritan Bay, some ten miles from the mouth of Matawan Creek, a nine-and-a-half-foot shark had taken one of those baits and been captured by a New York fishing party after what a newspaper called a "terrible battle."

The large shark possessed a huge jaw and teeth, and the fishing party believed it to be the man-eater that had consumed Stilwell and Fisher. With great excitement, they towed it back to Belford, New Jersey, eight miles from Matawan. New York and Philadelphia journalists and local residents crowded the docks to witness the shark being opened, to see if the bounty had been won. The shark was indeed a man-eater—a female bull shark, *Carcharhinus leucas*. But the men who cut open the bull were in for a surprise—twelve dead *Carcharhinus leucas* pups, each eighteen inches long and perfectly formed miniature adults, spilled out. While the capture of a gestating shark was notable, it held no value for the bounty hunters.

As the great white swam in the lower New York bays among the baited hooks, it was attracted to other lures. Fishing boats and sailboats and yachts, skiffs and steamers, trawlers and liners, plied the channels to the city. The shark had probably never shared the water with so many boats, large shadows that bewitched it with sonic and scent signals. Sharks are drawn to boats, scientists believe, by electromagnetic impulses emitted by ship equipment, by the metal flashing of propellers, by the skipping of oars across the surface, the leather workings on oars. Sharks crash into boats with exploratory bumps; and they are drawn by bait fish or recently caught fish. There is a contemporary account of an eight-foot blue shark leaping entirely out of the water and landing square on the snoozing form of an astounded young charter fisherman lying on the bottom of a boat, sleeping off seasickness while his friends fished for sharks. The young man awakened, fainted straightaway, and recovered to help his friends beat the shark to death.

Yet of all shark species, the great white is most notorious for attacks on boats, given its size and aggression and unique ability to crush a large hull. Shark researcher Xavier Maniguet refers mostly to the great white when he writes, "It is clear that a shark heading, even at a slow speed, for the hull of a boat can shatter it like a walnut. No wooden or plastic hull can withstand such a 'snoutbutt.'"

In Australia, sharks have long been known to bite gaping holes in hulls, rip off pieces of a boat, and leave large teeth embedded in the hull. In a particularly famous case from April 1946, a man and his son were fishing from a boat off the coast of New South Wales, when a twenty-foot shark took the line and then for no apparent reason charged the boat. According to the fisherman, the shark tore off the rudder, flung it high into the air, and "savaged it like a mad dog." In a final flourish, the shark made off with the rudder between its teeth.

Many men in boats have not been so fortunate. In June 1923, four miners were fishing from a reef on the south coast of New South Wales, when a school of sharks passed under the boat. "The boat shuddered, and the next instant a gaping hole was ripped in the bottom," the one surviving miner recalled. The boat heeled, filled with water, and wallowed, with the men struggling to cling to its side. One of the miners volunteered to swim two miles to shore for help. He had gone only about sixty feet, then he gave a cry and disappeared.

Late in the evening of July 14, a fisherman in the bay returned to shore with a battered boat and an eerie story. He had been cruising along when a big shark attacked his boat and tried to sink it. After a prolonged struggle, the fisherman prevailed in escaping from the shark, but not before he saw it close up: a great dark fish approximately eight feet long.

The great white that had escaped Matawan Creek, the big fish that had attacked five men in unprecedented frenzy, is as likely a suspect in that boat attack as the ocean could produce, yet it cannot be proven. What is known is that on that Friday the moon was nearly full, and the shark was intense with need, and as it cruised Raritan Bay there sounded a rich and confusing cocktail of scents and sonic bursts, boats and mammals.

North and east lay all the bays and harbors and beaches of New York City.

To Drive Away the Sharks

❧

She was tall and voluptuous and men's eyes followed as she moved on the beach that morning. The Atlantic was a clear and distant blue with sea foam lathering the sand under a round, full sky, but it was her form that men saw when she appeared, the aquiline nose and cheekbones and cascading hair of the vaudeville star Gertrude Hoffman. There was said to be something dark, irresistible, and ruinous to men in the lush figure of Hoffman. She had popularized the Salome dance in the early 1900s, unleashing its cousins, the striptease and the belly dance,

and the dance of the seven veils. She had been arrested for inde-
cent dancing (albeit for publicity reasons, rigged by her producer, William Hammerstein) and ordered to wear ankle-length
tights. Now the pearls and feathers of the stage were gone and
Gertrude Hoffman stood unadorned in a bathing costume.

At midmorning, the dancer stepped delicately into the
ocean and began to wade out. Thousands of bathers shared the
water with Hoffman at Coney Island and Brighton beaches and
all along the Brooklyn shoreline. Wednesday had hit ninety-
one degrees, the hottest day of the summer until Thursday,
when the mercury "aviated toward ninety-two," the weather-
men said. Friday, July 14 was another sizzler, and the Weather
Bureau in Washington declared no end in sight to the heat wave.

New Yorkers were escaping to the beach early. The Sea Beach
trains and electric streetcars rumbled in all morning from the
boroughs, and steamboats from Manhattan disgorged passengers
at Coney Island's Dreamland Pier. On the beach, a man and a
woman could escape the heat that had killed eight New Yorkers.
In Illusion Palace or the Village of Midgets or the Upside-Down
House (where furniture was nailed to the ceiling), a father or
mother could perhaps forget the infantile paralysis epidemic that
had taken seventeen more lives the previous day.

In the distant towers of Coney Island was a world in reassuring miniature, where visitors could replay and resolve to
their satisfaction the anxieties of modern civilization with the
help of a thousand fancies. It was said, "If Paris is France, then
Coney Island, between June and September, is the world." In an
age before television and the dominance of motion pictures,
Americans flocked to Coney Island to witness the events they'd
only imagined.

Yet nothing real or imagined by Coney Island's impresarios
in the American experience prepared visitors for the events of

that Friday morning on the beach. Shortly after wading out, Gertrude Hoffman slipped into the waves and began to swim, her slender arms arcing gracefully. She had swum several hundred feet off the foot of West Thirty-first Street, when terror stole her breath. A large, dark fin appeared in the water, moving swiftly directly toward her, whereupon the dancer believed she was about to be devoured by the man-eater of New Jersey.

Fortunately, *The New York Times* reported, Hoffman "had the presence of mind to remember that she had read in the *Times* that a bather can scare away a shark by splashing, and she beat up the water furiously." The large fin disappeared and Hoffman retreated to shore, where slowly her heart resumed its normal beat. Later, when she regained composure, the dancer wasn't sure if she had seen a shark or merely imagined it after reading the headlines in the morning paper. She was, the *Times* reported, "not sure . . . whether she had had her trouble for nothing or had barely escaped death." In any case, she was not eager to return to the water.

While Gertrude Hoffman's encounter in Coney Island was frightening, it was not at all unusual. Reports of sharks nearing the coast were multiplying. A shark panic unrivaled in American history was sweeping along the coasts of New York and New Jersey and spreading by telephone and wireless, letter and postcard. From the edge of the sea, an alarm sounded by the forces that had turned the sinking of the *Maine* into war had little trouble transforming a juvenile *Carcharodon carcharias* into a sea monster. Newsboys chased men down the street, hawking front pages right under their noses, and announced in Irish and Italian and Polish accents and high prepubescent voices to passing motorcars and horse carriages and the stone towers of Manhattan:

"Big, savage sharks infest coast!"

"Shark kills 2 bathers, maims 1, near New York!"

"Whole of Jersey coast infested with man-eating monsters!"

"Ten pounds of his flesh ripped off by sea monster!"

The *New York Herald* headline trumpeted six columns across the top, a size reserved for war or the "Second Coming": "Shark glides up shallow creek and kills boy and man, then tears another swimmer."

"Monster makes way through Raritan Bay and upstream mile and one-half."

"First little victim only 12 years old."

"Man who goes to rescue dies soon after being dragged from creature's teeth."

An average New Yorker in 1916 had seen little more of war than the simulations of the Boer War or the naval battle "War of Worlds" at Luna Park on Coney Island, but the *Herald* assured its readers, "No more spectacular raid on inland or coast waters ever was made."

The morning of Gertrude Hoffman's encounter, Thomas Richard, assistant steward of the Beau Rivage Hotel in Coney Island, was bathing in Sheepshead Bay at the foot of Emmons Avenue in Brooklyn, facing the other end of Coney Island, when fifty people breakfasting on the porch of the hotel yelled "Shark!" A group of bathers ran screaming from the water, but Richard was too far out to swim quickly ashore and saw a fin headed in his direction. As the fin closed in, he raced for a nearby motorboat and climbed in, drawing his legs out of the water a fraction of a second before the ripple passed where he had been.

Fear rounded the bays of New York from Gravesend Bay to Great Kills Harbor to the Rockaways. On Staten Island beaches there was a noticeable decrease in bathers—fewer still after employees of the Mount Loretto Home sighted a fin in Princess Bay, and, after a brief struggle, beached the bloodied corpse of an eight-and-a-half-foot shark. At Keansburg on Raritan Bay and Atlantic Highlands on Sandy Hook Bay—both sharing a shoreline with Matawan Creek—the bathers stayed on shore and basked in the sun. By Saturday, July 15, the weekend business of the bathhouse owners at Coney Island and Brighton Beach was in ruins. Police estimated fifty thousand Coney Island bathers had chosen to stay out of the water for fear of the man-eater. "Terror of Sharks Keeps a Million Bathers on Shore," the *New York World* reported.

The few who braved the surf could not have been reassured by the company. On long, deserted beaches, crowds frolicking in the water and cooling under umbrellas had been replaced by gangs of men with gaffs and spears, guns and harpoons—men with the high spirits of sportsmen, or the grim aspect of bounty hunters. "Bathing has come almost to a stop along the Jersey coast," *The New York Times* reported, "especially those areas where the man-eater has attacked, and a new sport, and public service, the hunting of sharks, has sprung up." A captain terrified a crowd at a Long Island dock by bringing ashore a monstrous seventeen-foot shark; only when he cut it open did he realize it was a plankton eater. In shallow water off Eldred's Bar near Rockaway Point in Brooklyn, eight men digging for sandworms saw a shark driving a school of weakfish toward shore—"a shark that was doing what sharks do every year when the weakfish appear," according to shark researcher Thomas B. Allen. In a fury the men killed it with oars, spears, spades, and eel-tongs.

Thus one of the most profligate shark hunts in history swept the coast. Fishermen slayed dozens of purported man-eaters and hauled their bloodied corpses to shore, where crowds watched the gigantic stomachs of the monsters slit open, revealing immense quantities of fish—but not the prize that paid: human flesh.

By that same Friday, swimmers were afraid to enter the waters of Chesapeake Bay for fear of man-eaters. The news on the front page of the *Washington Post* was presented as being as significant as the British assault on the Germans at the Somme. In headlines larger than those announcing the Mexican revolt, the Italian assault on the Austrians in Lagarina, the rush of Americans to join the army, or President Wilson's appointee to replace Charles Evans Hughes on the Supreme Court, the *Post* crowed: "Sharks cause panic. Man-eaters seen at numerous points along the Atlantic. New York and New Jersey shores guarded by armed men." That morning, a Baltimore swimming club made plans to hire a shark patrol for their Sunday race on the Chesapeake, and the Maryland State Police schooner *May Brown* confirmed that it had spied "big sea monsters" in Annapolis harbor. The "shark scare . . . threw fright into the many persons . . . who frequent the nearby shores of Chesapeake Bay and Severn River for bathing purposes," the *Baltimore Sun* reported.

Hysteria spread, afflicting the lowly and the mighty, as a single shark prevented people from entering the water along more than a thousand miles of the East Coast, from New England to Florida. Fishermen off Connecticut steered clear of Atlantic "monsters," and a Tampa, Florida, boater said the Gulf man-eaters were so thick he'd returned to port. A neighbor of Teddy Roosevelt said he saw a shark off the beach in Oyster Bay, Long Island, and called upon him to do something about it.

The shark became an American cause célèbre. Giant toothy sharks grinned from front-page photographs. Ruthless cartoon sharks stalked human prey on the women's pages, and editorial writers wagged about the death of the myth that sharks were harmless.

People signed up for special swimming courses that, according to Allen, were supposed to teach bathers how to outwit sharks. Swimming star Annette Kellerman offered her advice in both *The New York Times* and the *Washington Post* that one must simply keep an eye out for sharks—"you can always see them and dive under them if they rush up at you." Since the shark attacks "upside down," she explained, "you have a chance to get away, if the distance to shore . . . is not too far." A captain from Key West, Florida, who would later tutor Ernest Hemingway in deep-sea fishing, offered to kill the shark for free. The vice president of the Autocar Company on the Main Line of Philadelphia, who sported at Zane Grey's fishing camp in Long Key, Florida, said sharks, "not being very astute fish," would go for baited kegs every thousand feet. Letters to the editor advocated that Washington send the entire United States submarine fleet to destroy the shark. Another suggested the bait of a dummy stuffed with explosives and dressed like Lester Stilwell. Frank Claret, master of the Atlantic Transport liner *Minnehaha*, just arrived that week from London, said the largest of man-eaters were easy to scare away "by shouting as loud as possible, and by striking the water with one's feet and hands." The captain even suggested there was a new opportunity for fine dining, offering some recipes for shark, "not bad, if well curried." Moroney's Army and Navy Whiskey published a newspaper advertisement warning, "Keep away from those sharks at Atlantic City. They are café owners who are always 'just out' when you call for a highball made of Moroney's . . ." According to the *Philadelphia Evening Bulletin*, Hermann Oelrichs's famous bet had at last been settled; there was at last "proof sharks bite."

If the shark exposed an American impulse to make entertainment out of tragedy—an impulse as fresh as the San Francisco earthquake at Luna Park, a Coney Island production in three parts—in New Jersey the impact of the shark was real.

By the middle of July, thousands of citizens of New Jersey had showered telegrams and letters, editorials and telephone calls, on Trenton and Washington, begging the U.S. government and the state of New Jersey for help. Dozens of letters went directly to the White House, imploring President Wilson to take steps to rid the coast of the monsters. Hundreds of New Jersey citizens cabled Governor Tom Fielder with a collective alarm.

The economy of the Jersey shore was in a crisis. Tourists who had not yet had time to mourn or even understand the deaths of Charles Vansant and Charles Bruder reacted to the reported fatal attacks on yet another young man and a boy in New Jersey waters by packing—for home, or for the mountains. During the second week of July, the grand hotels, cottages, and guest houses from Cape May north to Spring Lake reported an average of 75 percent vacancies on some of the best beach days of the year. The threat of the shark prowling offshore cost Jersey hoteliers a quarter million dollars in lost reservations in a week. Combined with the growing fear of gathering in hotels and beaches and public places during an infantile paralysis epidemic, the economies of a dozen seaside towns were on the verge of ruin.

Twenty-eight trainloads of visitors on company excursions had canceled shore trips in recent days. The Asbury Park Hotel had closed, its full house sent packing, because of one infected child. Without summer tourist dollars, many communities would have trouble surviving the winter. The morning Gertrude Hoffman went for a dip, the governor of New Jersey was besieged by citizens' pleas for state authorities to kill the shark.

Governor James Fairman Fielder, a Wilson Progressive, forty-nine years old, a large, powerfully built man, stood before newspapermen from New York, Trenton, and Asbury Park in the governor's summer mansion in Sea Girt that Friday morning. Governor Fielder was one of the bright voices of the Progressive Era, men who believed man had mastered the animal kingdom and were close to perfecting mankind, and that government could fix anything.

The governor had called a press conference to make an announcement about the shark emergency. Fielder was a solid man in a crisis. Descended from a line of Dutch-English politicians and churchmen, he was widely admired for his unflappable temperament and was, in the words of Woodrow Wilson, his predecessor, "a man of proved character, capacity, fidelity and devotion to the public service."

Now, he announced to reporters, the state was facing a crisis for which no one had answers. Reflecting on the deaths of three New Jersey men and a boy, the governor gave his opinion that not one but many sea monsters were attacking the state's coastline at continuing peril to human life, yet there was "no possible action that the state could take that would lessen the evil." The governor had no idea what to do, for veteran fishermen and scientists couldn't settle on what the sea monster or monsters were, let alone offer a plan of action. Fielder had contemplated a massive hunt along the state's lengthy coast, but such an expeditionary force would have to be authorized by the legislature, which was out of session, and "even if the legislature could be called," he said, the "cost was prohibitive." The governor urged every coastal town in New Jersey to construct shark nets. If the irony occurred to him of a Progressive governor in the modern era asking for a man to step forward to slay a sea monster, Fielder did not express it. It was neither an armada nor a soldier-knight who was needed in this day and age, it was an expert. At the close of his brief address, Governor Fielder urged "the bathers . . . to be careful," and prayed someone would "come forward" with the knowledge to "drive away the sharks."

Friday morning in the White House, Woodrow Wilson was up before dawn and at five A.M. took breakfast with his First Lady. Somewhat frail at sixty years of age, the President preferred to rise later and work only three to four hours a day, but the war in Europe and the election had pressed him, he told the First Lady, to rise early and "steal up on them in the dark."

After breakfast the President retired to his office for an hour of correspondence, dictation, and brief meetings with a few key advisers. At eleven, the President, tall and graying in a tailored black suit, entered a Cabinet meeting to discuss "the shark horror gripping the New Jersey Coast." The citizens of New Jersey, New York, and other coastal states had sent a torrent of telegrams and letters to the White House beseeching the President of the United States to slay a man-eating sea monster.

On Capitol Hill that morning, New Jersey Congressman Isaac Bacharach of Atlantic City introduced a bill appropriating $5,000 for the federal Bureaus of Fisheries to cooperate in rounding up sharks for the purpose of "the extermination of man-eating sharks now infesting the waters of the Atlantic Ocean along the coast of New Jersey."

Joseph P. Tumulty, a Jersey City lawyer and the President's most trusted adviser since 1913, urged Wilson take bold and decisive action against sharks. Earlier that morning, Tumulty had cabled his friend, J. Lyle Kinmonth, editor of the *Asbury Park Press*, promising Wilson would "do anything in his power to . . . rid the Jersey coast of the shark menace."

Yet exactly what the President could do about a rogue shark was another matter entirely. William Redfield, secretary of the Department of Commerce, which oversaw lighthouses and fisheries, told the Cabinet that despite Congressman Bacharach's proposal, "the bureau of fisheries had been unable to offer any scientific explanation of the unprecedented attacks upon human beings." Bureau experts "reluctantly had been compelled to come to the conclusion that no certainly effective preventive measures could be recommended." Fisheries' only advice was "a shark catching campaign" and to warn bathers to stay in shallow water.

The President turned to his ablest Cabinet member and son-in-law, Treasury Secretary William Gibbs McAdoo, to lead a "war on sharks." Shortly after emerging from the Cabinet meeting, McAdoo called a press conference. Surrounded by Washington newspapermen, McAdoo announced that the U.S. Coast Guard and the Bureau of Fisheries would join forces to "rout the sea terrors." According to McAdoo, the coast guard cutter *Mohawk* would sail immediately to the Jersey coast to destroy any or all killer sharks, avenge four deaths, and save the bathing season.

On Saturday, July 15, the "U.S. war on sharks" was the biggest news in the *Washington Post* and front-page headlines across the world—in New York, Philadelphia, Chicago, and even London. "Wilson and Cabinet Make Plans to Prevent More Tragedies," the *Post* headline read. "Coast Guards Turn Hunters . . . Federal Cutters Also Are Ordered to Fish for the Monsters."

The Coast Guard "would be ordered to do what it could toward clearing the coast of the dangerous fish and preventing further loss of life." The U.S. lifesaving stations all along the East Coast would be involved, too, by order of the Treasury Department. According to the *Washington Post*, "no definite plan of action has been worked out, but the idea is to have the service aid in locating and when possible warn resorts of their proximity." On the front page of the *Washington Evening Star* was a political cartoon, "Uncle Sam's Latest Crusade," depicting a grim, machine-gun-toting Uncle Sam in a patrol boat flying a flag with the words "Death to Sharks."

That night the *Mohawk* stood at anchor in New York harbor, where it would remain. For in the days to come, a shark-extermination program along the 127-mile-long New Jersey coast would be judged "impracticable," and the campaign would be abandoned.

The federal government's final suggestion to New Jersey and its bathers was the same as Governor Fielder's: Install wire netting, and stay in shallow water. John Cole, director of all government lifesaving stations on the New Jersey coast, had a different opinion. "Where there are no nets, the best way to keep from getting bit is to keep out of the water," he said. "I wouldn't go in."

Something Peculiarly Sinister

⁓

The two men were going fishing in the bay, hoping to catch lunch or even dinner, if the fishing was good. In the early hours of Friday, July 14, the sky was cloudy, but the bay was calm. It was a splendid morning to be on the water. The men were friends and they had been lingering on the small wharf in the old port town of South Amboy, when Michael Schleisser, the smaller of the two, found an old oar handle lying on the wharf. The oar was snapped in half, the paddle gone, driftwood of a forgotten evening, an absent adventure. Schleisser picked it up and put it with his fishing gear.

"What do you need that for?" John Murphy asked his friend.

"Oh, it'll come in handy for something," Schleisser said.

Michael Schleisser was indeed good at cobbling things into something. He was brilliant with his hands. Schleisser was all of five-foot-six, a wiry man with a wide forehead and a long, tapering face and a handlebar mustache. Forty years old, he had emigrated from his native Serbia fifteen years earlier and had become one of the foremost taxidermists in the United States, specializing in turning out impressive trophies for hunters and fishermen. He was renowned as an animal trainer, and he was a big-game hunter who'd traveled the world and stalked the African veldt. In the backyard of his house in Harlem were a tethered black bear, gray wolf, red fox, and opossum, several large alligators in a tank, as well as an aviary, several turtles, a cage of white rats, and other animals. On the second floor were cases displaying mounted rare butterflies, racks of firearms, rows of animal heads, and stuffed animals from Asia, Africa, and South America. Michael Schleisser had trained or killed everything that moved, and was afraid of nothing.

John Murphy, a twenty-eight-year-old Bronx resident, knew his way around boats. He worked as a laborer for a steamship company. Together the men loved to fish Raritan Bay.

The launch was small, an eight-foot wooden motorboat, but ideal for two men fishing. Schleisser and Murphy sailed past Staten Island through Outerbridge Reach, entered Laurence Harbor, and finally reached Raritan Bay below Staten Island. They threw a six-foot net over the stern and began to trawl the bay with it. The net was great for snagging bait fish like tunny and menhaden. The boat chugged along smoothly, the net running six feet deep. After an hour, they had sailed far from the wharf at Amboy, and were motoring at the bottom of Raritan Bay, roughly four miles from the mouth of Matawan Creek.

Shortly before noon, the boat slammed to a halt. Scheissler and Murphy hit the floor, hands out to protect themselves. The force was such that the engine immediately sputtered and died. But the men knew they weren't having engine trouble. As Schleisser and Murphy righted themselves, they saw that something was caught in the net, something big. The boat began to move backward, stern first, against the waves. Water leaped the gunwales. The boat was being pulled backward fast, and dragged down. It was being pulled under.

Gifted with the ability to remain calm during a crisis, Schleisser, his heart raging, focused his gaze behind the boat. In the net he saw what he would later describe as "a big bifurcated tail flash out of water." He turned back to Murphy and shouted, "My God, we've got a shark!" The small craft moved backward rapidly. The rushing of the shark threw the bow high in the air and more water rushed over the gunwales. Murphy threw himself forward to keep the stern from being submerged. Schleisser searched the boat for a weapon. There was nothing at hand but their fishing rods and bait, and the broken oar handle. Had they intended to hunt the rogue shark, they would have taken out a larger boat, packed a harpoon, guns, and knives. Schleisser grabbed the oar handle and edged back toward the stern.

To his astonishment, the shark was rising out of the net and onto the stern, snapping its great jaws. The stern heaved downward, and Schleisser battled for purchase. He could see the fish's dark top and even its whitish underside—and the size of its teeth. Perhaps only a hunter as experienced as Schleisser could consider the creature attacking him without losing all hope. The mouth that Schleisser faced over the gunwales was wide enough to swallow him. Given his knowledge, he may have guessed it was a great white, perhaps the manhunter from the headlines. As the boat rocked wildly, the shark splashed water vigorously with its powerful tail. "The sea-tiger beat the sea into a foam," he later recalled.

Schleisser was in no position to surrender, for it soon became apparent that he and Murphy were the prey. The great white was trying to leap the gunwales to reach the two men, jaws agape. As the boat thrashed on the bay, Schleisser tried to steady himself to attempt a blow at the creature's head, but each time he set to swing the oar handle, "he was thwarted by the rocking of the boat."

Schleisser's plan was a dangerous one. He may have known of the shark's affinity for attacking oars or of the fury with which sharks around the world responded to confrontations with fishermen.

Finding his footing for an instant, Schleisser struck with all his strength. The first blow landed on the nose, the second about the gills. The shark responded furiously, rising directly toward Schleisser's arm. The great jaws missed their target, but the immense head struck Schleisser's forearm hard, its sandpaperlike skin opening cuts on Schleisser's wrist. There was blood now in the water. The shark thrashed wildly, entangling itself further in the mesh of the net. With a desperate rush it leaped onto the stern toward the men. Schleisser saw an opportunity and struck another heavy blow on the nose which partially stunned the shark. As it lay dazed for a moment on the stern, Schleisser struck it repeatedly on the gills and the head until the fish went slack and slowly slid into the net. Schleisser and Murphy fell back into the boat exhausted, near collapse. The shark was dead. They had beaten it to death.

Stunned, the men sat silently, unable to move or talk as the boat gently rocked on the bay. Moving slowly, they got the engine to turn over and chugged back toward Amboy, towing the dead shark.

When they reached the wharf at South Amboy, Schleisser and Murphy were greeted by the usual crowd of fishermen and onlookers who gathered when a boat arrived with an unusually large fish in tow. On this day, however, the murmurs of curiosity on the docks rose to levels of excitement beyond the usual discussion of the impressive size of the fish. For it was Michael Schleisser—a man with a reputation as a big game fisherman—who arrived at the dock, and the fish he had was no ordinary trophy. It was a shark, a large one.

Michael Schleisser and John Murphy clambered onto the docks with the ragged look of men who had nothing left to give. Wearily, Schleisser described the battle with the shark. The big-game hunter admitted the shark had attacked more ferociously than any African lion or any grizzly bear he had ever encountered. It was, he said, "the hardest fight for life I've ever had."

Eagerly, the men helped Schleisser and Murphy hoist the giant fish from its tow. It took half a dozen men to carry it. Michael Schleisser announced that he wanted a picture, and hastily, the massive shark was propped on a pair of sawhorses some seven feet apart. The taxidermist stood unsmiling behind his trophy, his torso nearly obscured by the height of dorsal fin. The fish's dark, unseeing eyes stared out in a kind of fury, and its jaw was propped open wide enough to take in a man's head. As the photographer snapped the picture, it was apparent to Schleisser and the other fishermen that the shark lacked the claspers of a male. Although it was too young to be carrying pups, the shark was a female.

The fisherman were taken aback since they traditionally assumed that man-eating sharks were males. In fact, while both genders are capable of devouring humans, females are in some respects more formidable. Equipped with extra girth to sustain and protect its eggs, the female white shark grows even larger than the male.

Throughout history the capture of a large shark has drawn the morbidly curious to witness the opening of the stomach to see if it contains human remains. That day the witnesses' curiosity was more than idle. Those who greeted Schleisser's boat were hoping the taxidermist had captured the man eater of Matawan Creek.

In the following days, while Michael Schleisser investigated the true nature of his trophy, John T. Nichols and Robert Cushman Murphy resolved to undertake their own search for the shark. Among the few men who grasped the identity and true nature of the shark that had terrorized New Jersey, Nichols and Murphy had appointed themselves the task of finding and killing it. On Wednesday, July 20, the scientists set out in their small launch into Jamaica Bay, which they had determined was a likely destination for a hungry shark that had demonstrated a northward progression of attacks—if it had not yet escaped to the sea. Murphy, a lanky six foot three, stood in the bowsprit of the small craft, a harpoon in one hand. At the wheel, John Nichols piloted the vessel and scanned the waters for a caudal fin on the surface—a signature of the great white, for Nichols and Murphy now had no doubt that it was a great white they were hunting. They expected the shark to be immense, thirty or possibly forty feet, and to reveal itself like a wide seam in the ocean. Nichols believed the shark that had killed four New Jersey men was "the only true man-eating shark," the species that his research had revealed was "according to Linnaeus, the Leviathan which swallowed Jonah." That the biblical story, apocryphal or not, was plausible impressed Nichols.

Nichols and Murphy were aware that the U.S. Coast Guard's war on sharks had been called off, and they now believed, as did

Hugh Smith at the U.S. Department of Fisheries, that the predator was a single great white shark.

Neither man was disposed by nature to pursue the ocean's largest and fiercest predator. Both loved the sea and its organisms passionately. But as Nichols concentrated on the horizon, he scanned the surface for the lone creature that inspired in him no affection, but, rather, a mixture of awe and dread. In the *Brooklyn Museum Science Bulletin* article that Nichols and Murphy collaborated on in April, they had written:

> There is something peculiarly sinister in the shark's makeup. The sight of his dark, lean fin lazily cutting zigzags in the surface of some quiet, sparkling summer sea, and then slipping out of sight not to appear again, suggests an evil spirit. His leering, chinless face, his great mouth with its rows of knifelike teeth, which he knows too well how to use on the fisherman's gear, the relentless fury with which, when his last hour has come, he thrashes on deck and snaps at his enemies; his toughness, his brutal nerveless vitality and insensibility to physical injury, fail to elicit the admiration one feels for the dashing, brilliant, destructive, gastronomic bluefish, tunny, or salmon.

Murphy would become a pioneering conservationist, an inspiration to Rachel Carson in her classic *Silent Spring*. He shared the Ancient Mariner's admonition of the preciousness of life. "And I had done an hellish thing/And it would work 'em woe: For all averred, I had killed the bird/That made the breeze to blow." But he had no qualms about killing a shark, even the rare *Carcharodon carcharias*. On a whaling voyage in the South Pacific, Murphy had noted that the whaleman's antipathy toward sharks was fierce, and came to respect it. The day a whaleman died, three blue sharks, about seven feet long, appeared under the stern, and "the old, old maritime conviction that these hated brutes had come expressly for the body was breathed about the ship . . . sharks are considered by sailors to be fair quarry upon which to practice all the barbarism of ingenious human nature," he wrote. "Indeed it is doubtful whether there be any creature that the average human being takes more pleasure in destroying."

Both men believed finding a white shark in the vicinity of New York City would be an epic accomplishment. "So far as we can discover [the white shark], it is throughout its cosmopolitan range in warm seas, a rare fish," they wrote. "It is occasional on the Atlantic coast of the United States as far north as Cape Cod, but we know of no definite record for Long Island." Rarer still was any evidence a great white shark had ever attacked a human being on the East Coast—evidence Nichols needed to persuade Dr. Lucas, and himself, that the New Jersey attacks were the work of a shark, a shark that needed to be killed.

Like Frederic Lucas, neither Murphy nor Nichols was inclined to believe any shark was a deliberate man-eater, but the past thirty-six hours had altered their view. In Matawan four days earlier, Nichols had been influenced by his meeting with Captain Watson Fisher, Stanley Fisher's father, the retired commander of the Savannah Steamship Line. Captain Fisher struck Nichols as an intelligent, reasonable man who shared Dr. Lucas's sentiments about sharks. Captain Fisher claimed that, in his fifty-six years at sea, he had never seen a shark attack a man and never knew of an authentic report of such an attack. Yet Fisher emphasized to Nichols his newfound conviction that his son was killed by a shark.

Retreating to the depths of the American Museum of Natural History in New York, Nichols had pored over rafts of old documents. By digging deep into the scientific literature of the nineteenth century, he found the proof he sought: documented evidence the great white shark had visited temperate waters and devoured human beings. It was in the 1880s, off the coast of Massachusetts, that a great white attacked and broke apart a fishing boat and proceeded to kill and devour most of the fishermen. Although the attack was far from shore, the white's presence in northern latitudes convinced Nichols. His research led him to believe that not only was Frederic Lucas wrong, but scientific and government assurances about the harmlessness of sharks were both uninformed and dangerous. New Jersey was correct to have "abandoned its swimming," he had told *The New York Times*, and now it was "time for New Yorkers to take warning. The garbage in New York Bay and chances of catching unsuspecting swimmers undoubtedly will bring the sea tigers into New York waters.

"It is the white shark which has been at work, and this is the second time in history this type has been seen north of Cape Hatteras," Nichols continued. "My own belief is that [this] single fish . . . has killed all four of the bathers and that if . . . it is killed the attacks will end."

Nichols made swift strides in his theory when, after returning from Matawan, he was able to persuade Frederic Lucas the victims were most likely attacked by a shark. Subsequently, in a humbling if not devastating moment, Dr. Lucas admitted on the front page of *The New York Times* that he had been wrong.

With the headline "Science Admits Its Error. No Longer Doubted That Big Fish Attack Men," the *Times* reported that "the foremost authority on sharks in this country has doubted that any type of shark ever attacked a human being, and has published his doubts, but the recent cases have changed his view."

So Nichols and Murphy set out into the waters of Jamaica Bay in their launch rigged to fish for the big shark. The scientists noted, to their dismay, that the weakfish and fluke in the bay had all but disappeared. Plants in Queens and Brooklyn daily discharged millions of gallons of raw sewage into the bay. The waste was slowly poisoning the clams and oysters—by 1921, the health department would abolish shellfishing in Jamaica Bay—but in 1916 the organic torrent from the city may have lured the shark.

They had armed themselves with several harpoons in preparation for an encounter with the big fish. Guns and knives were also aboard, to the extent they would matter. The scientists were under no illusions about their chances versus *Carcharodon carcharias* if it appeared in its full-grown size.

Forsaking sleep, they cruised the deep channel in Rockaway Inlet. In the daylight Nichols could see some distance through the water, paying special attention to sandbars, against which the sun would silhouette his quarry. Whereas the brown shark, the commonest large shark in the latitude of New York, Nichols noted, kept below the surface in the manner of the littoral species, its fin and tail seldom seen unless it was crossing a sandbar, the pelagic species like the white shark rode high in the water, announcing their presence like a surfacing U-boat.

Suddenly, on the second day, Nichols felt his heart protesting against his ribs. He had spotted a shark moving along the edge of the bar. Nichols carefully worked the sloop toward it, avoiding the shoals where he would go aground, and followed the winding course of the shark. Murphy narrowed his eyes as the sloop swung from one tack to another, and finally saw an elusive shadow moving a couple of boat lengths ahead. The light in the water could play tricks with the shadow, blowing it to monstrous size, but then the shadow slipped too far ahead to discern its true substance. Murphy tightened his grip on the harpoon and wondered if the iron would slow a white shark. Whaling in the South Atlantic, the power of five- and seven-foot blue sharks had astounded him. "We have seen one hooked, shot full of lead from a repeating rifle, then harpooned, hauled on deck, and disemboweled, yet it continued alive and alert for a long while, thrashing its tail and opening and shutting its weird expressionless eyes . . ."

As the huge shadow darted, Murphy readied himself for the possibility it may turn and shoot under the bowsprit, giving him but a fraction of an instant to strike. He knew well the consequence of a bad throw—he'd watch the iron graze the fish and "the pole stand quivering in the sand, while the shark darts away into deep water and is gone." He was not sure anymore if he knew the consequence of a good throw. For the local sharks, he knew it was a sure strike and "away goes the shark, spinning out the coil of rope and carrying the tub over the water with a rush." But what was a harpoon to an enraged three-thousand-pound fish: a bothersome needle? Should he pray it would come close enough for the guns and the knives? Or pray that it wouldn't?

When the shark came within striking distance Murphy surged forward, heart drumming, hoisting the harpoon, angling for purchase on the bowsprit. But the fearsome shadow was what Nichols and Murphy immediately recognized as a sand shark, *Carcharias taurus*, what is now known to shark biologists as the sand-tiger shark, a common, large, fish-eating species in the region, not known as an attacker of humans. With dismay the men exhaled, perhaps for a moment doubting their pursuit of a white shark. Lucas had warned them that almost every case of a captured purported man-eater he had investigated on the coasts of New Jersey or Long Island resolved to be "harmless, if ugly-looking, sand sharks."

The shark disappeared and the scientists spent the day and the night looking for larger shadows in the bay. Other sharks appeared, but nothing to arouse their interest. Nicholas and Murphy discussed leaving Jamaica Bay for the waters of Lower New York Bay and guarded against the unwelcome feeling that the trip was turning into a failure.

Nichols had hunted sharks many times for the gains of science and knew how a man squandered hours and days on the
water and grew sleepy and cramped and bored—until, when it
was least expected, a shark exploded from the deep. Murphy
had learned the same lessons in the South Atlantic, having
spent endless days stalking the great whales. But they didn't
have endless days now.

As the sun came up on the second day, Nichols and Murphy
trailed steel hooks on strong chains baited with the "tempting
morsel" of a cow's lung. Animal blood radiated and diffused in
the water as the launch rode the gentle bay, bearing the long
shadows of men, tired and bored, on the waters they had
known since boyhood that now seemed somehow alien.

Like a Tale from the Stone Age

❦

There was nothing left to do but cut open the fish to see what its stomach contents revealed, but Michael Schleisser disappointed his audience. Instead he recruited men to lift the huge creature into his automobile.

Back at home in his Harlem row house, Schleisser worked quickly, for the fish would decay rapidly. That afternoon, in the basement given over to a taxidermy studio, Schleisser began the enormous task of mounting the shark. It measured seven and a half feet long and weighed three hundred and fifty pounds. It was a dark, dull blue on top and white underneath. Schleisser cut the fish open and removed the stomach, whereupon a terrible odor filled the basement, and the taxidermist found himself sorting through a large, grisly pile of flesh and bones. There was a mix of large and small bones, and the bones appeared to be human. Schleisser weighed the flesh and bones together and they came to approximately fifteen pounds. As he studied the gruesome scene in the dim light of his basement, Schleisser came to believe he had caught the man-eating shark that had terrorized New Jersey for the first two weeks of July. As Schleisser began to mount the shark, that Tuesday, July 14, President Wilson had already suspended the war on sharks, and John Treadwell Nichols and Robert Cushman Murphy were making plans to hunt the predator in Jamaica Bay, unaware that an apparent man-eater had been caught. Schleisser, a showman at heart, felt no immediate need to inform the world. He wanted to confirm that the bones in the shark's stomach were human, and for that he required the assistance of a scientist. Schleisser resolved to ship the bones to the most famous scientist he personally knew, one whose word was beyond reproach. But first he made a phone call to his local newspaper, the *Home News*.

The newspaper was in a hurry to get the story out, but recognizing the publicity value of having the shark to display, the editors were willing to hold the story until Schleisser had completed his taxidermy. Four days later, Schleisser brought the stuffed and mounted shark to the offices of the Harlem newspaper. The next day, the *Home News* proudly devoted its front page to one of the most dramatic stories in its history, with the headline: "Harlem Man in Tiny Boat Kills a 7½ Foot Man-eating Shark."

"Like a tale from the stone age," the story began, "when men went forth single-handed, armed with nothing but a club, to slay ferocious beasts, is the story of two uptown men, one of whom, with the broken handle of an oar held off a monster man-eating shark after a terrific battle and finally killed it." There was the picture of Schleisser posing with the shark mounted across the sawhorses.

That day and the next, Thursday, July 20, the newspaper promised its readers "the monster will be placed in the window of the *Home News,* at 135 W. 125th St., where everyone will have an opportunity to see what a man-eating shark really looks like." Next to the man-eater, the *Home News* promised, would be a display of the large and small bones found in its stomach.

The box had arrived in the middle of the week at the American Museum of Natural History, addressed to the director, Frederic Augustus Lucas. It was not unusual for the museum to receive a box of dry bones, poison adders, or shrunken heads for that matter. This box received special attention because an accompanying note claimed that the bones the box contained had been retrieved from the stomach of the man-eating shark.

Lucas would have treated the claim with his usual skepticism had it not come from someone he knew and trusted. Michael Schleisser and Frederic Lucas were close enough that before Schleisser made a major exploration of Brazil, he requested and received a letter of introduction from Dr. Lucas to a curator at the U.S. National Museum. However, much as Lucas respected the taxidermy work Schleisser had done for the museum, the director remained suspicious that Schleisser was not purely devoted to science. "I am giving a letter of introduction to Mr. Michael Schleisser who is about to make a trip to the interior of Brazil," Lucas had written. "I have known Mr. Schleisser for a number of years and consider him reliable, although I rather feel that his expedition is largely on account of his love of exploration and partly for photographing."

The problem Schleisser confronted Dr. Lucas with was typical of the taxidermist: a discovery that was arguably scientific, but questionable, perhaps irresponsible, even sensational. Before him, unquestionably, was a pile of masticated human bones. Although the bones challenged his theory that sharks were unable to bite through human bones, Dr. Lucas was grateful to Schleisser for what he came to regard as a contribution to science, and wrote a note on museum stationery thanking the taxidermist.

> Dear Mr. Schleisser: I am very much obliged to you for your courtesy in letting me see the bones taken from the shark. They are parts of the left radius and ulna of one of the anterior left ribs. There is no doubt about this. They have, as you see, been badly shattered. Can you tell me the exact species of shark from which these bones were taken, or if you are in doubt, I am sure that Mr. Nichols would be very glad to call and determine the species exactly? Again thanking you for your kindness, I am, F.A. LUCAS, Director.

From Brooklyn and Staten Island and Greenwich Village they came. Thousands clambered aboard the trolleys to 125th Street in Harlem that Sunday. By the time John Treadwell Nichols arrived at the *Home News* office, a mob of thirty thousand people had gathered in front of it. Americans at the turn of the century were accustomed to behavior in crowds, for parades and public spectacles were commonplace. So that Sunday the mob formed a line, and began to pass before the window in orderly fashion. There were gasps and cries of "Monster!" Adults shuddered and turned away. Mothers pulled children to the side. Many refused to believe what they saw. The shark was monstrous to the point of being scarcely believable.

John Nichols pushed to the front and lingered, staring at the man-eater. His first glance eliminated all doubt. The preternaturally wide, torpedo-shaped body; the crescent caudal fin and long, narrow pectoral fins; the small second dorsal and anal fins; the bifurcated coloring; the large gill slits, broad conical snout, and black eyes; the huge teeth, distinctively triangular and serrated, and, unlike most sharks, the teeth in its top and bottom jaws almost symmetrical. The jaws were large enough to have taken human life—"yawning jaws and vicious teeth," a reporter called them. It was unquestionably *Carcharodon carcharias.*

Independent experts had determined that the bones taken from the shark's stomach were human. Physicians identified the eleven-inch bone as the shinbone of a boy—presumably Lester Stilwell's—and a section of rib bone as belonging to a young man, perhaps Charles Bruder. Dr. Lucas, however, maintained these judgments were "incorrect." The bones were certainly human, Lucas agreed, but based on the size of the shark and the condition of the bones, he claimed they were parts of the left forearm and left upper rib taken from the body of a robust man who had been "dead some time and not the result of any active attack." This was not proof, in Dr. Lucas's opinion, that a shark could bite clean through human bone, or that sharks attack man. This conclusion supported Dr. Lucas's lifework as well as his theory that the species of the attacker was unknown. In a letter to Bureau of Fisheries Commissioner Hugh Smith, Lucas declared that the great white with human remains inside was not the killer and unfortunately his colleague John Nichols "was not able to get any information other than that published in the newspapers."

Time, however, favored the young Dr. Nichols. Unknown to Lucas, Nichols, and their contemporaries, great whites live not only in the tropics but all over the world, and one of the largest populations is off the New Jersey–New York coast. This population is mostly juveniles, however, who take smaller prey and seldom stray close to shore.

On August 8, 1916, Hugh Smith wrote Frederic Lucas: "The excitement in this matter appears to have died down, much to the relief of this office, and I hope nothing will occur to resuscitate it."

By the end of that summer of 1916, the last summer before America entered the Great War, the great white shark had fallen from the front pages of the *Times* and the *Sun* and the *World.* The next spring, Woodrow Wilson told Congress: "The day has come when America is privileged to spend her blood and her might for the principles that gave her birth . . . the world must be made safe for Democracy." Even in the era preoccupied with "Over There" and "Lick a Stamp and Lick the Kaiser!" on to the time of flappers and radio, through the Great Depression and the Second World War and beyond, the shark would live on as an enduring presence in the American imagination.

On July 10, 1917, the one-year anniversary week of the attacks, President Wilson appointed Herbert Hoover to raise food production for the war effort, yet bigger news was that five hundred bathers fled screaming from the waters of Rockaway Park after swimmers spied a large fin near shore.

Over the next few decades, New York newspapers sounded what became an annual alarm, and the parents of Matawan forbade their children from swimming in Matawan Creek. The grand Engleside Hotel in Beach Haven was demolished for wood during World War II and, later still, the New Essex and Sussex Hotel in Spring Lake was converted to condominiums.

Today all evidence of the great white shark of that long-ago summer is gone. The carcass of the fish disappeared shortly after it was displayed in the window of the *Home News,* and some years later, a scientist spotted its jaw hanging in a window of a Manhattan shop at 86th and Broadway before it disappeared forever. Yet it was the legacy of this young, aberrant, perhaps sickly or injured great white to frame the way people perceive sharks. In 1974, Peter Benchley invoked the 1916 shark as the role model for his fictional white shark in *Jaws.*

By the end of the twentieth century, the deadly predator of 1916 immortalized by Benchley would begin to fade from popular culture. By the 1990s, the concept of the rogue shark had fallen out of scientific favor for lack of proof other than anecdotal material. Shark researchers even began to doubt Nichols's conclusion that the killer of all four victims in 1916 had been a single shark—or even, in all cases, a great white shark. Some suggest that a bull shark, *Carcharhinus leucas,* was the killer of Matawan Creek, as it is the only man-eating species that routinely passes into freshwater, whereas for *Carcharodon carcharias,* the trip would be extraordinary.

Indeed, by the twenty-first century, *Carcharodon carcharias* had assumed a new status as magnificent yet misunderstood sea creature, rare and accidental killer of man, and endangered species protected by the laws of numerous countries, including the United States. So radical was the change in attitude that in 2000 Peter Benchley pleaded with Australians not to destroy a great white that had killed a young swimmer. "This was not a rogue shark, tantalized by the taste of human flesh and bound now to kill and kill again. Such creatures do not exist, despite what you might have derived from *Jaws.* . . . Let us mourn the man and forgive the animal, for, in truth, it knew not what it did."

Hermann Oelrichs, whose 1891 reward was never collected, would have appreciated Benchley's view.

Still, in an era of fisheries that would eradicate it, science that would plumb all its mysteries, and global media that would reveal its every move, the great white endures in the depths where it has always reigned: in cautionary tales told by mothers and fathers, in whispers in the unconscious, in offshore shadows, and in ripples on a tidal creek.

Sources and Acknowledgments

Close to Shore was distilled during a period of two years from dozens of interviews; hundreds of contemporary newspaper accounts; turn-of-the-century diaries and letters, medical and scientific journals, birth and death records, census records, theses, films, and academic transcripts; research in more than twenty museums and libraries; and information from several hundred books on sharks, the oceans, tides, the history of science and medicine, man-eating animals, shipwrecks and sea monsters, Victorian love poems, Philadelphia, the Jersey shore, novels and plays of the era, and every aspect of American history and culture that I imagined would have affected the lives of people in 1916. These lives were shaped in the period shortly after the Civil War through the end of the Victorian period to the last days of the Edwardian era. Researchers April White in Philadelphia, Kelly Caldwell in New York City, and Melody Blake of *The Washington Post* were of invaluable help during the last few months of writing.

This would have been a book-out-of-water without George Burgess, ichthyologist, shark biologist, and Coordinator of Museum Operations of the Florida Museum of Natural History at the University of Florida in Gainesville. To George goes my endless gratitude for helping make sense of a shark that swam in 1916. As director of the International Shark Attack File

(ISAF), administered jointly by the Florida Museum and the American Elasmobranch Society, George studies contemporary and historic shark attacks as closely as anyone in the world. Anyone seeking information about shark attacks, or with serious information to impart about a shark attack anywhere in the world, should look at the ISAF Web site, www.flmnh.ufl.edu /fish/Sharks/sharks.htm. Those familiar with George's wisdom, humor, and state-of-the-science authority in the media will recognize it in this book; in the inflammatory sea of shark attack stories, he is the island of sense. Any mistakes or distortions in my descriptions of shark behavior are mine.

With George Burgess, I rode a boat up Matawan Creek, reconstructing the path of the shark, and attempted to fix the location of the steamboat dock attacks by global positioning system. George Burgess and I examined the sites of all four shark fatalities of 1916; his on-site estimate of the salinity of Matawan Creek was part of the evidence that led him, and me, to believe a great white shark could have passed up the creek. The National Oceanographic and Atmospheric Administration provided computer projections of the tide in Matawan Creek in July 1916, which confirmed that on the afternoon of July 12 the tide was nearing its highest level of the month, making possible the scene describing the moon's effect on the shark.

For my understanding of the cool coastal New Jersey currents that may have drawn the shark, I am grateful to Kenneth W. Able, director of the Rutgers University Marine Field Station in Tuckerton, New Jersey, the institution that overlooks the coast where Charles Vansant was killed. Ken's book, co-authored with Michael Fahay, *The First Year in the Life of Estuarine Fishes in the Middle Atlantic Bight*, was useful in helping me gain an understanding of the world in which the shark roamed. In an interview, Michael Fahay—a fisheries biologist with the National Marine Fisheries

Service Laboratory at Sandy Hook, New Jersey—helped me understand the movement of the Gulf Stream off New Jersey.

Among the many texts I relied on to understand the behavior of sharks, I would like to recognize a few here: *Great White Sharks: The Biology of Carcharodon carcharias*, edited by A. Peter Klimley and David G. Ainley; *Great White Shark: The Definitive Look at the Most Terrifying Creature of the Ocean*, by Richard Ellis and John E. McCosker; and *Sharks and Survival*, edited by Perry W. Gilbert. Although his rogue shark theory is now out of fashion, Victor M. Coppleson's *Shark Attack* provided a fascinating historic survey of shark attack. I am greatly in debt, as well, for my understanding of the variety of shark attacks to H. David Baldridge, author of *Shark Attack*. My thanks to Dr. Richard G. Fernicola, of Allenhurst, New Jersey, for his tireless devotion to this story over the years. His text, *In Search of the Jersey Man-Eater*, was especially illuminating in my study of the shark-attack wounds.

There are many books on sea monsters but none as good as *Monsters of the Sea: The History, Natural History, and Mythology of the Oceans' Most Fantastic Creatures*, by Richard Ellis, whom I owe thanks for my understanding of great white sharks in the lore of sea monsters.

My understanding of the ichthyologists and other scientists in the early twentieth century came from many sources, a few of which I would like to acknowledge here. I gained an understanding of Frederic Augustus Lucas, director of the American Museum of Natural History in New York in 1916, as a Victorian scientist grudgingly moving into the modern world from *Fifty Years of Museum Work: Autobiography, Unpublished Papers, and Bibliography*, published by the museum in 1933. The respect accorded Lucas as a museum administrator and "all-around naturalist" was evident in the introduction by Henry Fairfield

Osborn, a distinguished scientist who named *Tyrannosaurus rex.* Numerous contemporary newspaper accounts contributed to the profile of Dr. Lucas, and they also helped shape my portrayal of John Treadwell Nichols, the museum's curator of Recent Fishes. In describing John T. Nichols, I also relied on his desk diaries at the Museum of Natural History in New York, as well as his book, co-authored with Paul Bartsch, *Fishes and Shells of the Pacific World.* A rich portrait of Nichols exists in *A Gathering of Wonders: Behind the Scenes at the American Museum of Natural History*, by Joseph Wallace. Nichols's Romantic relationship to the sea is evident in his journal articles, press clippings, and also his 1922 book of poetry, *Sea-Rimes II.*

The ornithologist Robert Cushman Murphy's eminence is evident in numerous sources, including his obituary in *The New York Times.* I gained a sense of his personality from his classic books, *Logbook for Grace: Whaling Brig* Daisy, *1912–1913* and *Fish-Shape Paumanok: Nature and Man on Long Island*; his wife Grace Barstow Murphy's book, *There's Always an Adventure*; as well as his introduction to an edition of *The Swiss Family Robinson.* His conservation efforts on Long Island are discussed in Rachel Carson's *Silent Spring.*

The article on the sharks of Long Island that Nichols and Murphy co-authored in April 1916 for the *Brooklyn Science Museum Bulletin* was instrumental in establishing both men's knowledge about sharks and their relationship to each other. The journal article also established both younger men's respect for Dr. Lucas as a mentor, as Nichols and Murphy invited Lucas to contribute comments in the article on the great white. From Robert Cushman Murphy's papers, 1907–1973, and journal in the archives of the American Philosphical Society in Philadelphia, I learned of his especially close relationship with Dr. Lucas, his mentor, who sent him on the whaling brig *Daisy* with a letter "to be opened the day the first Albratross is seen." Lucas's moving role as a mentor to young scientists is well established by his letter: ". . . while I am too far on the wrong side of fifty to wish to be with you all the time, yet I would like mightily to be with you for a part of the time to see the Sea Elephants, the Penguins, and the glaciers of South Georgia. You will feel cramped and uncomfortable for a time, but you will soon harmonize with your environment and—what an experience for a young man!"

My deepest thanks to John Dillon of Sanibel, Florida, nephew of Charles Epting Vansant, the first known swimmer killed by a shark in American history. During several delightful days at his home, John and his wife, Jill, and brother, Larry, opened to me the private world of the Vansant family of Philadelphia. John Dillon's energy and scholarship as a genealogist have kept the Vansant story, and his uncle's place in history, alive. In particular, I relied on the *Condensed Vansant Geneaology* as well the family histories of the Eptings and Dillons. John's voice and love of family inform all the Vansant pages.

For my characterization of Charles Vansant's years at the University of Pennsylvania, I owe thanks to Mark Frazier Lloyd, director of the University of Pennsylvania Archives and Records Center, archivist Martin J. Hackett, and also James Curtiss Ayers. The Penn archivists tolerated my presence for weeks, and their expertise informs the Penn history in this book. The archivists gave me special access to Charles Vansant's Penn yearbooks— *The Records* of 1911, 1912, 1913, and 1914. My brief description of Vansant's years at Penn and the assertion that *This Side of Paradise* is an accurate reflection of those years is based on extensive research of turn-of-the-century university life as well as a reading of every page of the campus newspaper, *The Daily Pennsylvanian*, published during Vansant's four years. The mentions of Charlie, or "Van,"as his classmates called him, were few, but the feel of the times was abundant.

For Charles's academic record and school experiences before college, I would like to thank Tony Brown, Director of Alumni of the Episcopal Academy of Merion and Devon, Pennsylvania for access to the academy's archives.

For my understanding of Philadelphia society, I am greatly indebted to *The Perennial Philadelphians* by Nathaniel Burt, which paints a loving, incisive, and utterly convincing portrait of Old Phildelphians.

My descriptions of Beach Haven, Engleside and New Baldwin hotels, and the Engle family are drawn substantially from *Eighteen Miles of History on Long Beach Island* and *Six Miles at Sea: A Pictorial History of Long Beach Island*. Both volumes are by John Bailey Lloyd. My thanks to John for showing me his beloved island, the new Engleside Motel, and the site of Charles Vansant's death.

My portrayal of Dr. Eugene LaRue Vansant's medical practice is based on his papers contained in the archives of The College of Physicians of Philadelphia, and I wish to thank the curator of the Historical Library, Charles Greifenstein, and the reference librarian, Christopher Stanwood, for their assistance.

To fix Dr. Vansant's place in the medical history of the United States and the storied medical history of Philadelphia—necessary, I thought, to understand the moments he watched his son die despite the best "modern" medical knowledge—took wide-ranging research.

My thanks to Gretchen Worden, director of the Mutter Museum, the museum of medical history and education at the College of Physicians in Philadelphia, for an afternoon explaining the practice of turn-of-the-century medicine and showing me a typical doctor's office of the period as well as a variety of laryngological tools that Dr. Vansant would have used.

Louisa Vansant's personality shines through her letters from sailing ports around the world, especially her touching letter to Eugene from New York City dated Feb. 18, 1891. I obtained copies from John Dillon.

For my descriptions of turn-of-the-century Spring Lake, the New Essex & Sussex Hotel, and the New Monmouth Hotel, I would like to thank the librarians and curators at the Spring Lake Historical Society, who gave me access to their archives and exhibits. My description of Mrs. George W. Childs requires a special thanks to Dan Rottenberg, the Philadelphia writer who shared research on his forthcoming book on the Philadelphia banker J. Anthony Drexel, whose best friend was George Childs.

Woodrow Wilson's cabinet meeting about the shark was front-page news across America, and it is from these accounts the scene is derived.

My research in the small town of Matawan was made delightful by Ruth E. Alt of nearby Morganville, New Jersey, who with her husband Joseph runs something of a single-stop genealogical resource for the area that is truly remarkable. Ruth Alt's research and personal recollections of the boys at Matawan Creek—Lester Stilwell, Rensselaer Cartan, Johnson Cartan, Anthony Bublin, Charles E. Van Brunt Jr., Albert O'Hara, and Frank Clowes, as well as Constable John Mulsoff and retired captain Thomas V. Cottrell—were invaluable in creating the swimming-hole scenes. In addition to interviews and personal recollections, the sketches of the people in Matawan are drawn from stories in *The Matawan Journal* and *Keyport Weekly*, as well as Monmouth County census, birth, and death records. I am grateful to Helen Henderson for her interview about Matawan and for her fine pictorial book, *Around Matawan and Aberdeen*, which was extremely useful in its descriptions of the merchants, shops, and feeling of Main Street in the small town. Special thanks are due the librarians of the Matawan Aberdeen Public Library on Main Street for help with their archives, especially Virginia Moshen, for sharing her knowledge of the shark case; and Sarah Ellison, head docent of the Burrowes Mansion Museum in Matawan, home of the historical society, for showing me her town.

In my attempt to create a portrait of cultural life in early twentieth century America, the America of the Vansants and Bruders, the Fishers and Stilwells, I drew upon numerous sources. They include the first five volumes of *Our Times* by Mark Sullivan. *Our Times* was especially useful for my portrayal of the "Robber Baron" era, but it was a constant browsing companion as well for songs, schooling, automobiles, and a sense of being alive then. I also consulted *Only Yesterday: An Informal History of the 1920s,* by Frederick Lewis Allen, which begins in May 1919 with elements of life, like the hazards of driving a tin lizzie, still germane to 1916; *A History of American Life,* edited by Arthur M. Schlesinger, Sr., and Dixon Ryan Fox, which was the sturdiest of companions on social matters; and the book *1919* by John Dos Passos, which, though fiction, inspired fresh passes at the facts. *Remember When: A Loving Look at Days Gone By: 1900–1942,* by Allen Churchill, is a fine way for a reader, or a researcher, to acquire a glow of nostalgia.

In describing the Victorian era and its evolution to Edwardian times—the values and struggles with change that Eugene and Louisa Vansant brought to the beach—I relied on *Victorian America: Transformations in Everyday Life, 1876–1915,* by Thomas J. Schlereth. Useful as well was *Victorian Minds: A Study of Intellectuals in Crisis and Ideologies in Transition,* by Gertrude Himmelfarb. My portrayal of the relationship of Dr. Eugene Vansant and his son, Charles, is partly based on readings of *Dandies and Desert Saints: Styles of Victorian Manhood,* by James Eli Adams, and *Secret Ritual and Manhood in Victorian America,* by Mark C. Carnes.

The Internet proved an invaluable resource, from the many excellent Victorian scholarship Web sites to my online subscription to the *Encyclopaedia Britannica*. My understanding of the Jersey coast and shipwrecks was enhanced by an excellent Web site for New Jersey divers, www.njscuba.com.

For the opulence of the Gilded Age, especially the popularity of diamonds in New York City, I am in debt to the vivid history in *Gilded City: Scandal and Sensation in Turn-of-the-Century New York*, by M. H. Dunlop.

In my attempt to create the popular texture of the era— home, foods, fashions, railroads, automobiles, architecture, Victrolas, newsreels, pulps—I relied on contemporary newspaper accounts and a number of books. To re-create automobile journeys, particularly John T. Nichols's, I used *Scarborough's Official 1916 New York Automobile Association Tour Book for New York, New Jersey, Canada and the East*.

Finally, my thanks to the librarians and archivists at the American Museum of Natural History in New York; the Florida Museum of Natural History in Gainesville, Florida; the New York Public Library; the Free Library of Philadelphia; the Ocean County Library in Tom's River, New Jersey; the Asbury Park Library; the Matawan Aberdeen Public Library; the Spring Lake Historical Society; the University of Pennsylvania Library and archives; Temple University's Urban Archives; the Thomas Jefferson University Library and Archives; the Smithsonian Institution; the University of Miami Rosenstiel School of Marine and Atmospheric Science; the American Philosophic Society in Philadelphia; the Treasury Department in Washington, D.C.; the Library of Congress; and the National Oceanographic and Atmospheric Administration. The U.S. Coast Guard provided the log of the U.S. revenue cutter *Mohawk*, which fought the short-lived "war on sharks," as well as the records of Captain Carden and other officials of the Coast Guard.

Although there is a tendency to romanticize publishing houses and editors of the past, it is hard to imagine an editor in any time more devoted, intense, or talented than Charlie Conrad, executive editor of Broadway Books. This book could not have existed in its form of history, science, and narrative without his vision, passion, and literary gifts. I quickly learned I was not the only person kept up nights thinking about the best ways to tell this story, and for that, Charlie, I am most grateful. Becky Cole, assistant editor, pulled off the rare triple crown of being diamond-sharp, reassuring, and ever calm under pressure. Sharks don't float, but Becky did, ever protecting and perfecting this book. Special thanks to my agent, David Vigliano, whose genius is to see simultaneously into a market and a writer's soul. David somehow manages to follow me and lead me at the same time, always to the right place. Broadway Books was that place, and I owe a huge debt of gratitude to the people who made me feel like a swimmer with a dozen lifeguards: managing editor Rebecca Holland, marketing director Catherine Pollack, publicity director Betsy Areddy, jacket designer Patti Ratchford, text designer Richard Oriolo—whose designs I cherish—as well as the incredible cavalry-to-the-rescue copy editor Johanna Tani and typesetter Tina Thompson. My late father, William Capuzzo, a salesman for several New York publishing houses, would have been thrilled, as I am, by the efforts of the Random House West sales force.

My most heartfelt thanks go to my daughter, Grace, ten, a poet who listened to me read aloud; my daughter Julia, seven, an artist who decorated my office with drawings of sharks; and my wife, Teresa, whom I am lucky to have for yet another reason: She is a brilliant editor and wordsmith whose eye and ear shadow all these pages.

Selected Bibliography

The following is a partial record of the sources I consulted for the history and ideas in *Close to Shore*, offered to give a feeling for the range of material used and as a guide for those wishing to pursue the topics discussed in this book. Among the newspapers, circa 1916, I consulted were *The Asbury Park Press, The Baltimore Sun, The Home News* (Harlem, New York City), *The Keyport News* (Keyport, New Jersey), *The London Times, The Matawan Journal* (Matawan, New Jersey), *The New York Daily News, The New York Herald, The New York Sun, The New York Times, The New York World, The Philadelphia Daily News, The Philadelphia Evening Bulletin, The Philadelphia Inquirer, The Philadelphia Public Ledger, The Sunday Register* (Shrewsbury, N.J.), and *The Washington Post.* Dozens of magazines and journals were consulted, including the April 1916 *Brooklyn Museum Science Bulletin* article by John T. Nichols and Robert C. Murphy, "Long Island Fauna: The Sharks (Order Selachii)"; *Time* magazine; *National Geographic; Discover; Philadelphia* magazine; *New Jersey Monthly;* and many others, from *The Fishery Bulletin* to the *Journal of the American Medical Association.*

Able, Kenneth W. and Michael Fahay. *The First Year in the Life of Estuarine Fishes in the Middle Atlantic Bight*. New Brunswick, NJ: Rutgers University Press, 1998.

Adams, George Worthington. *Doctors in Blue: The Medical History of the Union Army in the Civil War.* Baton Rouge, LA: Louisiana State University Press, 1996.

Adams, James Eli. *Dandies and Desert Saints: Styles of Victorian Manhood.* Ithaca and London: Cornell University Press, 1995.

Ainley, David G. and Peter A. Klimley, editors. *Great White Sharks: The Biology of Carcharodon carcharias.* San Diego: Academic Press, 1996.

Allen, Frederick Lewis. *Only Yesterday: An Informal History of the Nineteen-Twenties.* 1931. New York: Harper & Row, 1964.

Allen, Thomas B. *The Shark Almanac: A Fully Illustrated Natural History of Sharks, Skates, and Rays.* New York: The Lyons Press, 1999.

Baldridge, H. David. *Shark Attack.* New York: Berkley Publishing Co., 1974.

Bartsch, Paul and John T. Nichols. *Fishes and Shells of the Pacific World.* New York: The Macmillan Co., 1945.

Bosker, Gideon and Lena Lencek. *The Beach: The History of Paradise on Earth.* New York: Viking, 1998.

Brands, H.W. *TR: The Last Romantic.* New York: Basic Books, 1997.

Brinnin, John Malcolm. *The Sway of the Grand Saloon: A Social History of the North Atlantic.* 1971. New York: Barnes & Noble Books, 2000.

Brown, Dee Carlton, editor. *The Record of the Class of Nineteen Hundred and Thirteen, University of Pennsylvania.* Philadelphia: The University of Pennsylvania, 1913.

Burt, Nathaniel. *The Perennial Philadelphians: The Anatomy of an American Aristocracy.* Boston: Little, Brown and Co., 1963.

Bynum, W.F. *Science and the Practice of Medicine in the Nineteenth Century.* New York: Cambridge University Press, 1994.

Capstick, Peter Hathaway. *Maneaters.* 1981. New York: St. Martin's Press, 1990.

Caras, Roger A. *Dangerous to Man: The Definitive Story of Wildlife's Reputed Dangers.* New York: Holt, Rinehart & Winston, 1975.

Carnes, Mark C. *Secret Ritual and Manhood in Victorian America.* New Haven and London: Yale University Press, 1989.

Champlin, John Denison, with editorial cooperation and an introduction by Frederic A. Lucas. *The Young Folks' Cyclopaedia of Natural History.* New York: Henry Holt & Co., 1905.

Chiquoine, Alexander Duncan. *The Record of the Class of Nineteen Hundred and Fourteen, University of Pennsylvania.* Philadelphia: The University of Pennsylvania, 1914.

Churchill, Allen. *Remember When: A loving look at days gone by: 1900–1942.* New York: Golden Press, 1967.

Colrick, Patricia Florio. *Spring Lake.* Dover, NH: Arcadia Publishing, 1998.

Cooper, John Milton Jr. *Pivotal Decades: The United States, 1900–1920.* New York, London: W.W. Norton & Co, 1990.

Coppleson, V.M. *Shark Attack.* Sydney, Australia: Agnus and Robertson, 1958.

Dos Passos, John. *1919.* Volume Two of the *U.S.A.* trilogy. 1932. Boston, New York: Houghton Mifflin Co., 2000.

Dreiser, Theodore. *The Financier.* 1912. New York: Meridian, 1995.

Dunlop, M.H. *Gilded City: Scandal and Sensation in Turn-of-the-Century New York.* New York: William Morrow, 2000.

Edwards, Hugh. *Shark: The Shadow Below.* New York: HarperCollins Publishers, 1997.

Ellis, Edward Robb. *Echoes of Distant Thunder: Life in the United States, 1914–1918.* New York: Kodansha International, 1996.

Ellis, Richard. *Monsters of the Sea: the history, natural history, and mythology of the oceans' most fantastic creatures.* 1995. New York: Doubleday, 1996.

Ellis, Richard and John E. McCosker. *Great White Shark: The definitive look at the most terrifying creature of the ocean.* New York: HarperCollins Publishers in collaboration with Stanford University Press, 1991.

Emery, Edwin. *The Press and America: An Interpretative History of the Mass Media.* Englewood Cliffs, NJ: Prentice-Hall, Inc., 1972.

Fernicola, Richard G. *In Search of the Jersey Man-Eater.* Deal, N.J.: George Marine Library, 1987.

Fitzgerald, F. Scott. *This Side of Paradise.* New York: Charles Scribner's Sons, 1970.

Flower, Raymond and Michael Wynn Jones. *100 Years on the Road: A Social History of the Car.* New York: McGraw-Hill, 1981.

Fox, Dixon Ryan and Arthur M. Schlesinger Sr., editors. *A History of American Life.* The 1948 thirteen-volume set abridged and revised by Mark C. Carnes. New York: Scribner, 1996.

Foy, Jessica H. and Thomas J. Schlereth. *American Home Life, 1880–1930: A Social History of Spaces and Services.* Knoxville, TN: The University of Tennessee Press, 1992.

Freeman, Michael. *Railways and the Victorian Imagination.* New Haven: Yale University Press, 1999.

Gilbert, Perry W., editor. *Sharks and Survival.* Includes *Treatment of Shark-Attack Victims in South Africa by David H. Davies and George D. Campbell.* 1963. Lexington, MA: D.C. Heath & Co., 1975.

Harris, Kristina. *Victorian and Edwardian Fashions for Women, 1840 to 1919.* Atglen, PA: Schiffer Publishing Ltd., 1995.

Henderson, Helen. *Around Matawan and Aberdeen.* Dover, NH: Arcadia Publishing, 1996.

Himmelfarb, Gertrude. *Victorian Minds: A Study of Intellectuals in Crisis and Ideologies in Transition.* 1952. Chicago: Elephant Paperbacks, 1968.

Hofstadter, Richard. *Social Darwinism in American Thought.* 1944. Boston: Beacon Press, 1992.

Hunter, Allan Jr., editor. *The Record of the Class of Nineteen Hundred and Eleven, University of Pennsylvania.* Philadelphia: The University of Pennsylvania, 1911.

Johnson, Paul. *A History of the American People.* New York: HarperCollins, 1998.

Kalfus, Ken, editor. *Christopher Morley's Philadelphia.* New York: Fordham University Press, 1990.

Kammen, Michael. *Mystic Chords of Memory: The Transformation of Tradition in American Culture.* 1991. New York: Vintage Books, 1993.

Kazin, Alfred. *On Native Grounds: An Interpretation of Modern American Prose Literature.* 1942. Garden City, New York: Doubleday Anchor Books, 1956.

Kendrick, A. Clements. *Woodrow Wilson: World Statesman.* Chicago: Ivan R. Dee, Inc., 1999.

Knudtson, Peter. *Orca: Visions of the Killer Whale.* San Francisco: Sierra Club Books, 1996.

Kynett, Harold H. Jr., editor. *The Record of the Class of Nineteen Hundred and Twelve.* Philadelphia: The University of Pennsylvania, 1912.

Lloyd, John Bailey. *Eighteen Miles of History on Long Beach Island.* Harvey Cedars, NJ: Down the Shore Publishing and The SandPaper Inc., 1994.

Lloyd, John Bailey. *Six Miles at Sea: A Pictorial History of Long Beach Island.* Harvey Cedars, NJ: Down the Shore Publishing and The SandPaper Inc., 1990.

Lucas, Frederic A. *Animals of the Past: An Account of Some of the Creatures of the Ancient World.* New York: American Museum of Natural History, 1929.

Lucas, Frederic A. *Fifty Years of Museum Work: Autobiography,*

Unpublished Papers, and Bibliography. New York: American Museum of Natural History, 1933.

Lukas, J. Anthony. *Big Trouble: A Murder in a Small Western Town Sets Off a Struggle for the Soul of America.* New York: Touchstone, 1977.

Lutz, Tom. *American Nervousness, 1903: An Anecdotal History.* Ithaca: Cornell University Press, 1991.

Maniguet, Xavier. *The Jaws of Death: Shark as Predator, Man as Prey.* 1991. Dobbs Ferry, NY: Sheridan House, 1994.

Martin, Richard and Harold Koda. *Splash! A History of Swimwear.* New York: Rizzoli, 1990.

Mathiessen, Peter. *Blue Meridian: The Search for the Great White Shark.* New York: Random House, 1971.

Maxtone-Graham, John. *The Only Way to Cross: The Golden Era of the Great Atlantic Express Liners—from the Mauretania to the France and the Queen Elizabeth 2.* 1972. New York: Barnes & Noble Books, 1997.

McPherson, James M., general editor. *"To the Best of My Ability": The American Presidents.* New York: Dorling Kindersley, 2000.

Morgan, Robert P., editor. *Music, Society and Modern Times: From World War I to the Present.* Englewood Cliffs, NJ: Prentice Hall, 1994.

Morrone, Francis. *An Architectural Guidebook to Philadelphia.* Layton, UT: Gibbs Smith, Publisher, 1999.

Murphy, Robert Cushman. *Fish-Shape Paumanok: Nature and Man on Long Island.* Philadelphia: The American Philosophical Society, 1964.

Murphy, Robert Cushman. *Logbook for Grace: Whaling Brig Daisy, 1912–1913.* Alexandria, Virginia: Time-Life Books, 1982.

Nash, Charles Edgar. *The Lure of Long Beach, being a detailed account of the traditions, history and growth of a grand little island off the New Jersey Coast.* Long Beach Island, NJ: The Long Beach Board of Trade, 1936.

Norris, Frank. *The Octopus.* 1901. New York: Penguin Books, 1994.

Nye, Russel. *The Unembarrassed Muse: The Popular Arts in America.* New York: The Dial Press, 1970.

Porter, Roy. *The Greatest Benefit to Mankind: A Medical History of Humanity.* New York: W.W. Norton & Co., 1997.

Prost, Antoine and Gerard Vincent. *A History of Private Life: Riddles of Identity in Modern Times.* Cambridge, MA: Harvard University Press, 1991.

Raby, Peter. Bright Paradise: *Victorian Scientific Travellers.* Princeton, NJ: Princeton University Press, 1997.

Roosevelt, Theodore. *Through the Brazilian Wilderness.* New York: Charles Scribner's Sons, 1926.

Rosenberg, Charles E. *The Care of Strangers: The Rise of America's Hospital System.* Baltimore: The Johns Hopkins University Press, 1987.

Scarborough's Official Tour Book, New York Automobile Association 1916, New York, New Jersey, Canada and the East. Indianapolis: Scarborough Motor Guide Co., 1916.

Schlereth, Thomas J. *Victorian America: Transformations in Everyday Life, 1876–1915.* 1991. New York: HarperPerennial, 1992.

Schneider, Dorothy and Carl J. *American Women in The Progressive Era, 1900–1920.* New York: Anchor Books, Doubleday, 1993.

Server, Lee. *The Golden Age of Ocean Liners.* New York: Todtri Productions Limited, 1996.

Solomon, Brian, with C.J. Riley. *Along the Rails: The Lore and Romance of the Railroad.* New York: MetroBooks, 1999.

Stevick, Philip. *Imagining Philadelphia: Travelers' Views of the City from 1800 to the Present.* Philadelphia: University of Pennsylvania Press, 1996.

Stover, John F. *American Railroads.* Chicago: University of Chicago Press, 1997.

Stutz, Bruce. *Natural Lives, Modern Times: People and Places of the Delaware River.* New York: Crown Publishers Inc., 1992.

Sullivan, Mark. *Our Times: The United States, 1900–1925, Volume I: The Turn of the Century, 1900–1904.* New York: Charles Scribner's Sons, 1926.

Sullivan, Mark. *Our Times: The United States, 1900–1925, Volume II: America Finding Herself.* New York: Charles Scribner's Sons, 1927.

Sullivan, Mark. *Our Times: The United States, 1900–1925, Volume III: Pre-War America.* New York: Charles Scribner's Sons, 1930.

Sullivan, Mark. *Our Times: The United States, 1900–1925, Volume IV: The War Begins.* New York: Charles Scribner's Sons, 1932.

Sullivan, Mark. *Our Times: The United States, 1900–1925, Volume V: Over Here, 1914–1918.* New York: Charles Scribner's Sons, 1933.

Taylor, Leighton, consultant editor. *Sharks and Rays.* New York: Time-Life Books, The Nature Company Guides, 1997.

Wagner, Frederick B. Jr., M.D., editor. *Thomas Jefferson University: Tradition and Heritage.* Philadelphia: Lea & Febiger, 1989.

Wagner, Frederick B. Jr., M.D. and J. Woodrow Savacool, M.D., editors. *Jefferson Medical College: Legend & Lore.* Devon, PA: published for Jefferson Medical College of Thomas Jefferson University by William T. Cooke Publishing, Inc., 1996.

Wagner, Frederick B. Jr., M.D. and Savacool, J. Woodrow, M.D., editors. *Thomas Jefferson University: A Chronological His-*

tory and Alumni Director, 1824–1990. Philadelphia: Thomas Jefferson University, 1992.

Wallace, Anthony F.C. *St. Clair: A Nineteenth-Century Coal Town's Experience with a Disaster-Prone Industry.* 1981. Ithaca: Cornell University Press, 1987.

Wallace, Joseph. *A Gathering of Wonders: Behind the Scenes at the American Museum of Natural History.* New York: St. Martin's Press, 2000.

Weigley, Russell F., editor. *Philadelphia: A 300-Year History.* New York: W.W. Norton & Co., 1982.

Whitman, Walt. *Whitman: Complete Poetry and Collected Prose.* New York: The Library of America, 1982.

Williams, Guy. *The Age of Miracles: Medicine and Surgery in the Nineteenth Century.* Chicago: Academy Chicago Publishers, 1987.

Williams, Susan. *Savory Suppers & Fashionable Feasts: Dining in Victorian America.* Knoxville, TN: The University of Tennessee Press, 1996.

Wilson, Edith Bolling. *My Memoir.* Indianapolis, IN: Bobbs-Merrill Co., 1938.

Wilson, Edward O. *The Diversity of Life.* New York: W.W. Norton, 1992.

Wullschlager, Jackie. *Inventing Wonderland: Victorian Childhood as Seen Through the Lives and Fantasies of Lewis Carroll, Edward Lear, J.M. Barrie, Kenneth Grahame, and A.A. Milne.* New York: The Free Press, 1995.

TWO KILLED AND ONE CRIPPLED BY SHARKS

Three Bathers on Jersey Coast Attacked by Man-Eaters at Crowded Beach.

MATAWAN, N. J., July 13.—Lester Stillwell, twelve years old, was killed by a man-eating shark while bathing in an arm of Raritan bay near here yesterday afternoon. Stanley Fisher, twenty-four years old, who went to his aid, was so badly injured in a struggle with the sea monster that he died while being taken to a Long Branch hospital. Joseph Dunn, twelve

SHARK KILLS 2 IN SUR

Boy and Young Man Victims Sea Monster.

NEW YORK HERALD, FRIDAY, JU

THIRD IS BADLY MANGLE

Sportsmen with Harpoons Kill Many Sharks in Chases in Great South Bay

the Deep Appears
ritan Bay, N. J.

Watch Monster's Tell-Tale Fins and Dive Deep for Safety at First Sign of Attack, Is Fair Sea Nymph's Advice—Gives Thrilling Story of a Shark Hunt in Jamaica. Exciting Chase Lasts for Two Hours.

By ANNETTE KELLERMANN.

WHETHER Carl Bruder was killed by the dreaded shark

MANY HUNT SHARKS ALONG THE COAST

Sport Has Become Popular as Result of Recent Raids by Man-Eaters.

STILLWELL'S BODY FOUND NEARLY BITTEN IN TWO

Little Hope Entertained for Recovery of Joseph Dunn, Whose Leg Was Badly Torn.

NEW YORK, July 14.—Shark hunting or fishing suddenly has become a popular sport along the New Jersey coast. In the waters of New York bay and along the ocean side of Long Island as a result of the recent raids by man-eating monsters from southern waters which have killed four persons. Re-

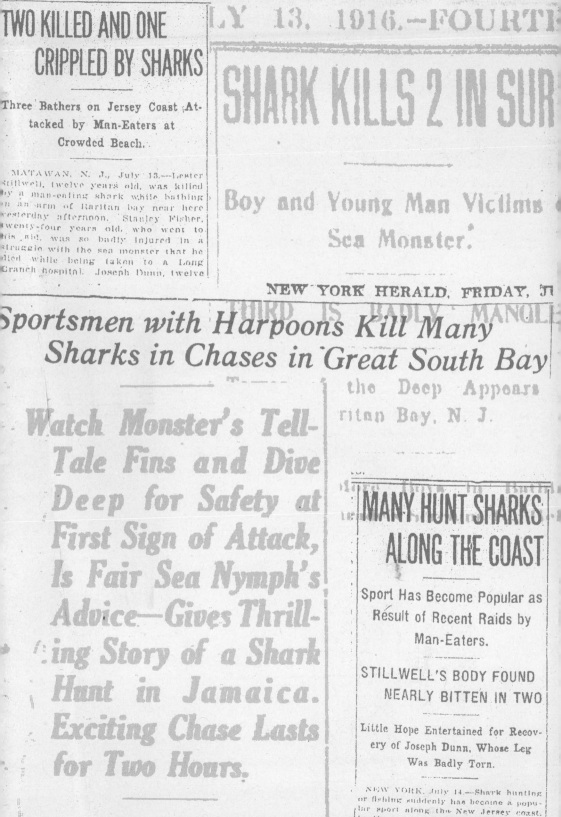